SERVICE OPPORTUNITIES FOR ELECTRIC UTILITIES: CREATING DIFFERENTIATED PRODUCTS

Topics in Regulatory Economics and Policy Series

Michael A. Crew, Editor
Graduate School of Management
Rutgers University
Newark, New Jersey, U.S.A.

Previously published books in the series:

Rowley, C., R. Tollison, and G. Tullock:
Political Economy of Rent-Seeking
Frantz, R.:
X-Efficiency: Theory, Evidence and Applications
Crew, M.:
Deregulation and Diversification of Utilities
Shogren, J.:
The Political Economy of Government Regulation
Hillman, J., and R. Braeutigam:
Price Level Regulation for Diversified Public Utilities
Einhorn, M.:
Price Caps and Incentive Regulation in Telecommunications
Crew, M.:
Competition and the Regulation in Telecommunications
Crew, M., and P. Kleindorfer:
Competition and Innovation in Postal Services
Thompson, H.:
Regulatory Finance: Financial Foundations of Rate of Return Regulation
Crew, M., and P. Kleindorfer:
Economic Innovations in Public Utility Regulation
Crew M., and P. Kleindorfer:
The Economics of Postal Service
Crew, M., and P. Kleindorfer:
Regulation and the Nature of Postal and Delivery Services

SERVICE OPPORTUNITIES FOR ELECTRIC UTILITIES: CREATING DIFFERENTIATED PRODUCTS

Edited by

Shmuel S. Oren
University of California, Berkeley

and

Stephen A. Smith
Santa Clara University

Kluwer Academic Publishers
Boston/Dordrecht/London

Distributors for North America:
Kluwer Academic Publishers
101 Philip Drive
Assinippi Park
Norwell, Massachusetts 02061 USA

Distributors for all other countries:
Kluwer Academic Publishers Group
Distribution Centre
Post Office Box 322
3300 AH Dordrecht, THE NETHERLANDS

Library of Congress Cataloging-in-Publication Data

Service opportunities for electric utilities : creating differentiated products / edited by Shmuel S. Oren and Stephen A. Smith.
p. cm. -- (Topics in regulatory economics and policy series)
ISBN 0-7923-9319-8 (hc). -- ISBN 0-7923-9320-1 (pbk.)
1. Electric utilities--Congresses. 2. Diversification in industry--Congresses. I. Oren, Shmuel S. II. Smith, Stephen A. (Stephen Allan), 1942- . III. Series: Topics in regulatory economics and policy.
HD9685.A2S44 1993
333.79'32'06--dc20 92-44559
CIP

Printed on acid-free paper.

Printed in the United States of America

TABLE OF CONTENTS

FIGURES

FIGURES (continued)

FIGURES (continued)

FIGURES (continued)

FIGURES (continued)

TABLES

TABLES (continued)

AUTHORS AND AFFILIATIONS

AKBARI, H., University of California, Berkeley, CA

ALVARADO, Fernando L., The University of Wisconsin, Madison, WI

BLUMSTEIN, C., University of California, Berkeley, CA

BOHN, Roger E., Tabors Caramanis & Associates, Cambridge, MA

BURNS, Robert E., Esq., The National Regulatory Research Institute, Columbus, OH

CAVES, Douglas W., Christensen Associated, Inc., Madison, WI

CHAMBERLIN, John H., Barakat & Chamberlin, Inc., Oakland, CA

CHAO, Hung-po, Electric Power Research Institute, Palo Alto, CA

CHEN, Tser-Yieth, Chung-Hua Institution for Economic Research and Institute of Management Science, National Chiao-tung University, Taipei, Taiwan

DARYANIAN, Bahman, Tabors Caramanis & Associates, Cambridge, MA

GLYER, J. David, Christensen Associated, Inc., Madison, WI

HAMM, Gregory L., Applied Decision Analysis, Inc., Menlo Park, CA

HODGES, R.W., Putnam, Hayes & Bartlett, Inc., Cambridge, MA

HSU , George J.Y., Chung-Hua Institution for Economic Research National Chiao-tung University, Taipei, Taiwan

JENSEN, Kenneth A., Barakat & Chamberlin, Inc., Oakland, CA

KAYE, R. John, University of New South Wales, Sydney, Australia

KEANE, Dennis M., Pacific Gas and Electric Company, San Francisco, CA

KOLBE, A.L., Putnam, Hayes & Bartlett, Inc., Cambridge, MA

MALCOLM, Wade P., Electric Power Research Institute, Palo Alto, CA

MANGO, Robert, Niagara Mohawk Power Corporation, Syracuse, NY

OREN , Shmuel S., University of California, Berkeley, CA

ROSENFELD, A.H., Lawrence Livermore Laboratory, Berkeley, CA

SIDDIQI, Riaz, Electric Power Research Institute, Palo Alto, CA

SIM, Steven R., Florida Power & Light (FPL), Miami, FL

SMITH, Stephen A., Santa Clara University, Santa Clara, CA

SULLIVAN, Michael J., Pacific Gas and Electric Company,
San Francisco, CA

TABORS, Richard D., Tabors Caramanis & Associates, Cambridge, MA

VARAIYA, Pravin P., University of California, Berkeley, CA

WILSON, Robert, Stanford Graduate School of Business, Stanford, CA

WU, Felix F., University of California, Berkeley, CA

Preface

This monograph is the proceedings of a symposium held at the University of California at Berkeley, September 12-14, 1990. It was sponsored by the Electric Power Research Institute (EPRI) and by the University of California University-Wide Energy Research Group (UERG). The symposium brought together researchers and practitioners from academia, the utility industry, private and public organizations and regulatory agencies to address various challenges and opportunities related to product differentiation in the electric power industry.

Electric utilities are evolving rapidly from commodity-oriented services to product-oriented services. Utilities are offering menus of service options tailored to the needs of different customers. Reliability is one important dimension of electric service that lends itself to such product differentiation., Options include lower rate curtailable services for industrial customers, higher reliability power for some commercial customers, and load control with rebates for residential customers., These specialized services are a first step toward the product differentiation goal of allowing all customers to choose the type of service best suited to their electricity needs.

The symposium provided a forum for in depth examination of the complex planning, development, and implementation issues associated with differentiated products. Its specific objectives were to:

- Review the state of the art in implementing reliability differentiated electric services.
- Address the entire process for developing and implementing reliability differentiated product menus including research, design, marketing, implementation, and evaluation.
- Consider technical, economic, and regulatory barriers to implementing reliability differentiated product design.
- Bring together individuals with a variety of theoretical and practical experience in electric power product differentiation.

This proceedings contains written versions of papers that were presented at the symposium with very minor editorial changes. Only a subset of the presentations are included in this proceedings, and the papers are grouped according to topics.

The symposium was co-sponsored by: Florida Power and Light Company, The National Science Foundation (Grant ECS-9016763), New England Electric Systems, Niagara Mohawk Power Corporation, and Pacific Gas and Electric Company. We would like to acknowledge the financial support provided by the sponsors and co-sponsors. In particular, we wish to thank Hung-po Chao and Riaz Siddiqi from EPRI and Richard Gilbert from UERG who made this symposium possible.

The program for the symposium was organized by an executive committee and session chairs. We wish to thank Douglas Caves, Greg Hamm, Peter Morris, Robert Wilson, and Felix Wu for their help in organizing the program. We also thank all the speakers, especially those who prepared written versions of their papers, and the participants for their insightful comments. Finally, we thank Laura Oliver of EPRI, who took care of all the large and small logistical matters that make a symposium successful.

The Editors

SERVICE OPPORTUNITIES FOR ELECTRIC UTILITIES: CREATING DIFFERENTIATED PRODUCTS

I. INTRODUCTION

WHY SERVICE DIFFERENTIATION? WHY NOW?

by

Hung-po Chao and Riaz Siddiqi
Electric Power Research Institute

The purpose of this paper is to offer a researcher's perspective on why we need to worry about service differentiation today. We shall draw lessons from the history and examine opportunities for the future. In closing, we will briefly describe an EPRI project, PRISM, which is designed to exploit some of these opportunities. We hope this will provide a basis for better understanding how to create services that meet future utility business and customer needs.

First of all, it is useful to take a brief look at the historical development of electric power systems and to see how the technological progress has facilitated service differentiation. Over many decades, the technological progress and economies of scale in power generation have contributed significantly to efficiency improvements in electric power systems. The development of high voltage AC transmission and interconnected and centrally dispatched systems enabled utilities to pool loads that vary randomly over time and geographical locations. Further, new generation technologies with different cost and operating characteristics offered utilities added flexibility to diversify fuel sources and to minimize cost by choosing an optimal technology mix. As a result, the cost of electricity declined steadily, and electricity markets expanded rapidly. All these developments took place when the public attitude was conducive to electrification.

In contrast, the impact of recent technological developments is characterized by economies of scope and market segmentation. New technological innovations, such as flexible AC transmission systems, distribution automation systems, smart meters, and home automation, enable utilities to better control the power systems and respond to specific market demands efficiently. With market competition and environmental constraints, the scope of electric power systems has been expanded to include the demand side. This offers utilities opportunities to integrate demand side and supply side options to provide a variety of services that satisfy specific market needs.

From a customer's perspective, the market for electricity has evolved from one that is simple and homogeneous to one that is sophisticated and diverse. Over a century ago when the industry was initially formed, electricity was used exclusively for street lighting. But this led to a rather inefficient utilization of expensive capacity with a load factor around 10%-15%, because the demand was concentrated in the evening hours. In an attempt to generate off-peak sales, utilities promoted electricity traction, heating and cooking.

Largely due to the development of electric motors and electronics, electricity became a highly flexible energy form with an increasing variety of end-use applications. Different customers have different needs. As the market grows more sophisticated and diverse, opportunities for profitable service differentiation arise. To exploit these opportunities, a utility needs to find out what customers in different market segments want and deliver differentiated services that yield the greatest value to those customers. Trying to satisfy all customers by offering an undifferentiated service at a uniform price is guaranteed to be a suboptimal strategy.

Next, let us mention the development of the interface between the utilities and their customers. A utility depends on meters to bill customers for electricity services. The development of metering technology affects the types of service that a utility can profitably offer. In the 1880s, before an electric meter was developed, electricity charges were based on the number of lights installed and filaments used. Only after the introduction of kilowatt-hour meters could a utility charge customers on the basis of marginal operating cost. More advanced meters, which feature kilowatts, kilowatt-hours and time-of-use, enable a more sophisticated rate structure including energy charge, demand charge and time-of-use pricing. In the 1990s, the advanced electronic meters allow for multiple functions and remote meter reading. These developments, merging with integrated communications networks and possibly fiber optics in the future, will greatly expand a utility's capability to offer customers differentiated services.

The 1970s represented a turbulent decade for the electric power industry, with double-digit inflation, two oil disruptions, two nuclear accidents, coal strikes, rapidly growing environmental regulations, the passage of PURPA, and increasing competition from natural gas. These developments broke a century-old way of doing business. The capital investment in generation by the electric power industry declined from $38 billion in 1983 to only $12 billion in 1989. For the first time in history, investment in power generation fell below that in transmission and distribution. This is a clear evidence that the generation segment of the business has entered a period of attrition. We can foresee that many utilities will depend on IPP's and bulk power markets for future energy supplies. Wholesale markets will assume a new role in utility business. Service differentiation will be equally in those markets as in the retail markets.

The increased competition, rapid technological change, tighter environmental constraints, and emergence of more sophisticated and diverse energy consumers of the 1990s challenge electric power companies to find new ways to ensure their survival and prosperity. Today's market requires that rather than delivering undifferentiated kilowatt-hours of electricity to a faceless and captive customer base, a utility must now work closely with its customers to identify, or better yet, anticipate, their energy-related needs. The utility must design products and services to meet those needs. If the utility is to survive, customers must receive (and perceive) value greater than that offered by competing providers.

The potential for service differentiation is virtually limitless. Utilities can explore differentiation systematically to expand their services. To more effectively serve a wide variety of customers' needs, the traditional electricity service can be differentiated along a number of dimensions: quality, time-of-use, reliability, and price stability, for example. Once a utility takes steps to differentiate the basic electricity product, a wide variety of new products and services become possible to take advantage of the differentiation of electricity.

As their use of differentiated electric services grows, customers will also need to more effectively control the delivery of this energy. Utilities are well placed to serve this need. For example, a utility can provide software or hardware to help a customer take full advantage of new service programs.

Utilities have extensive information about demand and supply of energy. They know the consumption patterns of their various types of customers. They know the cost, reliability and quality of the energy supplied. This information is of great value to customers striving to better manage their energy systems.

Many utilities can take advantage of their existing expertise and market presence to provide energy related services that go beyond energy sales, control and information. For example, if a utility has peak and off-peak rates that encourage the use of electric vehicles, it has an excellent opportunity to provide electric vehicles sales and service. Those utilities that can obtain emission allowance credits from conservation would be in an excellent position to sell energy efficiency.

All of these value enhancing new utility services are based on the same basic business; they build directly on a utility's skills and resources for providing energy. Additional opportunities exist for utilities to leverage their assets and to serve customer needs that go beyond energy service. For example, the technologies inherent in Smart House and distribution automation provide an opportunity to offer home security services.

In the evolving utility environment, the mandate to provide an undifferentiated electricity product is being replaced by the need to identify and satisfy specific customer needs. This means that product or service offering decisions become critical to utility planning and management. In contrast to the traditional focus on cost minimization, planning becomes a much more complex process that focuses on value maximization, and it must fully integrate technology and customer service. The traditional asset planning/operation cycle remains important, but it must be integrated with the product/service decisions. The real value of new technologies becomes obvious when their relationship to delivering high-value products and services to utility customers becomes clear.

Traditionally, reliability has been one of the most important criteria that measure the quality of electricity service. Existing outage cost studies indicate that different customers place very different values on service reliability, ranging from a few cents to tens of dollars per kilowatt-hour. Priority Service Methods (PRISM) is a project that helps utilities exploit these opportunities by providing methods for designing and implementing reliability differentiated service offerings that enable utilities to be more responsive to customers' needs.

Priority service is a special form of service differentiation that expands the quality dimension of electricity service. The key idea is to unbundle the basic electricity service into a menu of choices and to give customers an opportunity to select, from the menu, plans that best meet their individual needs. For instance, some customers would be willing to tolerate the inconvenience of more frequent power interruptions in exchange for a lower price, and others would be willing to pay a premium for even more reliable service than regularly provided. By allowing customers to make their own selection, priority service would enable the cost and availability of service to match more closely to their needs, thus lowering total costs.

What distinguishes the priority service concept from other demand-side management initiatives is its breadth. Instead of curtailing service to specific customers for a special rate, this approach presents customers with a menu of market options. A central element is a mechanism for providing information and incentive structures that can minimize both the cost and risk of implementation. A well designed implementation of priority service can benefit both customers and the utility.

From a broad perspective, service differentiation is an inevitable step in the evolution of the electric utility industry. As undifferentiated electricity service is being unbundled into a broad range of products, new markets are being developed and new business opportunities are arising.

Today, trying to satisfy all customers by offering a uniform energy product at an essentially uniform price is guaranteed to be an inefficient strategy. The utility business is characterized by increased competition, rapid technological change, tighter environmental constraints, and more diverse and discriminating energy consumers. To meet these challenges in the 1990s, utilities must be more innovative than ever before to create value enhanced new services that better serve their customers.

II. THEORETICAL FOUNDATIONS FOR SERVICE DESIGN

PRIORITY SERVICE METHODS

by

Robert Wilson*
Stanford Graduate School of Business

The advantages obtained from differentiation of products and services all stem ultimately from differences among customers. A product line serves customers better to the extent it includes products tailored to the preferences of specific market segments. Gains in efficiency from greater differentiation can be shared between customers and firms in various ways: in perfectly regulated or competitive markets the gains remain with customers, but in incompletely regulated or imperfectly competitive markets the firms can obtain profits from some degree of monopoly pricing, which of course also diminishes somewhat the gains obtained.

A main source of differentiation is unbundling a principal quality attribute of a product. Different customers value improvements in quality differently. Consequently, if a uniform quality is separated into a spectrum of lower and higher qualities offered at correspondingly lower and higher prices, then different customers prefer to select different qualities. Provided the previous standard quality and price are also offered, every

---

* Research support provided by the Electric Power Research Institute and the National Science Foundation (SES8908269).

customer's net benefits are improved by the opportunity to select from an expanded menu of service options.[1]

Efficiency gains from differentiation have long been of major importance in the regulated industries. For technical and historical reasons, regulated firms initially offered undifferentiated services of essentially uniform quality. Regulatory policies encouraged firms to emphasize supply-side economies of scale. Pricing was based mainly on cost recovery to exclude monopoly profits. This approach contributed to efficiency for the products actually offered but it ignored the additional efficiency gains obtainable from differentiation that adapts product designs to various market segments. Imperfect regulation, such as allowing rates of return to exceed the cost of capital, encouraged firms to emphasize capital investments and thereby indirectly to maximize quality attributes relying on capital-intensive technologies.

These regulatory policies were reversed during the past fifteen years, resulting in substantially altered incentives for firms in these industries. In part these changes are reflected in lower allowed rates of return on capital, and in part they are reflected in an overall relaxation of regulatory supervision and a general presumption in favor of deregulation wherever possible. In addition, in the power industry, environmental concerns and measures to economize on fuels have focused attention on the inefficiency of serving all customers in peak periods with fuel-intensive peaking generators and at prices below actual marginal cost.

These changes have produced a considerable emphasis on product differentiation generally, and unbundling of qualities especially. In the newly deregulated industries such as transportation, mail service, and telecommunications, this process has been accelerated by competitive pressures. Major gains have been obtained from differentiation of peak and offpeak services in these industries, and quality spectra have been introduced along several other dimensions. Airline service, for example, is

---

1 Chao and Wilson (1989).

differentiated according to time of advance purchase, duration of the trip, refundability of tickets, and frequency and annual mileage of travel, and class of service; mail service is differentiated according to speed of delivery and size or weight of the package; and telephone service is differentiated according to several measures of volume of traffic and switching services. Some of these innovations are motivated or accompanied by profitable price discrimination, but others reflect genuine efficiency-enhancing product differentiation.

In the electric power industry, unbundling has included differentiation between peak and offpeak periods, interruptible and curtailable service, variable or intermittent service such as cycling of appliances and standby and backup service, and increasing use of approximations to contingent spot pricing, such as real-time pricing. Each of these involves some degree of unbundling of the previously prevailing industry standard regarding uniform service availability at a uniform price, although in each case there are also other dimensions of quality that are relevant too.

In the following presentation, most of the discussion focuses on differentiation of service availability. Unbundling this quality dimension is especially important for the power industry. Partly this is because of the generation technology and the cyclic and stochastic features of aggregate demand. And partly this is because of the diversity among customers regarding the value they place on assured availability.

Power generation is capital and fuel intensive, so it is efficient to install peaking generators with lower capital costs and higher fuel costs to meet daily and seasonal peak loads that occur cyclically and stochastically. Nevertheless, for purposes of maintaining reserve capacity the cost of a peaking generator can exceed the cost of providing compensation to customers willing to forego service in times of extreme peak loads or equipment failures: in effect, a reservoir of customers accepting interruptible or curtailable service is a substitute for a reserve peaking generator.

More generally, the diversity of preferences among customers offers opportunities for the utility to improve all customers' net benefit from service. The explanation of how this can be done by differentiation of service priorities is our main topic below. A graphic presentation of the main ideas is provided in the Appendix.

Customers differ in two main ways. First, different customers have different demand functions indicating their maximum willingness to pay for successive units of power, depending on the time and circumstances. Second, for each customer, successive units of power are valued differently: typically a customer has a relatively high-value base load, perhaps a shoulder load, and then several optional loads that can be curtailed inexpensively. These successive load increments reflect enduses ordered in terms of their service values and costs of interruption. This is not the entire story, of course, since a customer's demand differs depending on whether it is viewed in the short-run or the long-run, where the latter includes the effects of optimal investments in appliances and processes. A customer may also incur fixed costs of interrupting and restarting a production process, whereas other activities (such as heating and cooling) can be interrupted briefly at little cost, as in the case of cycling.

The effect of these differences among customers and among enduses can be seen most clearly by considering an ideal system of contingent spot pricing in which a market-clearing price prevails at each time and circumstance. With such a system, each customer sets for each enduse a maximum price above which that activity will be shut down; this price may also depend on a price forecast if a fixed cost of shutting down and restarting is incurred. In practice, spot pricing has not been implementable in such a pure form, except for economy trades of bulk power at the wholesale level among utilities in power pools. One reason is the cost of continual monitoring of the spot price that is imposed on customers; another is the difficulty of organizing a market whereby customers can bid for service when supplies are scarce.

This is not a limitation, however, to the extent that customers' demands are fairly stable over time and among varying circumstances. That is, customers could pre-arrange via their service contracts as to the maximum prices they are willing to pay for their various enduses; these prices could be further conditioned on observable environmental factors such as the ambient temperature in the case of heating and cooling. Such a scheme involves longer-term contracts in which customers' power supplies are subject to the prevailing spot price estimated by the utility; moreover, each customer is charged the actual or expected spot price for the service provided. The optimal duration of such a contract depends on the stability (as measured by the serial correlation) of the customer's demand over time and the transaction cost involved in recontracting; if the serial correlation is high and the transaction cost is low then a relatively long contract minimizes the overall cost of transactions plus the expected losses from misallocation of power supplies due to changes in customers' preferences.[2]

Even this form of implementation is unnecessarily complicated in practice, and consequently a simpler version can be used that is based on differentiation of service priorities. The basic requirement for optimal allocation of scarce power supplies is that the highest value enduses should be the ones served from the supplies available. Thus, any allocation scheme is essentially a rationing rule in which each customer, enduse, or power unit is assigned a priority of service. They are then served in each contingency in order of their priorities until the available supply (or demand) is exhausted.

Practical implementations of such priority service use only a few priority classes. One reason for this is a general theorem that predicts that the loss from using only n priority classes, instead of many, is inversely related to the square of n.[3] This means that typically as few as four or five priority classes suffice to capture most, say more than 90 percent, of the potential gains from finer differentiation. Another reason, of course, is that it makes

---

[2] Chao and Wilson (1990).

[3] Chao and Wilson (1989).

dispatching simpler. Thus, the basic task confronting a customer is to assign each of his enduses to one of several priority classes, taking account of the differing prices and predicted power availabilities associated with the various priorities.

The utilities that have implemented various forms of priority service have adopted a variety of amendments to this basic scheme. First, customers prefer that other provisions be specified to pin down more exactly the charges and costs they are liable to incur, such as the warning time before a curtailment, the maximum number, magnitude, and duration of curtailments, and the penalty or buy-through price (perhaps specified merely as the contingent spot or real-time price) payable for noncompliance. Second, in some cases it suffices that the curtailment be determined by exogenous factors (such as temperature in the case of heating and cooling, especially in the case of cycled appliances).[4] In the others, it has been preferable to use a strict rationing rule, such as equi-proportional curtailment of customers.[5] One can also envision two priorities for each customer or enduse, one that affects curtailment and another that applies to the order in which service is resumed after a curtailment.

As mentioned above, the basic rule for pricing priority-differentiated services is that the price for each service option should be the same as the actual or expected contingent spot price for comparable service, were a spot price system used.[6] There is an alternative method, however, that is also useful. For simplicity, consider first the case that the utility offers a full range of options that allow each kilo-Watt to be assigned any service reliability r at a price $P(r)$. Suppose further that there is a fixed aggregate demand function $D(p)$ depending on the spot price p, whereas aggregate supply is stochastic and described by a function $F(s)$ indicating the probability that the supply exceeds s. In this case the marginal price $p(r)=P'(r)$ charged for the rth increment in reliability satisfies the

---

[4] Woo (1990a).

[5] Spulber (1990ab), Woo (1990b).

[6] Wilson (1989a). This same rule can also be used to price other services, such as standby and backup service, as well as long-term supply contracts.

equation $F(D(p(r)))=r$. To see why this is so, observe that (a) a kilo-Watt with service value v should be assigned the reliability r for which the net value $vr-P(r)$ is maximized, and therefore $v-p(r) = 0$; and (b) there are $D(v)$ units of demand with higher service values that are assigned higher reliabilities than r, and these must all be served with higher priority: consequently, consistency requires that supply exceeds $D(v)$ with probability r, which is what the equation states. More generally, if both demand and the supply S are stochastic then efficient rationing requires that $\text{Prob}\{S > D(p(r))\} = r$.[7]

Setting prices for several priority classes is somewhat more complicated, but the basic principle remains true that the marginal price of upgrading to the next higher priority should satisfy a similar relation. In each case, these formulas are equivalent to the general rule of charging the expected spot price for comparable service. As mentioned previously, however, practical implementations include several other provisions, such as warning times and limits on curtailments, and these must also be assigned charges that reflect the expected cost to the utility (and to lower priority customers who are disadvantaged by these limits accorded to this customer). Further, to meet revenue requirements the utility will usually need to employ some form of Ramsey pricing to fully recover its fixed costs of investments and operations. It can be shown that the efficient form of such a pricing rule is based on block-declining prices that offer quantity discounts in rough proportion to customers' demands.[8]

As with spot prices, the prices for service priorities can be used to construct criteria for capacity expansion. For example, in the extreme case that an increment to reserve capacity reduces the chance of curtailment only for the highest priority customers, customers' valuation of this increment is revealed by the price they are willing to pay for the highest service priority. More generally, priority service provides a wealth of new data that benefits long-range planning, particularly as regards customers'

---

[7] Chao (1990).

[8] Wilson (1989b, 1991).

willingness to pay for increments to the reserve margin that improve system capacity and reliability.

Priority service provides improved net benefits for all customers–lower bills for customers with low service values who welcome cheaper rates in exchange for greater risks of curtailment, and better assurance of interrupted power supplies for customers with high service values or fixed costs of interruption, who see the higher prices they pay as well worth the greater service reliability. These benefits are admittedly small for a utility with ample or excess capacity, but in an era when many utilities operate with slim reserve margins the gains can be large. Moreover, to the extent that regulatory agencies do not provide rates of return that fully recover the cost of capital, there are direct advantages to using a reservoir of curtailable demand as a substitute for peaking generators. Similarly, for a utility that occasionally buys from its regional power pool at prevailing wholesale spot prices, it may be cheaper to replace such purchases with curtailments.

Priority service can be construed as a first, partial step towards the ideal of fully differentiated contingent spot pricing. Indeed, taking account of transaction costs and the serial correlation of customers' demands, it may be as far as is practical and cost-effective for all but the largest industrial customers. It is more difficult to arrange dispatching for smaller commercial and residential customers, and in any case the gains are predictably less and perhaps less than the cost.

The long-term prospects for deregulation of power markets indicate that generation may become a substantially competitive market.[9] To the extent that occurs, competitive pressures will encourage firms to offer a greater array of differentiated options for major customers, as has occurred in the other deregulated industries. Service availability is a prime candidate for unbundling to accomplish this differentiation. Short-term economy trades will continue to be priced in a wholesale spot market, but for longer-term

---

[9] Joskow and Schmalansee (1984).

supply contracts it seems likely that some form of priority service or one of its many variants will become increasingly common. Cogenerators and customers relying on independent power producers already purchase standby and backup service under contracts with these features.

BIBLIOGRAPHY

Bohn, Roger, Michael Caramanis, and Fred Schweppe. "Optimal Pricing in Electrical Networks over Space and Time", *Rand Journal of Economics.* 15: 360-376, 1984.

Chao, Hung-po. "Priority Service and Optimal Rationing with Uncertainty", Electrical Power Research Institute, 1990.

Chao, Hung-po, Shmuel Oren, Stephen Smith, and Robert Wilson. "Priority Service: Unbundling the Quality Attributes of Electric Power", Report EA-4851, Palo Alto CA: Electric Power Research Institute, 1986.

Chao, Hung-po, Shmuel Oren, Stephen Smith, and Robert Wilson. "Selected Papers on Priority Service Methods", Report P-5350. Palo Alto CA: Electric Power Research Institute, 1987.

Chao, Hung-po, Shmuel Oren, Stephen Smith, and Robert Wilson. "Service Design in the Electric Power Industry", Report P-6543. Palo Alto CA: Electric Power Research Institute, 1990.

Chao, Hung-po, and Robert Wilson. "Priority Service: Pricing, Investment, and Market Organization", *American Economic Review*, 77: 899-916, 1989.

Chao, Hung-po, and Robert Wilson. "Optimal Contract Period for Priority Service", *Operations Research*, 37: 598-606, 1990.

Joskow, Paul, and Richard Schmalansee. *Markets for Power.* Cambridge MA: MIT Press, 1984.

Marchand, M. "Pricing Power Supplied on an Interruptible Basis", *European Economic Review*, 5: 263-274, 1974.

Spulber, Daniel. "Optimal Nonlinear Pricing and Contingent Contracts", University of Southern California, 1990a.

Spulber, Daniel. "Capacity-Contingent Nonlinear Pricing by Regulated Firms", University of Southern California, 1990b.

Tschirhart, J., and F. Jen. "Behavior of a Monopoly Offering Interruptible Service", *Bell Journal of Economics,* 10: 244-258, 1979.

Viswanathan, N., and Edison Tse. "Monopolistic Provision of Congested Service with Incentive-Based Allocation of Priorities'", *International Economic Review,* 30: 153-174, 1989.

Wilson, Robert. "Efficient and Competitive Rationing", *Econometrica,* 57: 1-40, 1989a.

Wilson, Robert. "Ramsey Pricing of Priority Service", *Journal of Regulatory Economics,* 1: 189-202, 1989b.

Wilson, Robert. *Nonlinear Pricing, Chapter 10.* New York: Oxford University Press, 1992.

Woo, Chi-Keung. "Efficient Electricity Pricing with Self-Rationing", *Journal of Regulatory Economics,* 2: 69-81, 1990a.

Woo, Chi-Keung. "Capacity Rationing and Fixed Cost Collection". Sausalito CA: Analysis Group, 1990b.

APPENDIX

GRAPHICAL PRESENTATION OF THE MAIN IDEAS REGARDING PRIORITY SERVICE

Figure 1. This figure illustrates that a typical customer prefers curtailments to complete interruptions. In the figure, the customer has a linear demand function and can choose between a two-thirds probability of curtailing half his load and a one-third probability of interrupting his entire load. Because curtailment affects only his lower value enduses, he prefers the curtailment option. The gain and loss from curtailment as versus interruption are shown in the figure relative to the line representing the

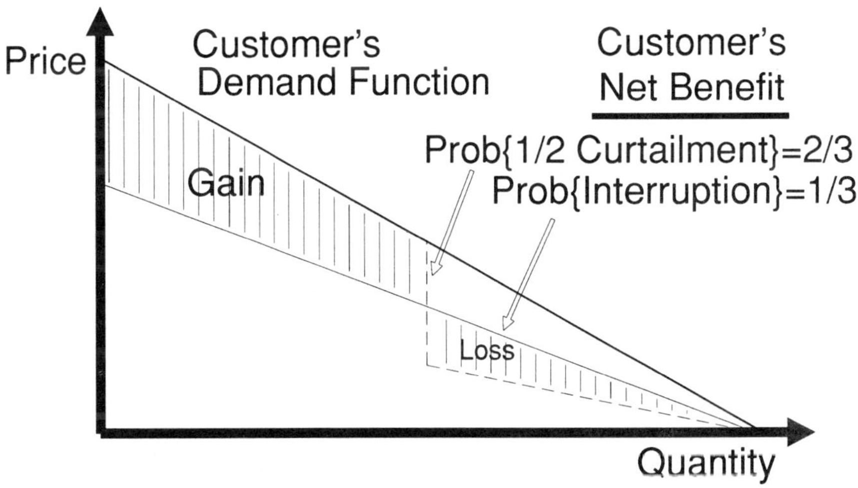

Figure 1. Customers Prefer Curtailments to Interruptions

average value of enduses obtained from the interruption option: the gain exceeds the loss because curtailment affects only the lower-value enduses.

Figure 2. This figure illustrates that for each particular enduse a customer prefers higher service reliability, even at a somewhat higher price, if the value of serving that enduse is higher. For example, the high reliability option provides the maximum net benefit when the service value is high. The three slanted lines indicate the net value as a function of the enduse's service value, for each of three service options (low, regular, and high reliability). High reliability is presumed to cost more but the slope of the line is steeper due to the lower frequency of service curtailments.

This figure also illustrates the advantage of unbundling service reliabilities. If the customer has several enduses with different service values, then he prefers to select different service options for each one.

Figure 3. This figure illustrates how the utility can price unbundled service reliabilities. When the service qualities are bundled, the uniform price p provides a single service reliability r for all customers and all enduses; that is, supply exceeds demand a fraction r of the time. By offering three reliabilities at different prices, so that the average reliability is still r, the utility can provide a menu of service options to customers. Some enduses obtain the high reliability r_1 at the high price p_1, provided others accept the low reliability r_3 at the low price p_3.

Figure 4. This figure is like Figure 3 except that it points out that an efficient menu of service reliabilities and associated prices should have the property that the marginal charge for higher reliability should be the same as the expected marginal price of service.

Figure 5. This figure shows how the marginal price $P'(r)$ of a marginal increment in service reliability is calculated from the utility's aggregate demand function and from its probability distribution of supply, in the special case that demand is not stochastic. This price is set so that the demand at this price is less than supply with probability r. Also shown is

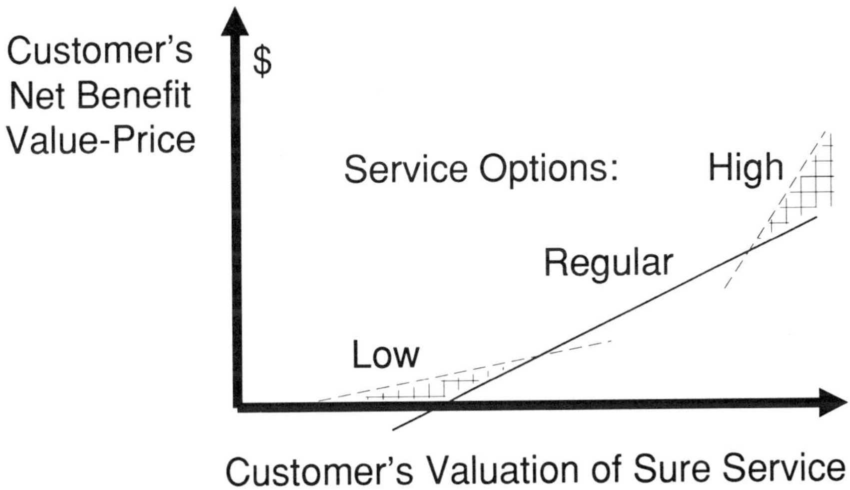

Figure 2. Unbundling Service Reliability An Individual Customer's Gain

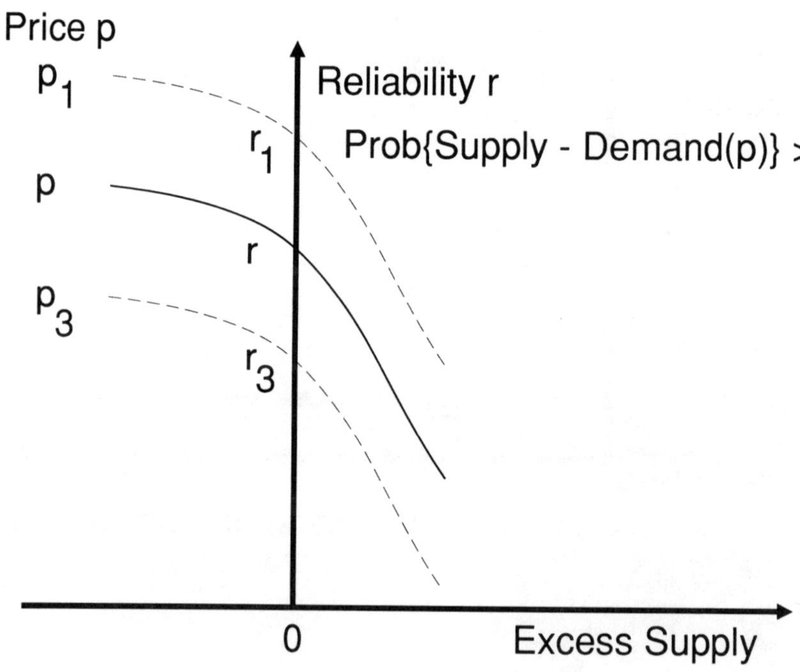

Figure 3. Illustration of Unbundling of Reliability

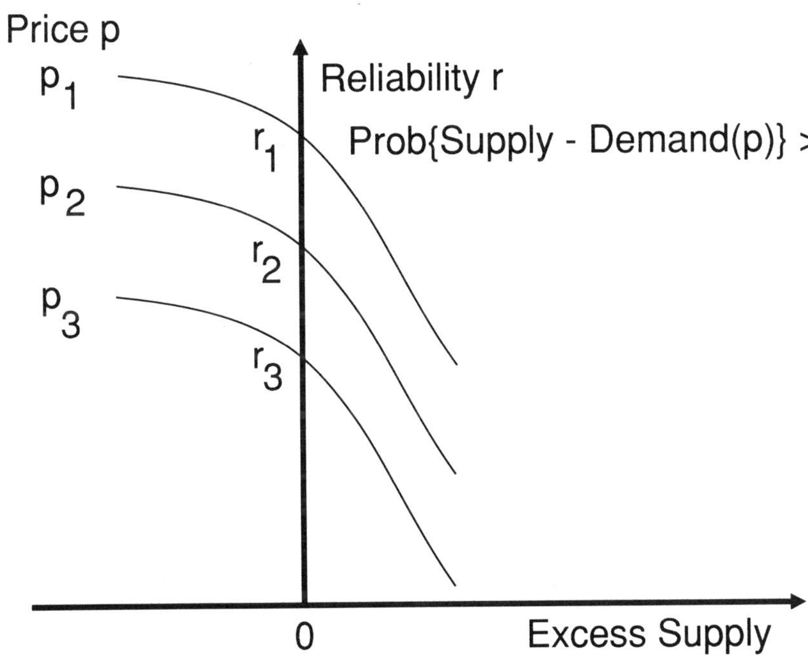

Figure 4. Example: Marginal Charge For Reliability at r_2 is $P'(r_2) = p_2$

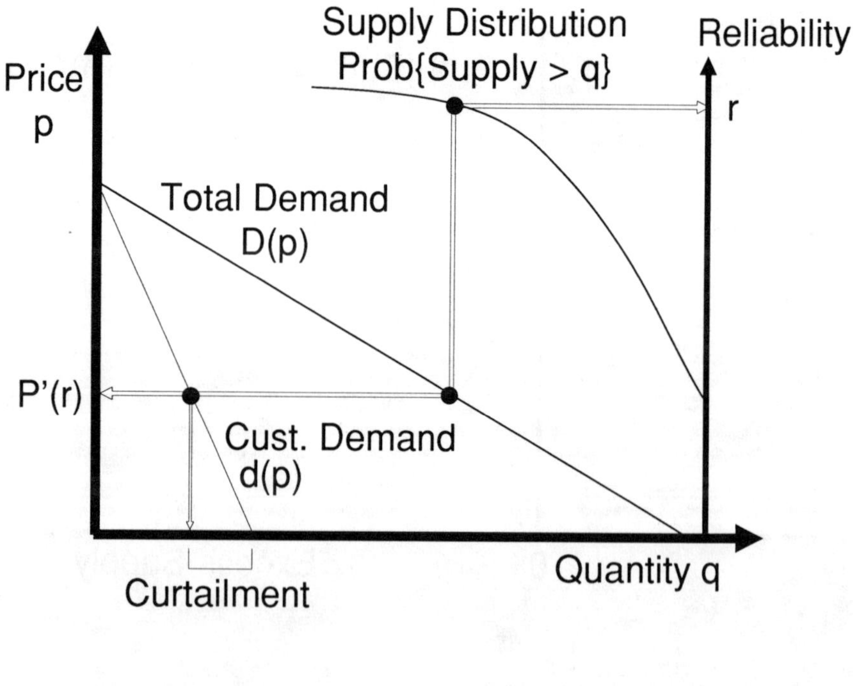

Figure 5. Calculation of Marginal Price of Reliability

how this determines the magnitude of an individual customer's load curtailment when the actual supply is the quantity $q=D(p)$: the customer is curtailed to the load $d(P'(r))$, where $d(p)$ is his demand function, $p = P'(r)$, and r is the original forecasted probability with which the aggregate supply q can be provided.

Figure 6. This figure interprets the charge for a given service priority as the expectation of the spot price that would be paid for the same conditions of service delivery. Each enduse has an associated service value interpreted as the maximum (or 'reservation') spot price at which the customer would purchase service for that enduse. When the spot price is higher than this reservation price, he would forego service. Priority service allocates available supply to meet the same service conditions, so the charge for the priority that provides service in the shaded area is the same as the expectation of the spot price averaged over this area.

Figure 7. This figure shows a more elaborate representation of the calculation of the marginal charge for each of three reliabilities r_1, r_2, and r_3 at corresponding prices. The calculation is represented in terms of the probability distribution of net supplies, and the induced probability distribution of the spot price that this implies. The condition that characterizes an optimal pricing scheme is that each service reliability r_i is the probability that the spot price is less than the cutoff spot price p_i associated with that reliability; in turn, this is the probability that supply exceeds demand at this spot price.

Figure 8. This figure illustrates that the net effect of priority service is to charge each customer for the lost service values imposed on other customers by serving this customer–and in turn these other customers recoup their losses via the lower charges they pay for their lower priorities. In the figure, a (high) priority 1 customer pays the expected spot price for his service conditions; consequently, in each event in which he is served (i.e., when the spot price is less than p_1) he is paying the increment in the spot price at p_2 that represents the service value of a curtailed enduse for a

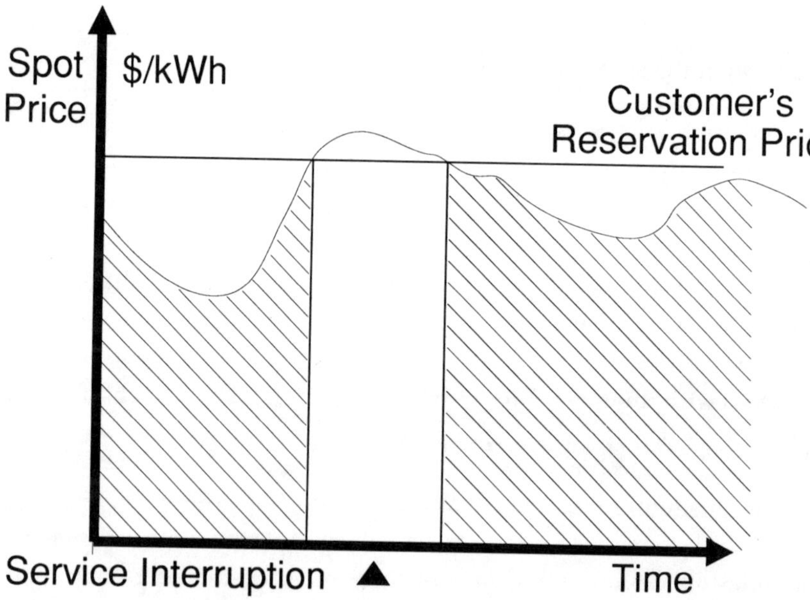

Figure 6. Priority Charge = Expected Spot Price for Same Service Conditions

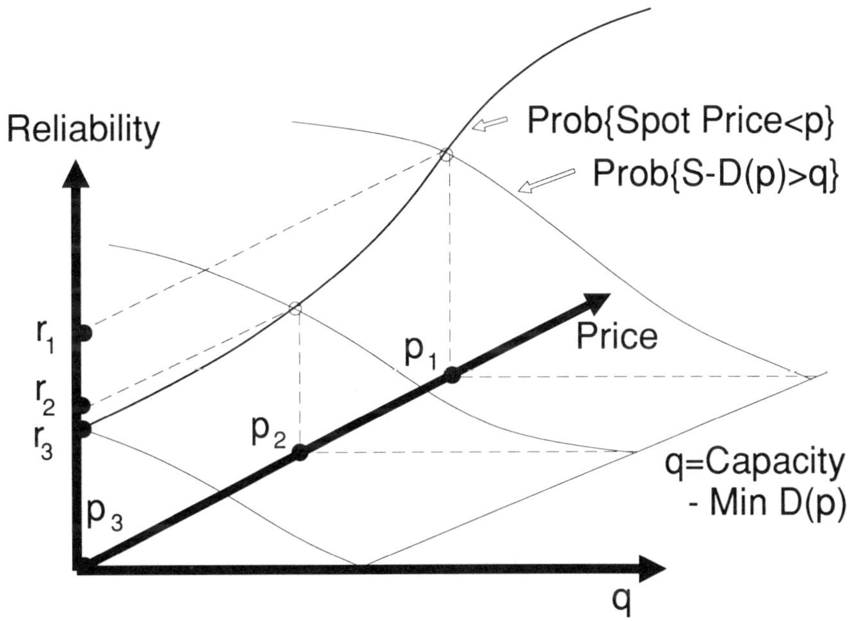

Figure 7. Calculation of Marginal Charge for Reliability

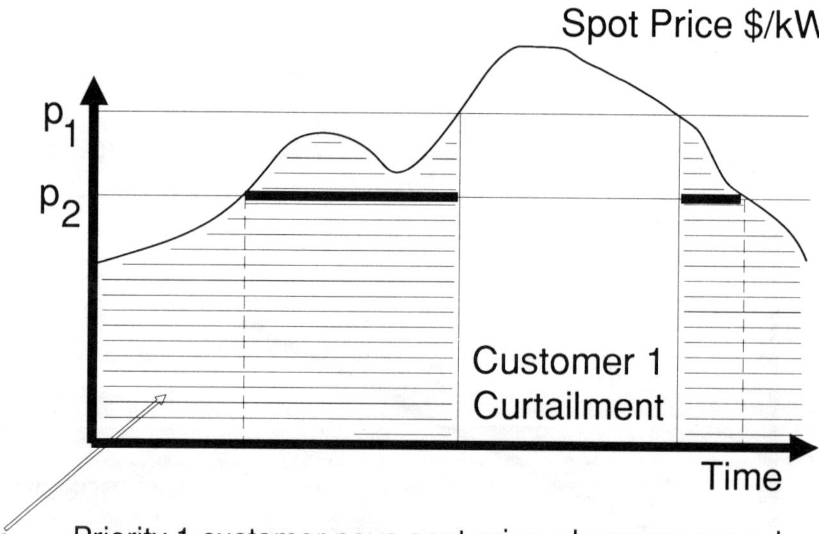

- Priority 1 customer pays spot price whenever served <==> Pays reservation price of Priority 2 customer whenever customer 2 is not served.

Figure 8. Priority Charge Compensates Lower Priority Customers

customer selecting (lower) priority 2 for which the cutoff spot price is $p_2 < p_1$.

Figure 9. This figure shows that the net gain from priority service is positive for every enduse, as compared to random rationing of scarce supplies, provided the utility's net revenue remains unchanged. A low valuation enduse benefits because the lower price more than compensates for more frequent curtailments, and a high valuation enduse benefits because the reduced frequency of enduses more than compensates for the higher price. Enduses with valuations in the middle also gain because the greater efficiency with which supplies are rationed provides a 'dividend' from the utility that enables the price paid for the old unbundled service reliability to be reduced.

Figure 10. This figure re-interprets Figure 9 in terms of the utility's aggregate demand curve. With random rationing of supplies, the linear demand curve $D(p)$ yields the total surplus that is the area between marginal cost and the line representing the expectation of the realized demand values, say $rD(p)$ where r is the average service reliability with random rationing. In contrast, priority service enables enduses with high service values to be served with high reliability and those with low service values to be served with low reliability, as indicated by the curve that indicates the expected surplus obtained for each unit of demand. The net gain from using priority service is positive because the area representing the 'gain' exceeds the area representing the 'loss' compared to random rationing, due to the fact that more frequent curtailments are imposed on the enduses with the smallest service values.

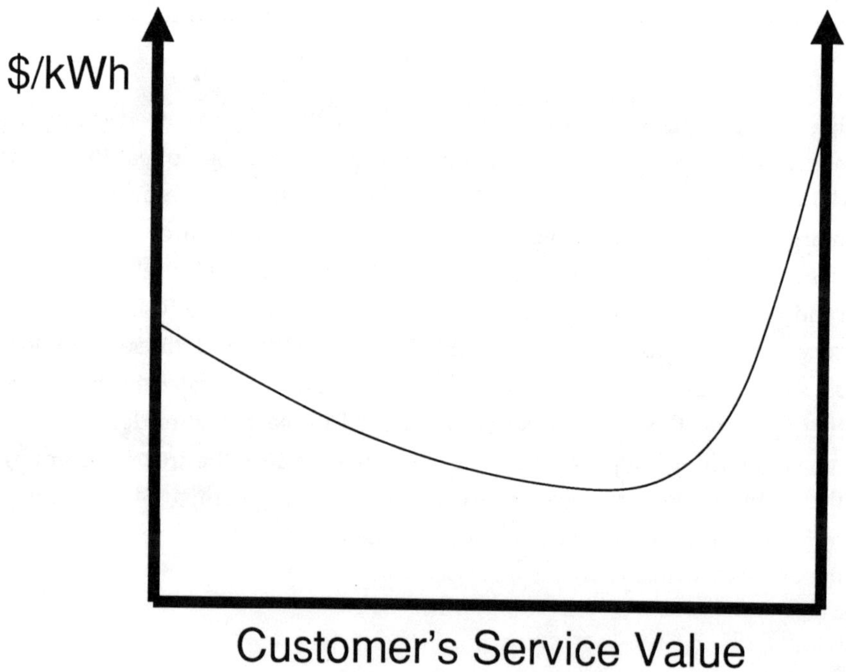

Figure 9. Net Gain from Priority Service Compared to Random Rationing if Firm's Revenue Unchanged

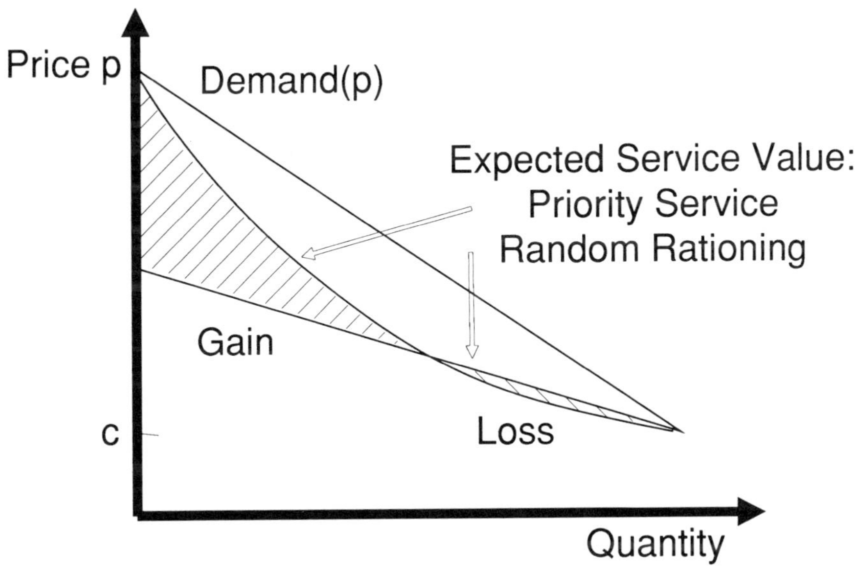

Figure 10. Net Gain from Priority Service

REAL TIME PRICING: BRINGING ADDED VALUE TO UTILITY PROGRAMS

by

Bahman Daryanian, Richard D. Tabors, and Roger E. Bohn
Tabors Caramanis & Associates

INTRODUCTION

Real Time Pricing (RTP) brings information concerning the time-varying costs of electricity generation, transmission, and distribution to the consumer. There are, at the present time, a number of experimental rates and implemented RTP rates in the United States and elsewhere. The paper which follows presents the results of an experiment[1] designed to test the economic advantage of RTP used to schedule Electric Thermal Storage (ETS) systems in the NYSEG service territory during the winter of 1989-90. A complementary experiment is being conducted with ETS (cool storage) on the Consolidated Edison of New York system with actual RTP based control during 1992.[2] These experiments represent the first full test of all but the

---

[1] The experiment and its results has also been reported in: "An Experiment in Real Time Pricing for Control of Electric Thermal Storage Systems". *IEEE Transactions on Power Systems*, vol. 6, no. 4, pp. 1356-1365, November 1991.

[2] For additional information on this experiment, see: Tabors Caramanis & Associates, "Real Time Pricing of Commercial Cool Storage: Interim Report", November 16, 1990.

billing component of RTP. While others have provided RTP information, none have developed, implemented, and evaluated RTP based customer response algorithms.

OVERVIEW

The objectives of the first phase of the real time pricing (RTP) experiment carried out by Tabors Caramanis & Associates (TCA) in the winter of 1989-90 and 1990-1991 in the New York State Electric and Gas (NYSEG) service territory were to:

1. Develop experimental rates based on the hourly generating costs or opportunity costs of generation of NYSEG;

2. Develop the mathematical response algorithms for use in RTP control of scheduling the charging of electric thermal storage (ETS) systems in selected commercial buildings in the NYSEG service territory; and

3. Implement a fully automated hardware and software system for:

    - communicating hourly prices from NYSEG, weather data from the National Weather Service, and building energy use data from the sites, to the TCA's computer control system located in Cambridge, MA,

    - applying the control algorithms for the control of ETS in the individual buildings,

    - sending charging schedules to on-site controllers in the buildings themselves, and

    - calculating utility costs for an ETS under time-of-use (TOU) based control, RTP based control, and for a similar building without ETS.

This paper reports on the experiment which was carried out at three commercial sites in the NYSEG service territory.

- Brewster 1: The one story office component of a commercial Service Center. The system contains a 12,614 gallon Megatherm pressurized water tank whose charging was controlled by a dedicated logical controller programmed to operate against TOU rates.

- Brewster 2: A single floor store front in a shopping mall. The system contains a 400 gallon unpressurized Hydrokinetix storage system controlled by its own simple outdoor reset plus time clock. The logic operated against TOU rates.

- Plattsburgh: The office portion of a small manufacturing facility. The system utilizes earth storage by heating a bed of sand and allowing natural convection to bring the thermal energy to the surface of the concrete slab floor. The existing system charged only based on time and surface temperature.

Table 1 presents a summary of the sites and Figure 1 presents the overall system architecture of the RTP based control system. Each site was monitored for indoor and outdoor temperature and for status of the heat storage system. In the Brewster 1 site, extensive monitoring was already underway. The data were captured and transmitted to the control computer system in Cambridge. At both Brewster 2 and Plattsburgh, an integrated data logger and controller were installed,

The control computer system in Cambridge integrated data automatically. This included maintaining the pricing information, contacting the weather service for forecasts of next day conditions, and contacting the individual sites for current temperature and storage system status. The scheduling algorithms were run in Cambridge and the calculated charging schedules were downloaded to the individual sites.

The integrated system was developed to be fully automated. The differences between thc experimental system and a fully implemented system lie in two areas:

- In the experimental system NYSEG cost data was generated in the control room in real time but was delayed in transmission by 24 hours. The prices used in the experiment were stored and then retrieved out of phase by one week. Actual operation of the experiment was carried out *as though* the data were being received in real time.

- In a fully implemented system the data gathering function, the calculation of schedule, and the control of the building storage system charging would be on-site rather than split between the site and a central control computer as was the case in this experiment.

Table 1

SUMMARY OF SITES

Specification	Brewster Office Bldg.	Brewster Store Front	Plattsburgh Office
Size	27,000 sq. ft.	1,100 sq. ft.	4,000 sq. ft.
Activities	Office; repairs	Retail store	Office
Storage type	Pressurized water	Unpress. water	Earth storage
Storage size	12,500 gallons	400 gallons	
Approx. capacity of storage	10,000,000 Btu 2,900 kWh	300,000 Btu 88 kWh	Undefined
Energy mgmt syst (pre RTP)	Andover controls	Simple thermostat	None used
Storage control logic (pre RTP)	Outdoor reset + timer	Outdoor + timer	Timer only
Heat used Jan to March	112,000 kWh	8,700 kWh	14,900 kWh (+12,000 kWh baseboard)

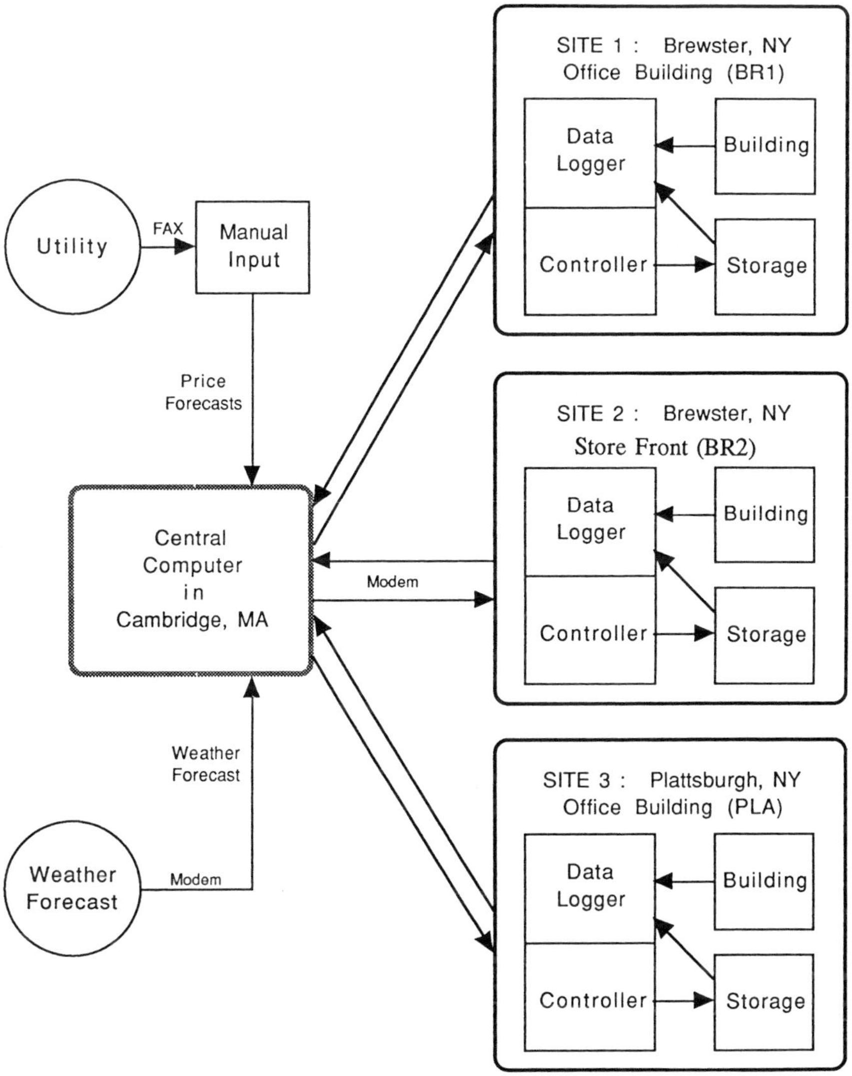

Figure 1. Overall System Architecture of the RTP Control System

SETTING OF REAL TIME PRICE

Implementation of RTP

In the development of a real time price based rate there are a number of design parameters which influence the rate structure. Two critical considerations are period definition and update cycle length. Period definition refers to the length of time for which a given RTP holds. Update cycle length is the amount of time between successive price calculations. Within each update cycle the prices may change, hourly, for instance, but the prices have been fixed ahead. The closer and/or shorter the update cycle and the more periods within each cycle, the closer the real time prices can match the utility's marginal costs. On the other hand, customer ability to respond and the costs of metering may depend on the period definition and updated cycle as well. A common pairing of update and cycle is the 24 hour update in which hourly prices are set a day ahead. In this experiment the period and update cycle were both one hour. This is the finest level of detail for which utility cost data were available and since customer response and communications were fully automated, use of an hourly RTP had little additional transaction cost.

The choice of period and update cycle are a function of conditions at both the utility and the customer. Experience in this experiment indicated clearly that significant advantage was gained by moving to hourly updates as, with significant inter-utility and inter-pool sales, the day ahead forecast proved to be quite different on an hour by hour basis from the actual utility opportunity costs as described below. In addition, with automated response logic, joint utility customer value is maximized by moving to shorter update cycles. There is little reason to "protect" customers from changing prices when the benefits of response are greatest here and when the technology (hardware and algorithms) of response is available.

Given the above discussion, we developed an RTP rate with an hourly update cycle.

The ideal real time price is:[3]

RTP at time t	=	marginal generation fuel cost at time t
	+	marginal generation and network maintenance cost
	+	marginal cost of network losses at time t
	+	generation and network quality of supply cost at time t

The first three components, fuel costs, maintenance costs, and losses costs, are relatively straightforward. The quality of supply can be thought of as that price increase needed to maintain the balance of supply and demand at the time of shortage. In practice the quality of supply for generation is estimated as a capacity cost, a gas turbine for instance, distributed across only those hours in which there is a probability of loss of load. The quality of supply for the transmission and distribution (network) system is directly analogous. There is usually an additional component of the real time price that makes it non-ideal but is necessary because of the current embedded-cost based regulatory system. This component is designed to account for differences in revenue recovered between an RTP rate and an embedded cost rate.

Our objective was to design an experimental RTP rate such that the following four conditions were met:

---

[3] For a complete discussion of the theory of Real Time Pricing or Spot Pricing, see: Fred C. Schweppe, Michael C. Caramanis, Richard D. Tabors, and Roger E. Bohn, *Spot Pricing of Electricity*, Kluwer Academic Press, Boston, 1988.

There has yet to be a clean definition/differentiation between RTP and Spot Pricing. In the reference above we make the distinction that a Spot Price is a marginal cost based rate that varies in real time and is, therefore, a special case of RTP. This name arises because of the similarity between this and Spot Markets in other commodities. A number of rates called "real time rates" currently in place contain these same characteristics and thus any distinction has, in use, disappeared.

1. The RTPs elicit the same customer behavior as pure marginal cost rates.

2. The rate design is acceptable to the regulators as well as simple and easy to implement and explain to the participating customers.

3. Customer specific revenue neutrality exists if the customer does not respond to RTP, i.e., does not change his/her consumption patterns from what it was under TOU rates.

4. If the customer responds to RTPs, his/her bill will change by an amount that does not exceed the savings (positive or negative) to NYSEG from his/her behavior under RTPs vis a vis TOU rates.

The final RTP rate design consists of hourly MARGINAL COSTS adjusted by the marginal cost of line losses plus a constant REVENUE RECONCILIATION adder. Specifically:

$$RTP(t) = MC(t)_{adj} + [TOU - AMC]$$

where

$$AMC = \text{Average Marginal Cost}$$

$$MC(t)_{adj} = MC(t) \times [\text{Marginal Losses at Time t}].$$

New York State Electric & Gas (NYSEG) is part of the New York Power Pool (NYPP); the ideal starting point for calculation of an RTP would be the pool system lambda or resource marginal energy costs corrected for area reliability constraints. In the absence of a pool lambda the NYPP based NYSEG lambda is the best available proxy. The three conditions relevant to NYSEG are:

1. NYSEG primarily sells to NYPP during hour t

$$MC(t) = NYSEG_{F\&OM} + (\text{Average NYPP Buyers}_{F\&OM} - NYSEG_{F\&OM})/2$$

2. NYSEG primarily buys from NYPP but is not deficient during hour t

$$MC(t) = NYSEG_{F\&OM} - (NYSG_{F\&OM} - \text{Average NYPP Seller}_{F\&OM})/2$$

3. NYSEG buys from NYPP and is deficient during hour t

$$MC(t) = (\text{Average Marginal NYPP Seller}_{F\&OM} \times 1.1) + 3 \text{ mills/kWh}$$

Marginal losses are estimated as a linear function of NYSEG system load [2 × B × system load] by assuming that total losses are adequately modeled as a quadratic function of load. The value of the coefficient B used is 0.000037 per MW.

Two adjustments were made to these hour-ahead pool prices. First, since all customers were low voltage (660 volts or lower), an hourly adjustment was made for distribution system losses. Following the theory of spot pricing of electricity, this was calculated as a percentage of the high voltage price, rather than an absolute number. The percentage usually varied between 9 and 16 percent, depending on how heavily loaded NYSEG's distribution system was at that time. Second, an approximate adjustment of 10 mills per kWh was made for revenue reconciliation.

Forecast of RTP

Forecasts of RTP are needed for optimizing the charging of the electric thermal storage systems. As described above the RTP was based on a forecast of NYSEG's NYPP lambda. While several different forecasting methods were considered including using a unit commitment model and a historical/statistical model, it was decided that the most accurate forecasts available were those generated by system operators and control room personnel of NYSEG. They were already forecasting prices on a day-ahead basis under contract obligations, using a three or four multi-hour time period. They agreed to provide forecasts of hourly prices on a day-ahead basis for this RTP experiment. Because of other contract obligations, the NYSEG operators were at times forecasting the costs for the next hour, 45 minutes ahead of the hour. This forecast, or quote, is verbal and non-binding and only communicated if the other contracting party requests it. For the experiment, the operators simply recorded this hour-ahead price forecast. An entire day of forecasted hour-ahead prices as well as the actual prices were recorded on a form and faxed to TCA along with the day-ahead price forecast and the day-ahead hourly load forecast sent to NYPP.

It was decided for this experiment not to send the forecasts in real time to Cambridge in order not to overburden the utility's personnel. However, it was determined that in practice this information could be generated and sent to the RTP sites on an hourly basis. Since it could have been technically feasible to transmit the prices in real time, the experiment was conducted as if "day-ahead" forecasts were received the previous day, and "hour-ahead" forecasts were received 45 minutes before the hour, *using the previously week's data as if it had been received in real time.* This was done by hiding the data, in a file, then sending it to the storage control programs one hour at a time.

The use of one week old data for a current day's price determination:

1. Maintained the correct statistical profile of costs;

2. Removed the burden of the hourly data communication responsibility from the operators while allowing them to practice one hour-ahead marginal cost (MC) forecasting;

3. Allowed the team to study the value of information in the various forecasts with respect to each other, the perfect forecast, and various TOU rate structures; and

4. Did not allow the ETS results to show the true interaction between weather (which influences building load) and prices. This was further investigated statistically and using simulation.

RTP and Forecast Results

The actual real-time prices exhibited a great deal of variation throughout the experiment. The highest price recorded during the experiment was 99.4 \$/MWh (1 \$/MWh = 1 mill/kWh), the lowest was 15 \$/MWh. The average price was 33.8 \$/MWh. Although the highest prices occurred during the TOU on-peak period (7 am to 10 pm), low prices (in the range of 25 to 30 \$/MWh) occurred during this period as well. During the TOU off-peak hours (10 pm to 7 am plus Saturday and Sunday), the highest price that occurred was around 75 \$/MWh. Prices on Saturday and Sunday varied almost as much as during the week, with weekend prices often as high as their weekday counterparts. The maximum price increase from one hour to the next was 59.7 \$/MWh and the maximum price decrease from one hour to he next was 49.1 \$/MWh. Evaluation of the price patterns show that prices can vary substantially from hour to hour, day to day, and week to week.

The tremendous short-term variation in prices is due in part to short term purchases/sales within NYPP and between NYSEG or NYPP and its neighboring utilities that take place at this time scale. The sales are hour by hour deals negotiated by utility system operators to meet load at the lowest possible costs. One system will offer to sell another system power at an estimated but non-binding price. The price represents the operator's best guess of the cost of producing electricity by the seller's system. The price that is actually paid is the actual price calculated by the pool at the end of the hour in which the transaction took place. There are other kinds of short-term sales that affect the hourly price, including sales to other pools and wheeling transactions.

Analysis of prices indicates that NYSEG's native load is generally not a good predictor of the real time price. Figure 2 shows that price can vary a great deal given a certain load. For example, the prices at the 1,400 MW load level have a 32 \$/MWh range (low of 25 and high of 67 \$/MWh). The higher loads display higher variations. Note that prices were adjusted to account for losses. This has the effect of increasing prices at every load level with prices associated with higher loads being adjusted upward slightly more.

The monthly price duration curves, as seen in Figure 3, show that even though December had generally higher prices than January, February or March, approximately 50 percent of January prices were higher than December's. Price duration curves, analogous to load duration curves, show how often different prices were achieved. December had higher prices due to the extremely cold weather during the month, 1,206 degree days versus 738 for January and 701 for February. The low prices on the December curve are partly due to the Christmas holiday season.

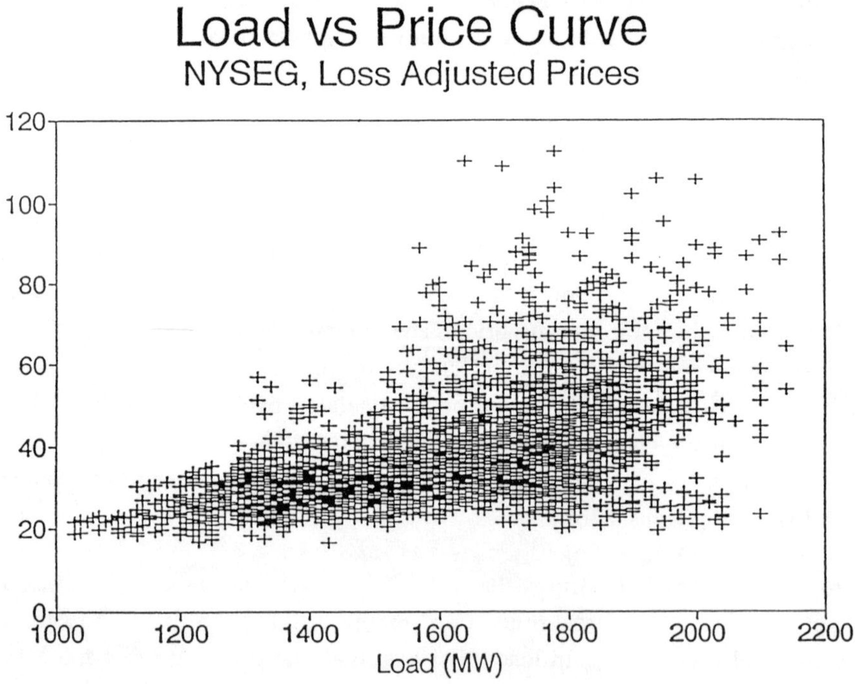

Figure 2. Load Versus Loss Adjusted Prices for NYSEG

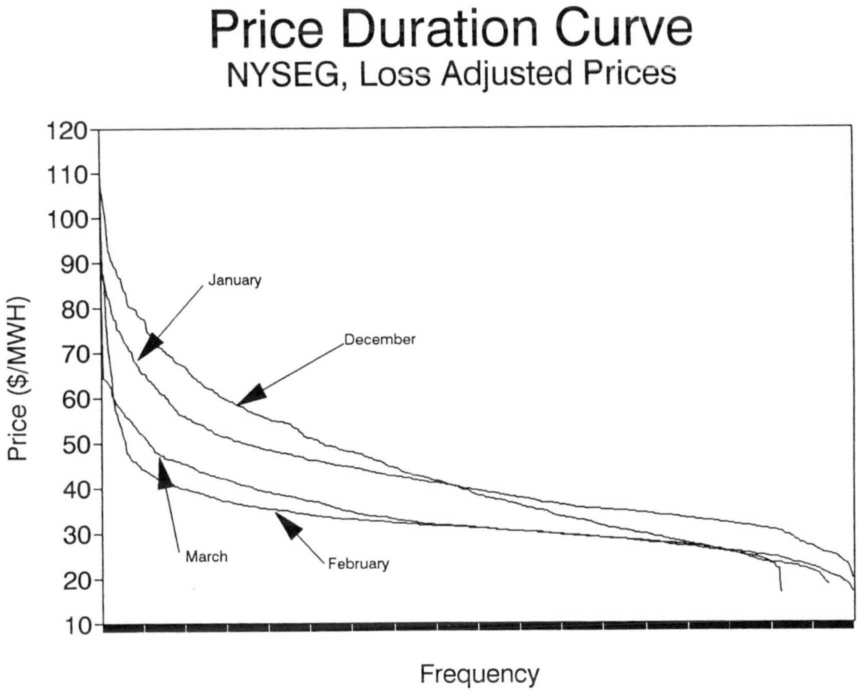

Figure 3. Month Price Duration for NYSEG

In the experiment, the hour-ahead forecasts were the prices used for billing. The rationale for using the hour-ahead forecast is that customers should know the price of electricity when it is being used. This price, however, is only an estimate of the actual cost to the utility. Thus, the more accurate the forecast, the more accurately it reflects the actual cost of producing the electricity, and the scheduling of the storage charging will be more optimal.

The precision of the forecasts varied quite a bit. Figure 4 shows a week of forecast versus actual prices. During days when the actual price changes were small, both the day-ahead and hour-ahead forecasts were close to actual. During days when the price changes were larger, the day-ahead forecasts were generally not very accurate. The hour-ahead forecasts intermittently captured the price variation. For this experiment operators based their forecasts on judgment. Under full implementation of an RTP system, a short term price forecasting model could be developed analogous to a short term load model.

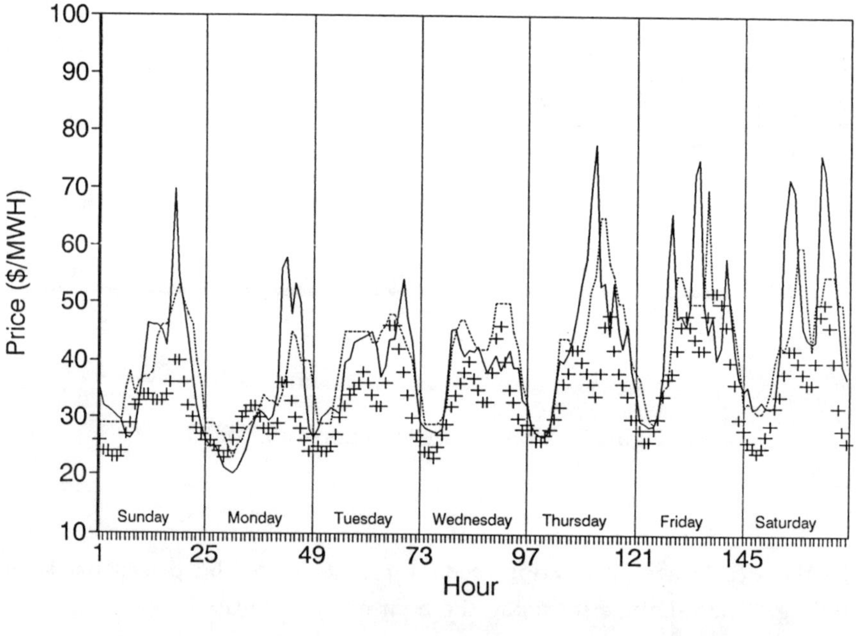

Figure 4. Forecast Precision – Forecasts versus Actual Prices for a Week

CONTROL/RESPONSE

Control System Design

Existing control systems for ETS under TOU rates are based on two simple rules. The first rule is to allow storage charging only during the off-peak periods. This response rule is optimal for the building owner, but not for the utility, since the TOU rate structures do not reflect the true day-to-day and hour-to-hour variations in the cost of electricity. The second rule is to use the current day's outdoor temperature as a predictor of the next day's heating/cooling load. Present "outdoor temperature reset" mechanisms use a linear relationship to adjust the storage limits for nightly charging according to the outdoor temperature; the lower the temperature, the higher the storage limit is set. Since outdoor temperature provides only a crude forecast of tomorrow's load, a more economic utilization of storage requires a more sophisticated load forecasting method.

In order to respond near optimally to RTP, the HVAC control system for a building with thermal storage must have the capability to sense its current status and predict its future heating (or cooling) loads. Based on the future prices, the control system then decides on a least-cost schedule of electricity usage to satisfy its thermal demands. Optimal response requires daily variations in the storage charging periods in order to account for the hourly changes in loads and prices. The utility cannot control the storage of many customers because daily customer requirements vary depending on occupancy, scheduling of holidays, physical performance of the storage system, and other building specific factors, some of which cannot be predetermined.

The RTP based control system design relies on locally distributed intelligence, whereby the utility calculates the real time prices, and makes these available to the customers, whose computers then sense and optimize the response schedule for their individual buildings. All the data gathering and computational capability resides in the building being controlled. However, for reasons of efficiency, the RTP controls for this experiment were implemented on a single PC located in Cambridge, Massachusetts. This made the system operations more flexible in debugging the software and monitoring the sites.

An important feature of the present RTP based control system is that it is designed as a retrofit to the building's existing control systems. Price and weather information are gathered electronically, the building status is sensed, and a near-optimal storage charging schedule for the building is calculated and activated automatically all under computer control. The additional computer technology required for RTP control, beyond the existing building control system, is an IBM-AT class computer, modems for communications, a data logger/controller unit, and a few additional sensors to measure the status and performance of the HVAC system. This system architecture is shown in Figure 1.

The elements of RTP control were in place by late 1989, and all three sites were under RTP control by early January 1990. Before each site was placed under RTP control, information about the site was gathered by the data logger. Next, the site was controlled by the central computer under the same TOU strategy that was previously used at the site. This testing allowed us to understand the dynamics of each site and to check out the field equipment. The sites remained under RTP control, with the control system being continuously improved, through March 30, 1990, when they were returned to TOU control. Data was continuously logged from each site until May 5, 1990. Each day, price information was sent via fax from the NYSEG control room to Cambridge beginning on November 1, 1989, and continuing through March 31, 1990. Weather information was received electronically beginning on December 1, 1989 and continuing throughout the experiment.

Control System Implementation

The hourly least-cost storage charging schedule was downloaded into the controller unit of the hardware at the sites. At specified times in the schedule, the controller reset the storage temperature band limits, and thereby, activated the storage heating elements, controlling the timing and the amount of storage charging. The space conditioning temperature profile and heating demands of the occupants were sensed by the system but were not altered in any way. Each building's conventional HVAC thermostat control system determined independently when to draw heat from the storage system (the case of the earth storage in Plattsburgh is described later) in response to conventional thermostatic control (Brewster store front) or the Andover EMS (Brewster office building). Therefore, the size and the pattern of the actual daily heating load were not altered by the RTP based control system.

Operation of RTP Based Control System

The central computer in Cambridge supervises and automatically implements all the site data retrieval and storage, control computations, and site scheduling. It coordinates placing of calls to the sites, the weather service, and to a price subdirectory/file. The optimization programs, also residing in the central computer, determine the near-optimal storage charging schedules which are uploaded to the sites.

The central computer initiates execution of required programs by means of an automatic event management program, according to a time stamped schedule located in an "action" file. The required files and the timing of their execution are automatically put into the action file at various stages of the daily operations. In a typical data logging and control session, the event manager executes a data retrieval program at a predetermined time. This in turn places a communication call to the specified site and receives a table of half-hourly measured data most recent 48 hours in the case of Brewster office building and 24 hours in the case of Brewster store front and Plattsburgh office building). At each of the sites, the data logger collects the measured data on a continuous basis, does the initial processing (time averaging, integration, etc.), and places them in a half-hourly table. The data logger at Brewster office building keeps the last two weeks of data, but only 24 hours of data are kept for the Brewster store front and Plattsburgh office building.

Immediately after downloading data from each site, the data is reformatted and appended to a data file, that provides a historical performance database for each site. The data are time stamped and are accessible on-line whenever needed. They are used as inputs to the calculations. Based on the schedule of the action file, but independent of the communications with the sites, the central computer executes two programs which retrieve price and outdoor temperature forecasts from a price subdirectory and a weather service company, respectively. The most recent price data that have been received by fax are manually put in the price subdirectory. The price program checks this subdirectory once a day. The weather information is downloaded to the Cambridge central computer twice a day at approximately 7 am and 7 pm. The price and weather programs reformat and time stamp the data and put them in a data file which are accessed whenever the optimization programs are executed.

The event manager next calls the corresponding optimization program which determines a least cost storage charging scheduled. This program accesses the historical data files, price file, and the forecasted site temperature files. The current storage status, which is the initial condition for the control algorithm, is input from the recently appended historical data file. The program also extracts the hourly heating load and site temperature data of the last day; and in conjunction with the predicted future site temperature and predetermined load pattern shapes, computes forecasts of the next two days' hourly heating loads.

The price and building load forecasts are used in a two-stage procedure to calculate a storage charging schedule. The first stage assumes deterministic conditions and produces an optimal schedule for the next 48 hours or more. The second stage considers the uncertainty in future prices and heating loads, and modifies the schedule heuristically.

The charging schedule is actually a schedule of maximum and minimum storage temperature limits, which act as an adjustable hysteresis band. The storage heating elements are activated or deactivated depending on the value of the actual tank temperature relative to the temperature band.

The heating elements are turned on by placing the temperature band above the maximum allowable storage temperature. Conversely, placing the temperature band below the minimum allowable storage temperature turns off the heating elements.

After a charging schedule for storage is determined for the next two or three days, the first 18 hours of the schedule are written to a file and communicated to the site. The on-site controller switches relays on or off according to the residing schedules. These relays in turn control the electrical heating of the storage.

In routine operating mode the central computer in Cambridge calls each site six times a day (every four hours) on a predetermined schedule and retrieves the stored data from each data logger. If no connection is made, the computer immediately tries to call again. After a limited number of tries, the computer terminates the process and tries again at the following hour. The site communications are set up such that only one site is called during a single hour.

Control Algorithms

The control algorithm is composed of two stages. First, using the multi-day price and load forecasts, a deterministic linear program is solved to calculate an optimal schedule, assuming the price forecast and load forecast are completely accurate. The non-simplex algorithm used takes advantage of special features of the problem and is much faster than a standard LP.[4] Second, a heuristic procedure takes into account the uncertainties and inaccuracies of all forecasts and determines, hour by hour, whether charging should be done during that hour. If the forecasts were perfect, then the heuristic simply gives the same results as the deterministic optimization. More often, the procedure reacts to unexpected changes

---

[4] Daryanian, B., Bohn, R.E. and Tabors, R.D., "Optimal Demand-Side Response to Electricity Spot Prices for Storage-Type Customers", *IEEE Transactions on Power Systems*, vol. 4, no. 3, August 1989, pp. 897-903.

(either increases or decreases) in the prices and loads. It calculates a "threshold" price and compares it with the hourly price (hour-ahead forecast) and depending on the actual storage status adjusts the schedule determined in the first stage.

For each optimization run, the deterministic algorithm uses the day-ahead price and load forecasts to solve for a deterministic optimal storage charging schedule. The hour-ahead price forecasts are then used as inputs to the stochastic heuristic, which modifies the storage charging schedule by considering the deviations in prices and storage behavior from their predicted values. The actual hourly marginal cost data are used in the evaluation and cost analysis.

The *deterministic algorithms* were run every four hours for each site. In principle these could be run each time significant new forecast information is available. The algorithms execute in less than a minute on a 12 MHz 80286 machine so that computational time was not a significant issue.

Brewster Office Building and Brewster Store Front: The hourly load forecasts, the day-ahead price forecasts, and the current storage temperature are inputs to the deterministic algorithm. Embedded in the algorithm is a state equation for storage at each site. The state equation relates the energy in the storage at each hour, to the storage energy level and the energy inputs and outputs of the previous hour. The coefficients for the state equation are determined through regression analysis using the accumulated site data. The state equations were updated twice during the lifetime of the experiment.

Although the optimization problem is structured as a linear programming problem, the algorithm uses a fast non-simplex method. The solution of the algorithm is the optimal storage charging schedule for approximately the next 72 hours, given that the input prices and the loads are accurate and will not change. Any savings or costs beyond the 72 hours are ignored. The algorithm computes an initial solution which is based on meeting the heating requirements at each hour by heat generation at the same hour without any storage action. Next the algorithm searches in a structured fashion for the most expensive hour in the time horizon and substitutes that hour's electricity usage by that of a less expensive hour without violating any storage and production constraints. It continues searching for the next most expensive hour and repeats the scheduling until no more savings are possible.

Plattsburgh Office Building. Due to the difficulty of measuring the heat outflow from the earth storage, the deterministic algorithm for Plattsburgh has a different and simpler form. The problem arises from the fact that the earth storage is not enclosed, which results in continuous heat transfers among the ground, the storage, and the building driven by their respective temperatures. Historical data was used to estimate a linear relationship between desired average daily temperature difference between indoor and outdoor, and the number of hours required to activate the heating element or mats under the sand and cement floor. The algorithm employs this relationship to decide the number of hours needed for charging, by using the forecast of the outdoor temperature for the next day. The algorithm then selects the least expensive hours for charging. The control is based on the measured temperature of the bottom floor slab. Similar to the water storage cases, the heating elements are activated by setting the temperature hysteresis band above or below the maximum and the minimum allowable temperatures.

The deterministic algorithm would have sufficed if the day-ahead price forecasts made by the utilities were used as a basis for billing of the customer. However, the billings are based on the hour-ahead price forecasts in order to capture more of the benefits of RTP for the utility. Thus, the second stage of the algorithm, a *stochastic heuristic algorithm,* takes into account the uncertainty of the future prices and the heating loads at the two Brewster sites. The heuristic determines the threshold price below which the deterministic algorithm asks for storage charging. Then comparing the actual hour-ahead price forecast and the actual level of the tank temperature to the threshold price and to the forecasted deterministic tank temperature level, the heuristic determines a new schedule of storage charging hours. If the price communication from the utility is automated and hour-ahead prices are available on time, only the first hour would be implemented, and the entire scheduling computation would be repeated every hour. However, for this experiment it was operationally feasible to consider the hour-ahead prices four hours at a time and repeat the scheduling computation once every four hours for each site.

In the case of Plattsburgh, the stochastic heuristic has a slightly different form. Again, similar to the water storage system, a threshold price is calculated based on the highest price below which the deterministic algorithm allows the charging of the storage. However, instead of using temperature, the earth storage status is measured in terms of the actual number of hours charged compared to what was determined by the deterministic algorithm. Therefore, at each hour, the heuristic compares the hour-ahead price to the threshold price and depending on the actual number of hours already charged decides whether it should charge during the next hour. If the answer is affirmative, the hysteresis band is set above the maximum allowable slab temperature. Because of the very slow dynamics of the earth storage system, and because of the time delay in the transfer of the heat from the heating mat to the slab, heating elements may not be activated for hours.

Load Forecasts

Because the loads were weather sensitive, the basic input to the load forecast was the weather forecast. The weather forecast used was from the Limited-Area Fine Mesh model of the National Weather Service. All of the forecasts were produced through the use of the Model Output Statistics technique and were supplied by Weather Bank, Inc. of Salt Lake City, Utah. The forecasts contain probability of precipitation, thunderstorm probabilities, three-hourly temperatures, three-hourly surface dew points, surface winds, etc. The control algorithm, however, only uses the temperature forecast. The weather information was automatically updated via modem twice a day and contained temperature information for the next 48 hours.

The weather forecast for Albany, NY was used as a proxy for Brewster and Burlington, VT was used for Plattsburgh.

The control algorithm requires an estimate of the hourly heating load for the duration of the time horizon in order to perform the optimization. The forecasting method uses a two step process. First, the next day's total load is estimated based on the next day's forecast of outdoor temperature, previous day's total load, and the day of the week (weekdays and weekends). Second, the forecasted *total* load is distributed into forecasted hourly load according to the percentage of the total load that historically occurs during each hour. The hourly percentages form a normalized daily load pattern.

Since load forecast data are inputs to the deterministic algorithm, it was necessary to extend the load forecast for 24 hours to a total of 72 hours. It was assumed that the outdoor temperature would be repeated for the future days, and consequently, the load forecast was simply assumed to be in effect for another day. A future improvement will consider differentiation of weekdays from weekends.

RESULTS

Introduction

All three sites were under NYSEG's TOU based rates before the inception of the RTP control experiment. Recall that the conventional TOU control system is based on a time clock which enables charging of the storage system during NYSEG's off-peak rate period (between 10 pm and 7 am weekdays and at any time on weekends). Thus, at 10 pm each weeknight the storage heating elements would turn on and begin heating the storage medium (water for the two Brewster sites, and sand for the earth storage site). Heating continues until a target temperature is reached, corresponding to a target energy level. This target is based on the "outdoor temperature reset" formula, in which the contemporaneous outside temperature is used as a proxy for the next day's heating load. Thus, the colder it gets outdoors, the hotter the storage tank is heated. It was found that these systems tended to be very conservative, i.e., the storage systems were heated more than was generally necessary to meet the next day's demand.

In this experiment, the TOU and RTP control schemes are the same during discharge (removal of heat from storage for use in the buildings). The existing building heating system determines when and how much heat is needed, and pumps hot water out of the storage tank to meet this need. The fundamental differences between RTP and TOU control are two-fold:

1. The *amount* of energy stored each night is determined in a more complex way under RTP, based on a weather forecast, and

2. The *timing* of energy storage is determined in a more complex way, based on the hourly real time prices and an optimization program. Note that customer comfort was not affected since the building heating system was controlled by the building occupants and in Plattsburgh customer comfort was improved. The goal of the RTP control is to use less expensive electricity without affecting comfort.

Each site was operated under TOU control, then switched to RTP control in the first week of January.

Brewster Office Building (BR1)

Figure 5 shows the hourly behavior of the Brewster office building for Tuesday, March 6, 1990. The weekly behavior for week 9 (Saturday, March 3 to Friday, March 9, 1990) is shown in Figure 6. During that week, the site charged 10,944 kWh. The exact times of charging are shown by the thin, mountainous line in Figure 6. The diamond line at the top shows the tank temperature in degrees Fahrenheit, a measure of the tank energy level.

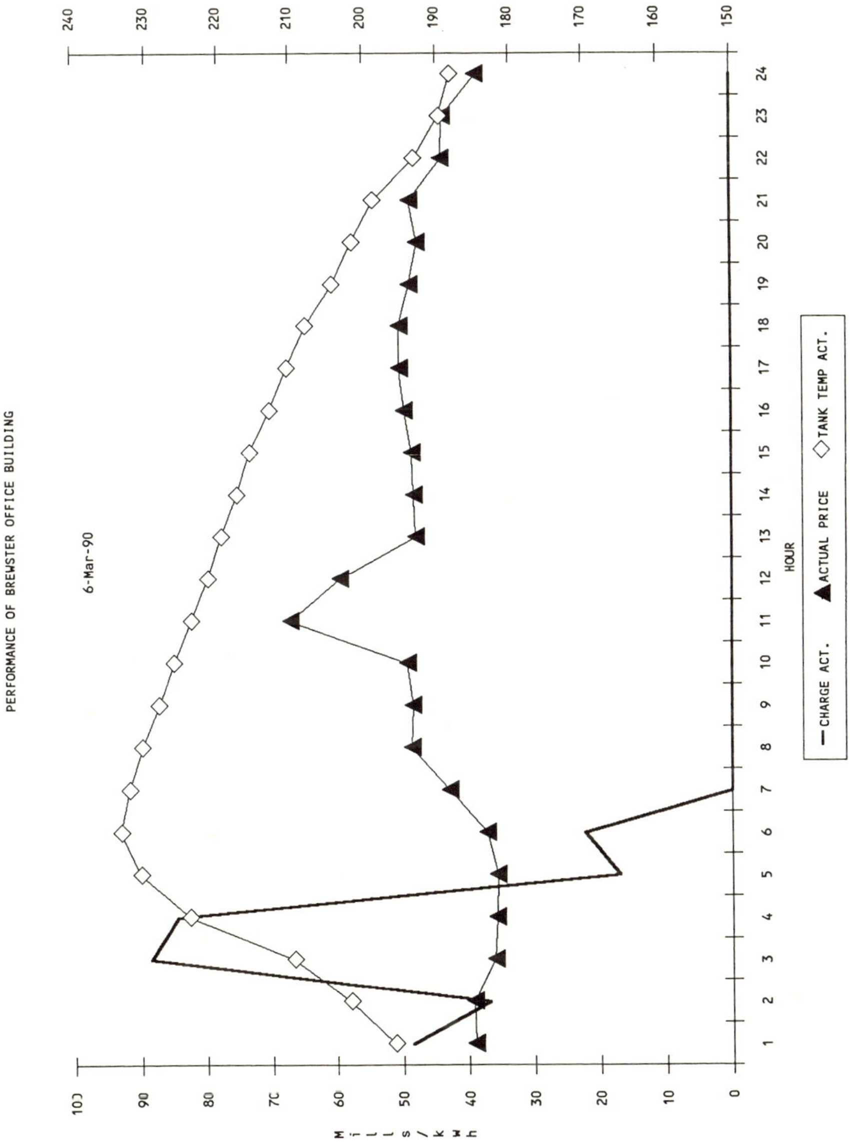

Figure 5. Hourly Graph of Brewster Office Building

During each night as electricity was used, the tank temperature rose quickly and dramatically. The rate of decline of tank temperature during the day is a function of building load, which in turn is a function of outdoor temperature and other factors. Although building load is not shown on this graph, it was tracked, forecasted, and considered in the optimization.

During the weekend, the highest temperature was reached Sunday morning, at approximately 245°F, and the lowest temperature was reached late Sunday at about 200°F. The daily working range (maximum and minimum) of tank temperature decreased progressively from Monday until the lowest tank temperature was reached on Wednesday evening (170°F) just before charging started. The previous peak of tank temperature was reached on Wednesday morning at 223°F. *Therefore, due to the large size of the storage, there was significant inter-day storage carry-over from the less expensive weekend hours to expensive weekday hours.*

The dark triangles in Figure 6 show the actual real time prices as they unfolded during the week. This information was available only ex post; the system operated with hour-ahead price forecasts of these numbers. Despite this, charging decisions tracked the times of lowest prices quite closely. For example, on Saturday and Sunday the system waited until the early morning hours for the lowest prices instead of charging at 10 p.m. The system also acted to optimize as much as possible across days. For example, Tuesday night/Wednesday morning had only four low-priced hours, and the system charged for only a few hours that night. This led to the decline in tank temperature to its lowest level the following day, followed by an increase to 220°F on Thursday morning when prices were lower than Wednesday morning.

Decisions of this type were based on hour-ahead price forecasts, and therefore not completely optimal ex post. Charging schedule was also influenced by the load forecast and the status of the storage system at the time of scheduling.

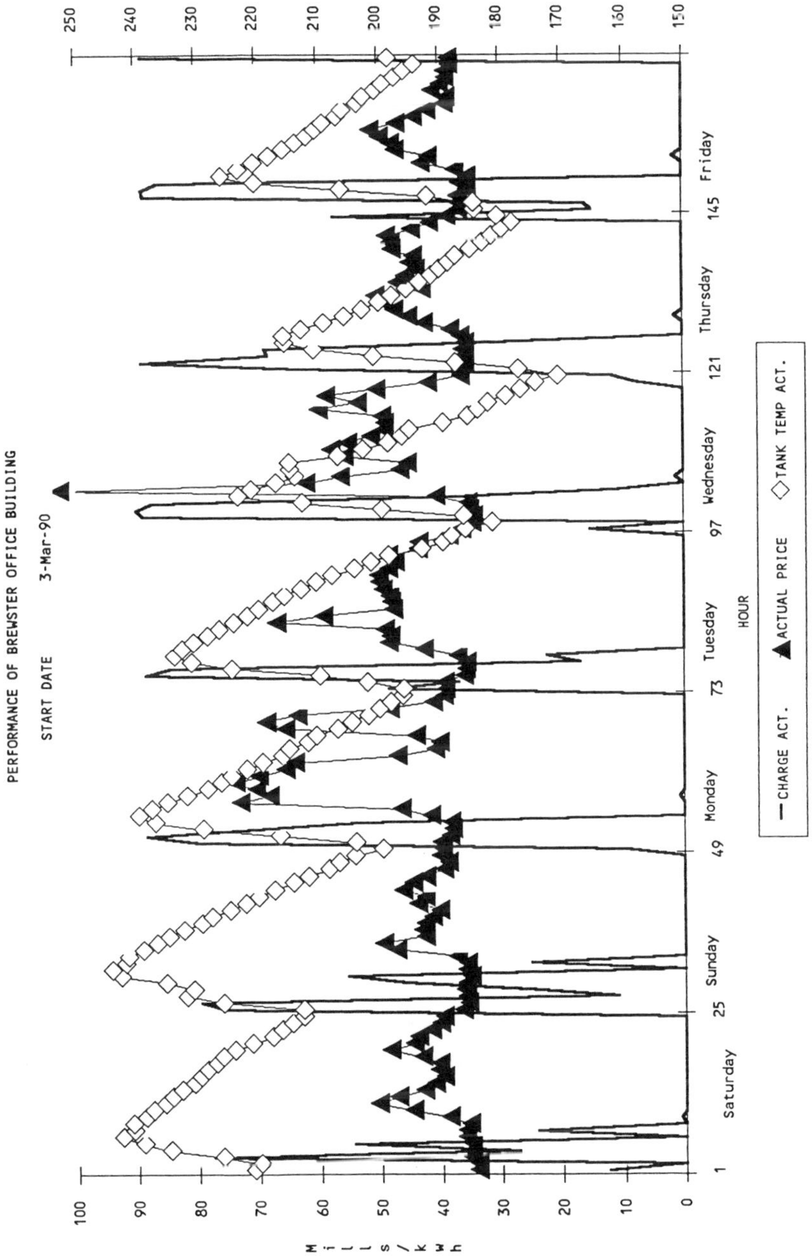

Figure 6. Weekly Graph of Brewster Office Building

The measures of performance of RTP control are the improvement in performance of RTP control over conventional TOU control and the improvement over a conventional heating system with no storage. The behaviors of the "No Storage" case and TOU based control during the weeks in which RTP control was actually running were simulated. The simulation method slightly overstates the effectiveness of conventional TOU control, resulting in a conservative estimate of performance.

The No Storage results are based on the simulation of an equivalent heating system with no storage system. The underlying assumption is that in a No Storage system, the heating loads are met concurrently at the time they occur. Thus, the No Storage electricity usage pattern for a particular week was proportional to the heating load pattern. Actually, the heating load pattern for a week was scaled so that its total sum for the week equalled the total actual electricity usage under the RTP control.

The TOU control simulation assumes TOU off-peak operation at maximum hourly charge where the storage maximum temperature is based on the "outdoor temperature reset", and a 10°F temperature dead band. The "outdoor temperature reset" rule used in the simulation was based on the regression analysis of the actual TOU operations early in the experiment. The heating load used in the simulation was based on the actual heating load measured during RTP control. The time horizon was a week, 10 p.m. Friday to 10 p.m. the next Friday. The initial tank temperatures used in the simulation were equal to the actual tank temperature measured at the start of the corresponding weeks. The resulting electricity usage pattern was again scaled so that the total simulated electricity usage was equal to the actual total electricity usage under the RTP control.

The TOU percentage saving is calculated by subtracting the total RTP cost from the total TOU cost and dividing it by total TOU cost. The calculation of the No Storage case is similar. The total costs are the costs to the customer if the corresponding price is used for billing. Demand charges were not considered. Prices are adjusted for losses but not for revenue reconciliation. (In the actual RTP operations, a 10 mills/kWh revenue reconciliation adder was used.)

Figure 7 shows estimated savings from RTP control on a week by week basis. During the first three weeks the control algorithms were still being modified. The results are shown as a percentage rather than absolute dollars. The figure shows a 2 by 2 comparison that was performed each week and can be interpreted as follows:

	Evaluated By:	
Baseline for comparison	Hour ahead prices	Actual hourly prices
RTP versus no storage at all	Column 1	Column 2
RTP versus storage with TOU control	Column 3	Column 4

The most useful comparison is column 3: how much was saved by RTP control over conventional TOU control of the same storage system, measured using the prices seen by the customer (one hour-ahead forecasts of the actual hourly RTP). This savings is expressed as a percentage of the cost of operating the system under TOU control. Thus in week 9, RTP control saved approximately 11 percent over TOU control. Major improvements to forecasts and other equations used in the control of the Brewster office building were made during the first three weeks of the project. Minor improvements continued to the last week of the project.

The week by week savings show variations for a number of reasons. Most importantly, some weeks had RTP prices which gave greater opportunities for savings. For example, if the prices were perfectly flat for a week, then neither conventional TOU nor RTP control of the storage system would give any benefit for that week. Similarly, if the least expensive hours fall between 10 p.m. and 2 a.m. every weekday, the RTP control will choose the same hours as conventional TOU control. In addition, some of the week to week differences are due to pure chance. Simulating the same week with a slightly different starting conditions might give somewhat different results due to the effect of temperature dead-bands. These results will average out over time.

Increased accuracy in hour-ahead price forecasts results in numbers closer to those in columns 3 and 4. For evaluation of performance under RTP control, the total seasonal savings should be more meaningful than the weekly savings, because the different factors affecting the results will average out.

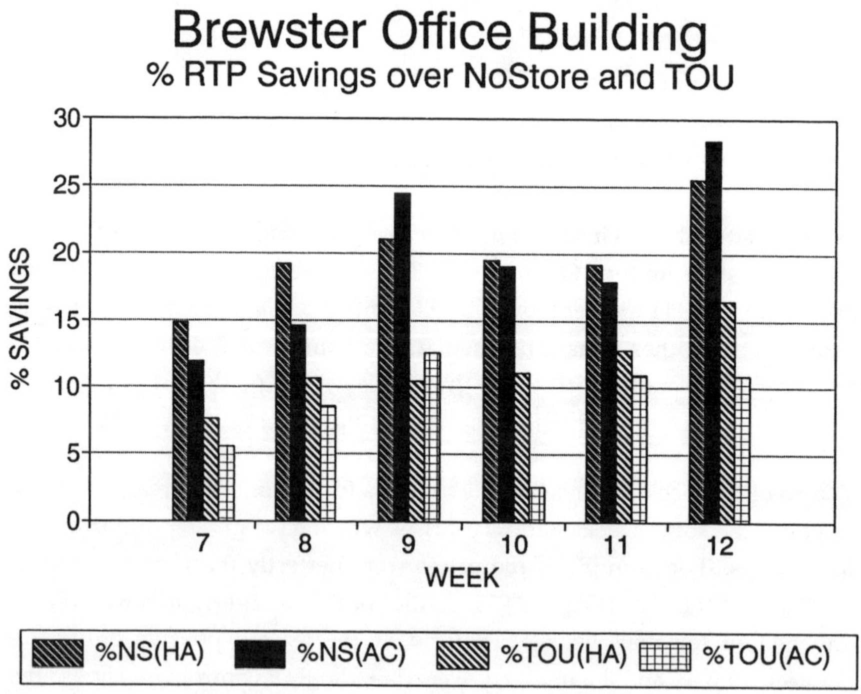

Figure 7. Week by Week Saving for Brewster Office Building

The savings resulting over the 12 weeks of RTP control during which approximately 112,000 kWh of electricity were used are shown below.

As can be seen in Table 2, the savings to the utility of RTP control of the electric thermal storage system were almost double those of TOU control. Since the cost of electronics and communications was a small fraction of the hardware costs of storage plumbing and tanks for this site, the results suggest that RTP control is a cost-effective enhancement to the storage system.

Table 2

TOTAL SAVINGS FOR BREWSTER OFFICE BUILDING
FOR WEEKS 1 TO 12

Types of Costs	Utility Costs Provide Service	Percent Savings Over No Store
Costs with No Storage	$3979	--
Costs under TOU control (estimated by simulation)	$3636	8.6
Costs under RTP as incurred (measured by actual RTP)	$3360	15.5
Costs which would have been incurred under RTP if a perfect hour-ahead price forecast available (est.)	$3141	18.5

Overall Results

The RTP/ETS experiments carried out in the NYSEG service territory during the winter of 1989-90 were successful in demonstrating the economics and the feasibility of RTP based control of thermal storage. These results can be seen first in terms of the technical feasibility of RTP and the operation of real time cost analysis and RTP setting, second in terms of the development and implementation of algorithms for controlling ETS loads at customer sites based on RTP, third in terms of customer satisfaction and finally in terms of its potential extension to other areas of process storage.

For setting prices, forecasted and actual hourly cost information was generated by NYSEG staff in the control room which was then translated into an hourly price to customers. An estimate of revenue neutrality was made *ex ante* and included in the price forecast. It was shown that actual revenue neutrality could be achieved with rolling price adjustments. This result is important for two distinct reasons, the first related to operations, the second to the benefits of customer behavior.

From the perspective of utility operations, it was demonstrated that within the routine operations of a New York State utility the information required to provide both hourly and daily forecasts of the marginal cost of operations is available and can be provided on a routine basis. For this experiment the daily and hourly price information was generated and recorded in real time and faxed one day late to the central computer in Cambridge. The logical next step would be to move to a stand alone computer system in the NYSEG control room into which the forecast and actual costs could be input. This computer could then call either a central computer in Cambridge or a set of distributed control systems at customer sites. Moving from the delayed RTP to an actual hourly real time price, would then be a logical and completely straightforward step. The next step of integrating the cost forecasting and price calculations into an existing or a future control system computer in the control room would require a larger level of effort, but is feasible.

The use of hourly prices rather than day-ahead prices provided significant improvement in the benefits of RTP to the utility and customer. These benefits result in part from the operating characteristics of NYSEG and in part from the better matching of customer price to utility cost. Because NYSEG is a net seller into the NYPP and to other regional utility customers, its opportunity cost is not a function if its generating cost but rather of its (and the NYPP's) opportunity cost or resource cost. This cost varies significantly between hours and can be only roughly forecast a day ahead. In the NYSEG case, the ability to forecast the price one hour ahead is significantly better than the ability to forecast a day ahead.

A corollary to the above is that the quantity and quality of customer response *from the perspective of the savings to the customer and the utility* is a function of the accuracy of the cost forecast (upon which customer response and the customer bill are based) relative to the actual real time cost to the utility. The more accurate the price forecast relative to the actual, the larger are the combined benefits of RTP to the utility and customers.

The second overall result of the experiment was to demonstrate the feasibility of automatic control of customer storage loads using RTP based signals. The experiment demonstrated the feasibility of automatically retrieving price and weather information, implementing for each site a simplified building demand forecasting model, developing a near-optimal charging schedule and then modifying that schedule to reflect hourly prices. Both water storage systems successfully demonstrated each of these characteristics. The inherently different storage and discharge characteristics of the earth storage system showed our ability to monitor and control the charging of the system and led to significantly improved customer comfort with a minor reduction in cost.

The third result from this experiment was in terms of customer satisfaction with the operation of RTP. As hypothesized before the experiment, those customers using the water storage system were indifferent to RTP control in that their comfort level was unchanged, only their bill was reduced. The RTP based control logics provided sufficient energy to the storage tanks to guarantee adequate supplies to the buildings at all times. In the case of the earth storage system, customer comfort was dramatically improved through the length of the experiment.

The dollar benefits of the RTP experiment were substantial. Operating savings of the larger of the two water based systems (Brewster office building) were increased by nearly a factor of two over the same system operating on conventional TOU-based control logics, with the customers unaware of *any* change in comfort. Another way to state the savings is that RTP control averaged an eight percentage point reduction in system costs, over and above the savings of approximately ten percent achieved under TOU control. Figure 7 presents the week by week system savings. By comparing the savings based on the hour-ahead forecast with the saving based on the actual price (after the fact) it is possible to see the value of improved hourly forecasts on the level of savings achievable with RTP. The more accurately prices can be forecast, the greater the savings possible with RTP.

The savings at the smaller water storage site (Brewster store front), as shown in Figure 8, were also impressive in percentage terms, but were small in absolute terms because the customer's total bill was not large. For this site, it is likely that any implementation of RTP would combine the control of several individual storage systems so as to take advantage of economies of scale in communications and logic. The Brewster store front was one of about 30 identical systems in a strip mall. Potentially all 30 could be independently controlled by a single on site PC with a corresponding increase in gross benefits.

Control of the earth storage system resulted in lower savings than those seen in the water systems, but resulted in increased customer comfort and satisfaction with the heating system. In the earth storage system there are only limited savings possible given the slow thermal constants of the system and the fact that the system is passive, i.e., the heat is released when it reaches the surface of the slab. The contribution made by the RTP experiment results primarily from being able to forecast the building desired load for the next day based on a forecast of temperature. Given this information the quantity of heat needed in the slab to achieve this level of dissipation the following day could be calculated and then programmed. Based on this forecasting ability, customer comfort levels could be maintained, but there was little effect from rescheduling the charging into specific hours of low cost. The actual savings from RTP in the Plattsburgh system were hard to evaluate because of the need to simulate how it would have operated under conventional control. Conventional control tended to overhead the system when outdoor temperatures were warm, and under-heat the system when outdoor temperatures were cold, leading to corresponding swings in indoor temperature and comfort. However, when we simulated the behavior of the TOU system, we gave it credit for correctly choosing the total energy to use over a week, and only altered the timing during the week of that use. This led to a calculation of little or no monetary savings of RTP over TOU, which probably understates the true savings. In addition, several potential improvements to the scheduling algorithm were identified and could probably lead to further savings.

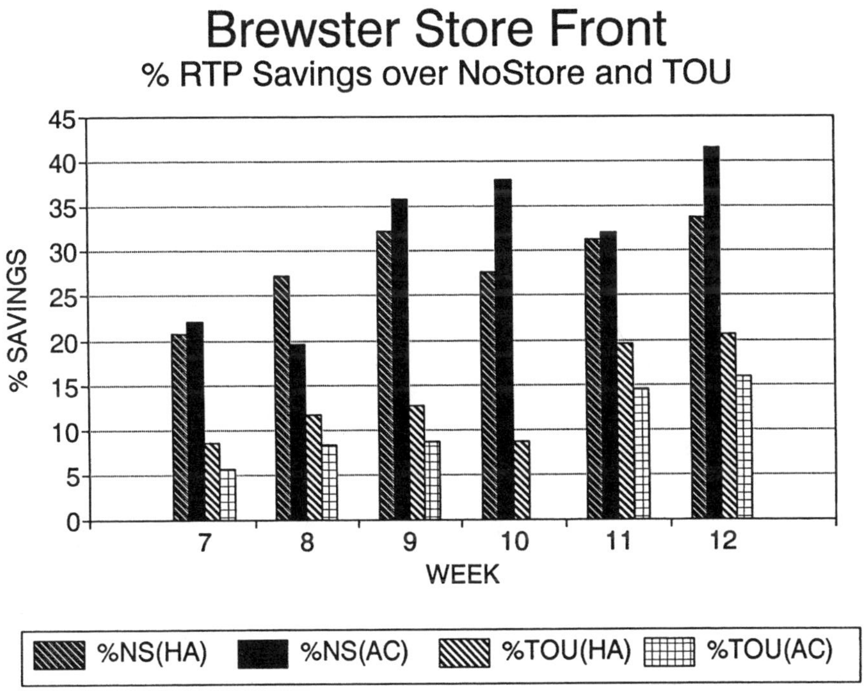

Figure 8. Week by Week Savings for Brewster Store Front

The savings achieved during the course of the experiment reflect a number of events and improvements. For example, the Brewster store front and Plattsburgh office were not fully operational until mid-February. Various small improvements were made at all three sites at various times. Thus, as shown in Table 3, the savings increased over time.

Table 3

AGGREGATE SAVINGS OVER DIFFERENT PERIODS*

Time Period	Brewster Office Building	Brewster Store Front
Weeks 1 to 12 (Total)	7.6%	---
Weeks 7 to 12	8.9%	9.0%
Weeks 9 to 12	10.2%	10.4%

During the experiment, many additional potential enhancements were identified but not implemented. The most important of these include:

- Better price forecasts
  - Time series forecasting methods to supplement NYSEG calculations
  - Price adjustments, based on statistical model, several times per day
  - Enhanced price extension formulas

- Automatic tuning of site parameters
  - Adaptive load forecasting
  - Adaptive estimation of state equations
  - Wider range of allowable tank temperatures, giving more storage capacity

- More research on parameters used in heuristics
  - Temperature dead bands
  - Time horizon length
  - Frequency of recalculations

- Event-driven scheduling of recalculations

It is not possible to estimate the impact of these changes on savings, without further experimentation or simulation. However, based on the weekly results and the data in Table 3, the range of likely savings in the next generation of this experiment is between 10 and 20 percent (RTP over conventional control).

Electric thermal energy storage systems are examples of a much more general phenomenon in both the industrial and commercial sectors, that of process storage. The relevant conditions are that there exist some excess capacity of production and storage, i.e., that the potential for scheduling exist, that the load have a daily and/or weekly cycle and that it be forecastable even though stochastic. The magnitude of the savings reported in this paper would be the same for any process storage system of the same magnitude facing the same relative rate structure. As was demonstrated in this experiment, for any customer, the more variable the prices, the greater are the benefits of using RTP based control over TOU based control.

In summary, the experiment showed that RTP can be implemented effectively as a means of controlling commercial building heat storage systems. All of the components, except actual billing, needed for a fully operational RTP system were undertaken as part of this experiment, and all were fully functional. Unlike the majority of other experiments which provide only real time rates to customers, this experiment demonstrated the feasibility and desirability of automated response to RTP.

The numerical benefits of RTP were significant relative to the savings of ETS under TOU control. Operating savings on the larger of the two water based systems (the Brewster office building) were increased by nearly a factor of two over the same system operating on conventional control logics and TOU rates, with the customers unaware of *any* change in comfort. These results confirm that automated control based on RTP is an effective and efficient means of providing additional value added to existing utility programs such as ETS and forms the basis for development of new strategies for utility/customer economic efficiency.

III UNDERSTANDING THE CUSTOMER'S NEEDS

MODELING CUSTOMER PREFERENCES; LESSONS FROM EXISTING MODELS AND DATA

by

Douglas W. Caves and J. David Glyer
Christensen Associated, Inc.

The underlying premise of product differentiation is that utility customers have different needs and that overall welfare can be increased if the utility serves these needs with an array of properly priced services. Our question is, "Does the existing evidence provide any support for this premise?" We discuss this issue by examining the evidence related to five key questions regarding customer preferences.

QUESTION 1: ARE CUSTOMERS LIKELY TO RESPOND TO THE OPPORTUNITIES OFFERED BY PRODUCT DIFFERENTIATION?

Consider customer participation in current programs that have priority service features–Interruptible/Curtailable (I/C) rates and Real-Time Pricing (RTP). Over a hundred U.S. utilities have instituted I/C rates (Ebasco, 1987). An EPRI study of a sample of these utilities indicates that participating customers generally curtail loads when requested. Analysis of customers on I/C rates shows load reductions during curtailments ranging from 23% to 60% for curtailable rates and from 80% to 100% for interruptible rates. Figure 1 shows the percentage reduction in load, with the

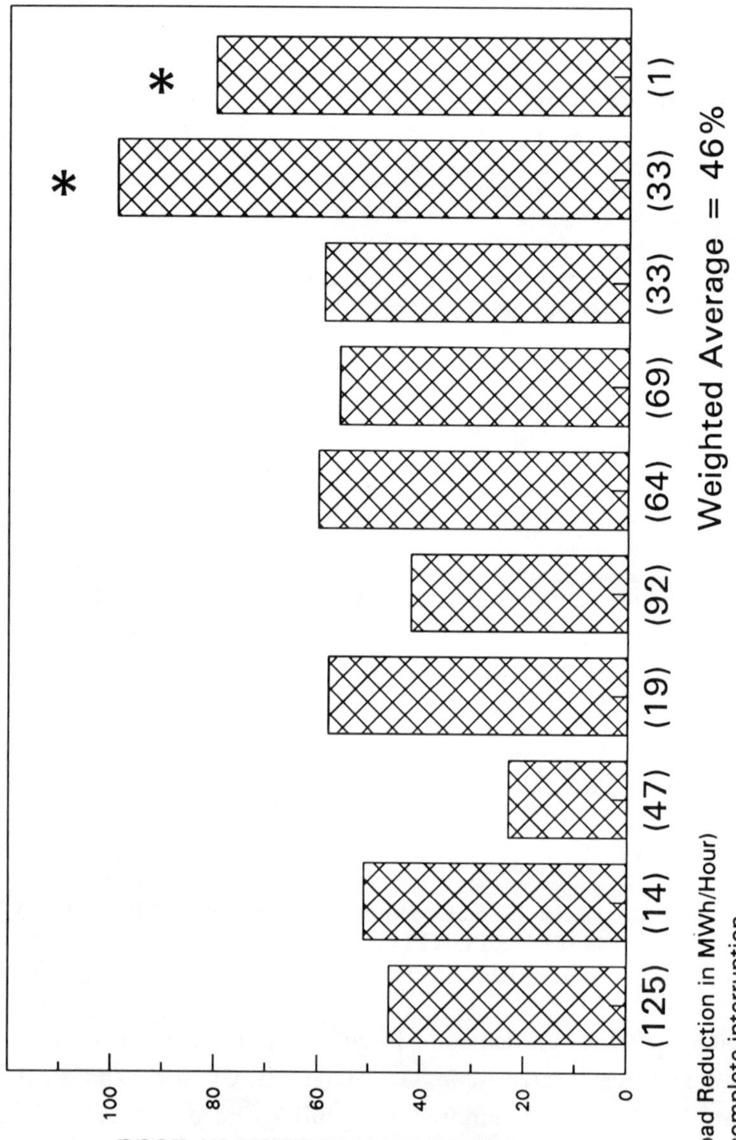

Figure 1. Load Reduction as a Percent of Expected Load at Selected Utilities with Curtailment Program

amount of the reduction in total MW listed below the bars (Caves, Herriges, and Windle, 1988).

Real-Time Pricing programs are much less common but are beginning to supply very useful information on customer response.[1] Consider the RTP experience at Niagara Mohawk Power Corporation (NMPC) with the Hourly Integrated Pricing Program (HIPP). This program attracted 17 large commercial and industrial customers with loads totaling 180 MW. Figure 2 shows the estimated response for the typical large C&I customer to HIPP's marginal cost-based real-time prices. Hourly prices on the range of 3 to 4 times the standard on-peak rate brought forth load reductions on the order of 35% (Caves and Neenan, 1990).

The above evidence from existing interruptible and real-time pricing programs clearly illustrates that some customers will participate in Priority Service programs and that they will alter usage patterns in response to prices or curtailments dispatched with short notice.

QUESTION 2: WHAT ARE THE COSTS TO CUSTOMERS OF TOTAL OUTAGES THAT MAY ARISE UNDER SOME FORMS OF PRODUCT DIFFERENTIATION?

Outage costs are important for three reasons. First, outage costs are a key component in the design of rates and dispatch algorithms for priority service programs. Second, outage costs indicate the range of preference variation among customers. Third, outage costs are useful in planning for optimum system investment.

Figure 3 shows results from a recent EPRI survey of outage cost studies along with the results of two very recent survey studies. These studies show

[1] For general review and background see Tabors, Schweppe, and Caramanis (1989) and Schweppe, Caramanis, Tabors, and Bohn (1988).

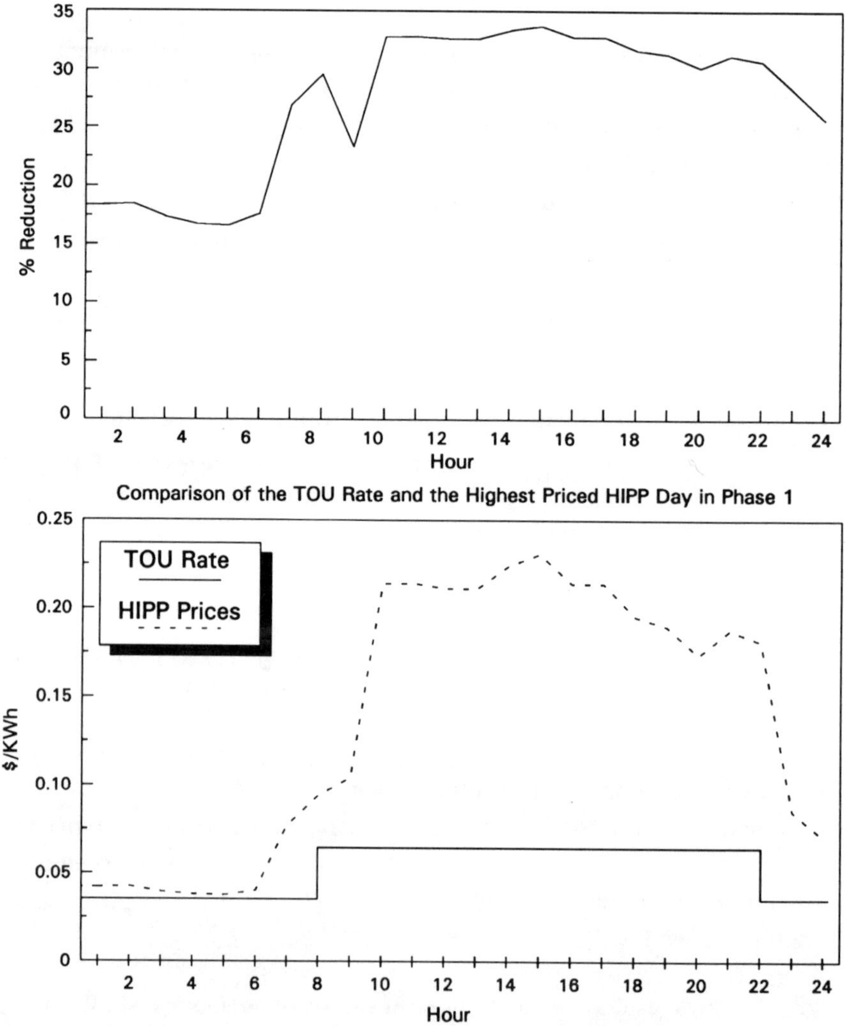

Figure 2. Typical Respondent Performance: Percentage Load Reduction in Response to HIPP Prices on Highest Priced Day

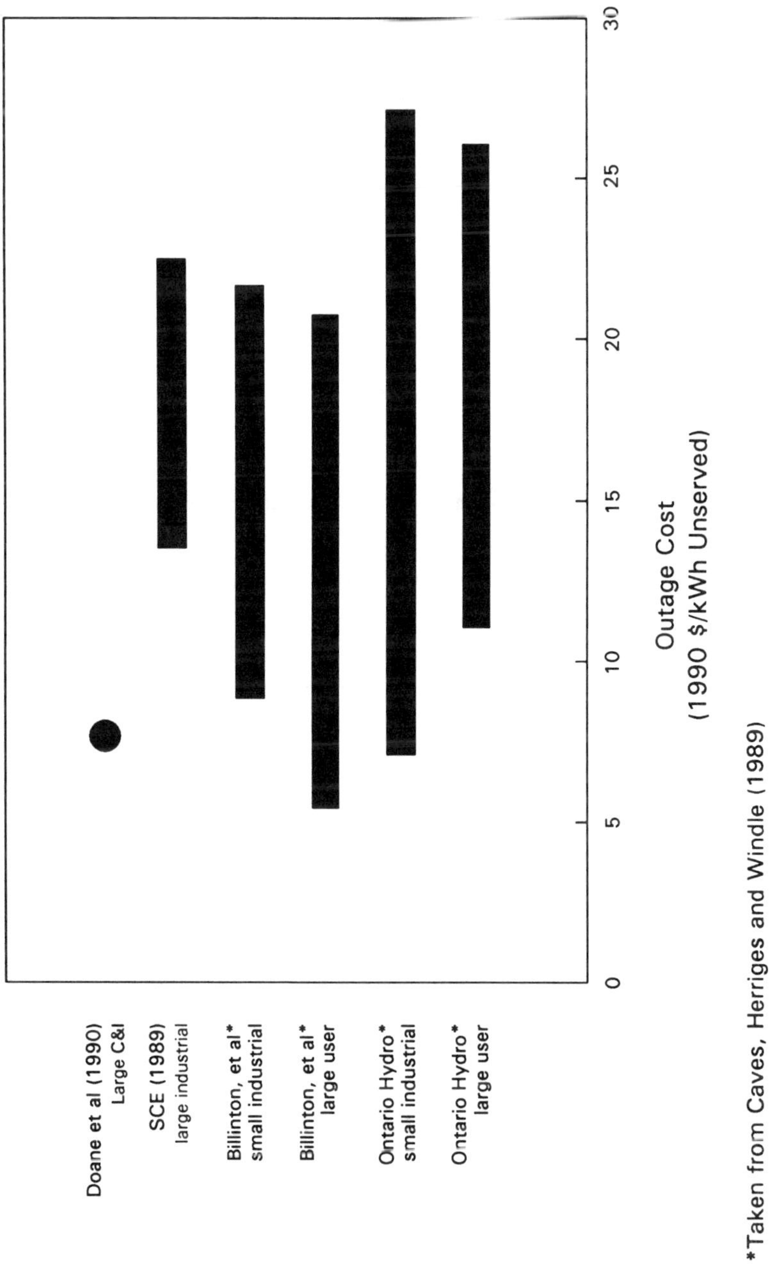

Figure 3. Outage Cost Estimates for a One Hour Interruption

considerable variation across studies. However, there is general agreement that *average* total outage costs exceed $5/kWh for industrial customers. The two most recent studies put average total outage costs in the $7-23/kWh range.

The range of results illustrated in Figure 3 makes it difficult to pin down a value for average total outage costs, but the data make it abundantly clear that such costs are much higher than current electricity prices.

Given this observation, why do we observe customers participating in programs that may involve either enforced curtailments or load changes in response to real-time prices that are rather modest in relation to the quoted outage costs? One reason is that some customers have outage costs that are below the average. A second reason is that most programs involve only partial outages rather than the total outages that characterize the survey responses. And finally, in comparison to suffering a mandatory total outage, the opportunity to respond voluntarily to a price is a highly flexible option for the customer. The following questions examine each of these three possibilities in light of existing data.

QUESTION 3: DO CUSTOMER PREFERENCES DISPLAY THE RANGE OF VARIATION THAT IS CONSIDERED BASIC TO PRODUCT DIFFERENTIATION?

Customers display a wide range of preferences. For example, data from a recent survey (Doane, McClelland, Schulze and Woo (1990)) showed that outage costs for large customers range from less than 2 to over 20 dollars per kWh of unserved energy. Figure 4 shows the frequency distribution of customers' total outage costs. Similar variation was observed in customer's responses to real-time prices in the HIPP experiment at NMPC. Estimated elasticities showed considerable variation among customers and across time periods for the same customer. Figure 5 illustrates some of this variation. High elasticity customers would drop load by 45 percent in response to the

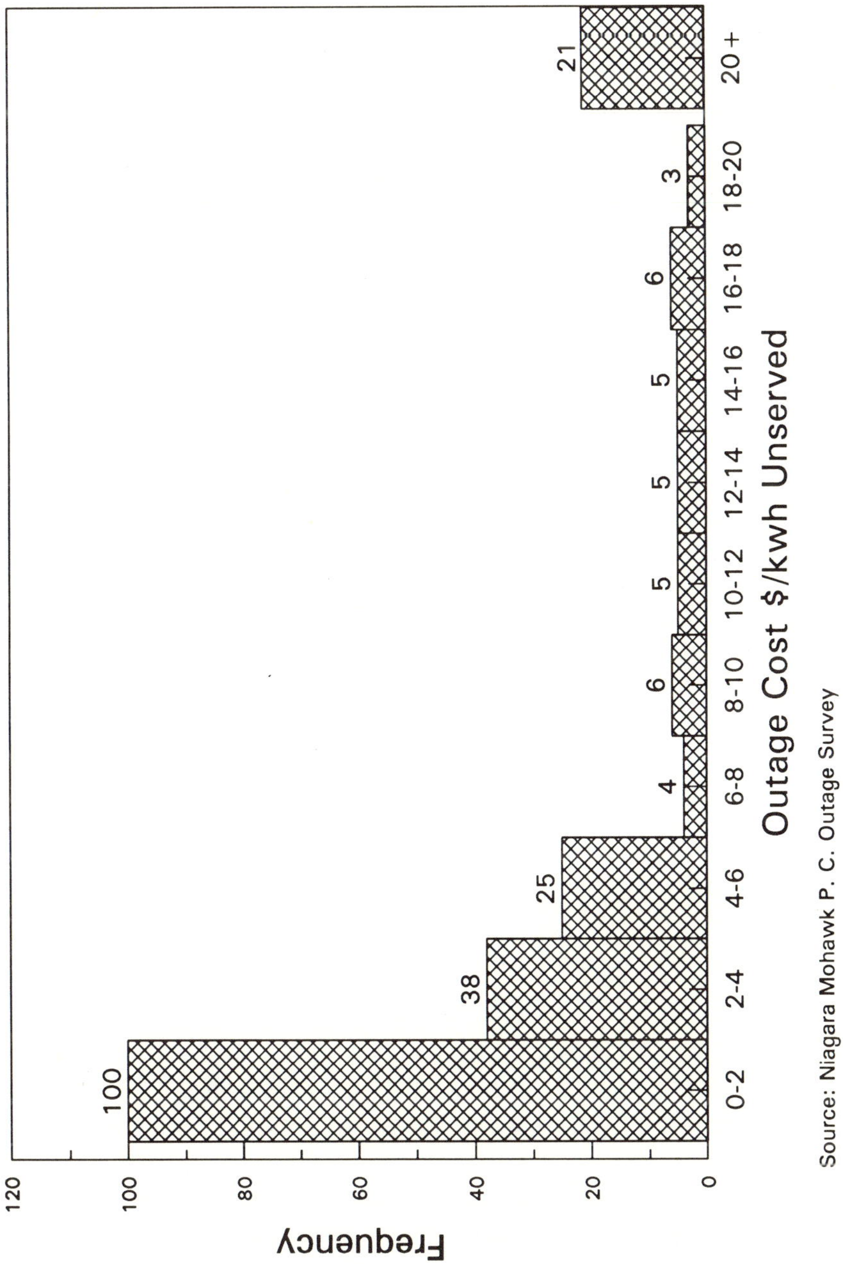

Figure 4. Distribution of Outage Costs Across Customers

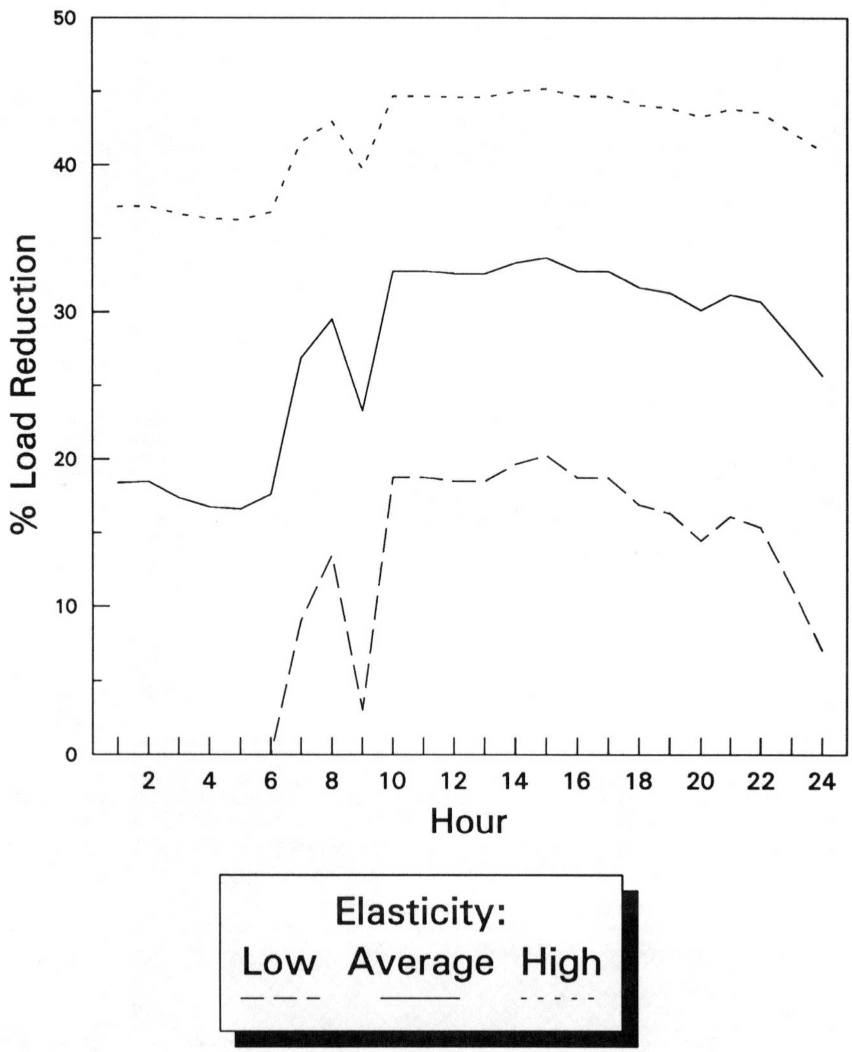

Figure 5. Percentage Load Reduction in Response to HIPP Prices on Highest Priced Day

price profile shown in Figure 2, while lower elasticity customers would drop load by 18 percent. Moreover, this range understates the full range of variation. There are times when the data indicate near zero elasticities for some customers. At these times customers have virtually no flexibility and show little response even to high prices.

Hence, the data provide considerable support for the notion that customer preferences display a wide range of variation that could support product differentiation.

QUESTION 4: WHAT ARE THE COSTS TO CUSTOMERS OF PARTIAL OUTAGES THAT MAY ARISE UNDER SOME FORM OF PRODUCT DIFFERENTIATION?

The outage costs cited above are for total outages, whereas most proposed forms of products differentiation envision taking advantage of customers' differences in valuations of partial outages. Unfortunately, there is virtually no survey research on partial curtailment costs. Therefore, to assess the impacts of partial outages, we turn to a simulation model of customer demand for electricity that has been developed as part of the PRISM project.

Like all models, the PRISM demand model involves some simplification of actual behavior. Nonetheless, it encompasses all of the features that are basic to assessing response under programs with dispatchable events including: customer uncertainty over timing of events and/or prices, daily variation in customer preferences, revisions in preferences as events are revealed, and occasional constraints that leave the customer relatively inflexible. The model can simulate customer behavior under numerous programs that involve uncertain events, such as random outages, curtailments or interruptions, real-time prices, or interruptions with buy-through options. Given data on customer loads and elasticities, the model simulates the effect of any of these uncertain events on loads and on customer welfare. Hence, it can be used to assess the welfare effects of partial outages of any size.

For our simulations of partial outage costs, the key question is what elasticities to use. To illustrate the computations, we use average elasticities from the analysis of real-time pricing data at Niagara Mohawk. This is appropriate because real-time pricing customers are routinely curtailing their loads in response to high prices received with short notice.

The simulation model was applied to a month of hourly loads for a typical industrial customer with a peak kW of 3,200 and average on-peak usage of 2,180 kW. Partial outages were simulated by selecting a Firm Power Level (FPL) and curtailing the customer to this level for a six hour period. The requisite load changes and the customer's resulting welfare loss were then calculated. Because loads vary from day to day the impact of this partial outage in terms of load reduction and cost to the customer will vary from day to day. Hence, the simulation was run 20 times with the partial curtailment falling on a different weekday each time.

Figure 6 provides a schematic illustration of the welfare analysis of a partial outage on two days, when the customer has demand curve D_1 on Day 1 and D_2 on Day 2. On Day 1 (Day 2) the customer would use Q_1 (Q_2) units of electricity at the standard price, P. Constraining the customer to the FPL implies a large reduction in usage on Day 1, with corresponding welfare loss shown by the triangle between the demand curfew and the FPL above the standard price. On Day 2, curtailment to the FPL results in a smaller reduction in usage and a much smaller welfare loss.

The results of using the PRISM model to simulate this level of partial curtailment over all potential weekdays are summarized in Table 1. The curtailed load averaged over all the potential curtailment days is 624 kWh/hour, which implies a 30% reduction from typical usage levels. There is considerable variation across days as indicated by the standard deviation and the maximum and minimum values. Dividing the welfare cost by the load reduction provides a measure of the partial outage costs in terms of dollars per kWh unserved; this averages $1.19/kWh. The simulation reveals considerable daily variation in partial outage costs which range from $.04 to $5.57/kWh unserved.

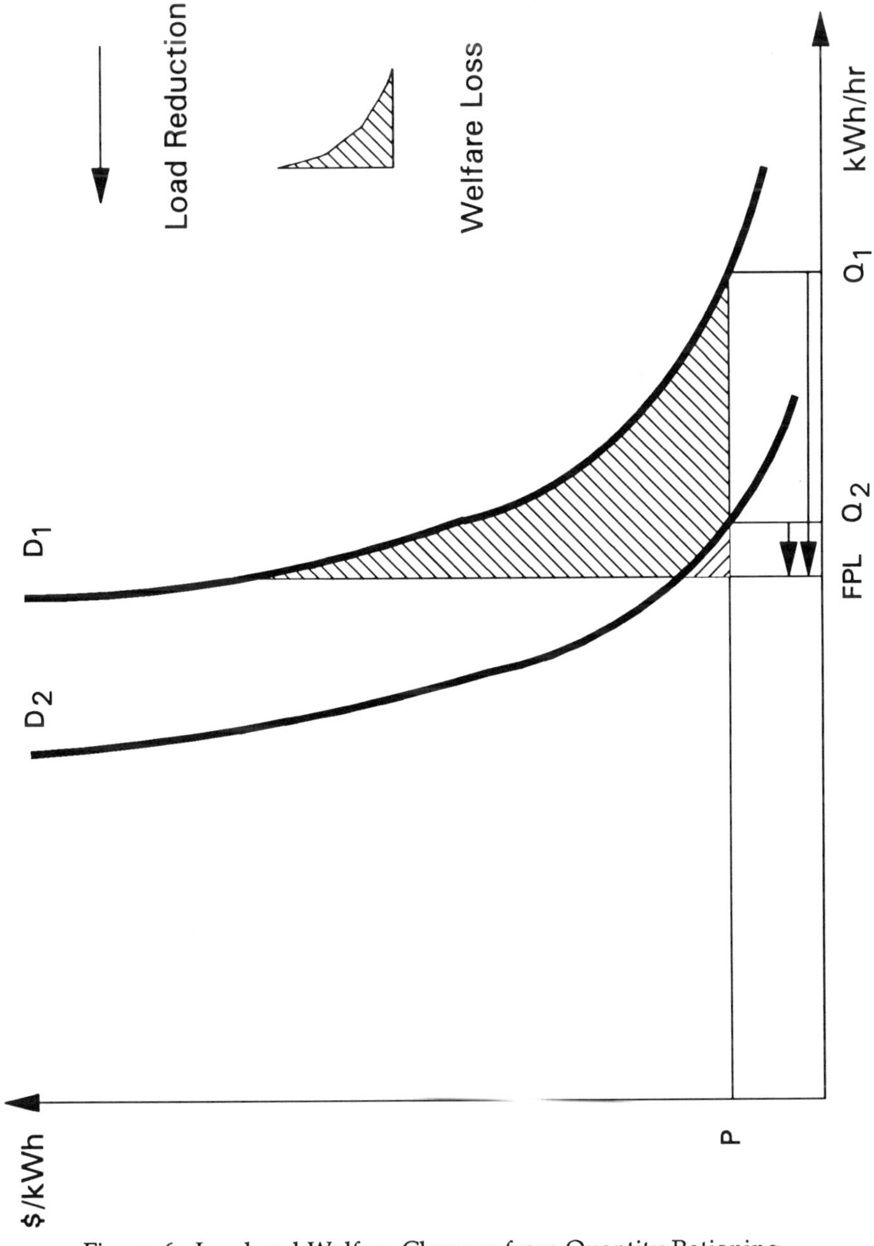

Figure 6. Load and Welfare Changes from Quantity Rationing

The partial outage costs are not directly comparable with the total outage costs of Figures 3 and 5. This is because there is not a direct link between the average elasticities used in the simulation and the unknown elasticities of the customers in the survey samples. Nonetheless, it is notable that the partial outage costs are generally on the low end of the estimated range of total outage costs, which is to be expected because customers will sacrifice their lowest valued uses first in a partial outage situation.

Table 1

LOAD REDUCTION AND WELFARE LOSS FROM QUANTITY CONSTRAINT

Typical Industrial Customer, Summer Afternoon
Max Demand = 3,200 kW, Avg. Demand = 2,200 kW
6 Hour Curtailment

	Load Reduction kWh/Hour	Welfare Cost, $	$/kWh Unserved
Quantity Constraint			
mean	624	4461	1.19
std. deviation	468	11126	1.35
minimum	12	22	0.04
maximum	1450	44248	5.57

QUESTION 5: CAN FLEXIBILITY ENHANCE THE VALUE OF PRISM PROGRAMS TO THE CUSTOMER?

The curtailment scenario described above indicated that using even partial outages to meet quantity constraints can sometimes be very costly to customers. Are there ways to increase the customer's flexibility and thereby reduce vulnerability to costly events? The price system provides maximum flexibility for the customer, allowing wide latitude in the choice of quantities utilized. To illustrate the implications of price flexibility we conducted a second set of simulations using exactly the same customer baseline loads and elasticities.

This set of simulations used a six hour real-time price instead of a six hour forced curtailment to stimulate load reductions. The real-time price was chosen to be that which yielded the same *average* load relief, 624 kWh/hour, as the quantity constraints. This real-time price turned out to be \$.50/kWh for a customer whose standard rate was \$.075/kWh. Again, there were 20 simulations, each one featuring the \$.50 real-time price on a single, different day and the standard prices on all other days. This pricing scenario might correspond either to a program with a dispatchable TOU price or to an interruptible program with a buy-through price.

Figure 7 provides a schematic illustration of the welfare effects of price rationing. The customer welfare cost is given by the area of the two shaded triangles. These two triangles will have a smaller area than the area of the two triangles in Figure 6.[2]

Table 2 contains a summary of the pricing simulations together with the results of the parallel curtailment simulation repeated from Table 1.

While the average load relief is the same in the two sets of simulations, the pricing program grants flexibility that is of tremendous value to the customer. The customer's average welfare loss under the pricing program is \$.13/kWh, only 11% of the \$1.19/kWh cost of the enforced partial outages.

---

2 In Figure 6 each load decrement under D_2 increases outage cost by less than the reduction in costs from each equal load increment under D_2 until loads on each curve correspond to P_R. To put the curtailment and pricing scenarios on the same footing, we assume that the pricing program carries a customer credit that is equal to the expected utility revenue gain at the FPL of FPL*(P_R – P).

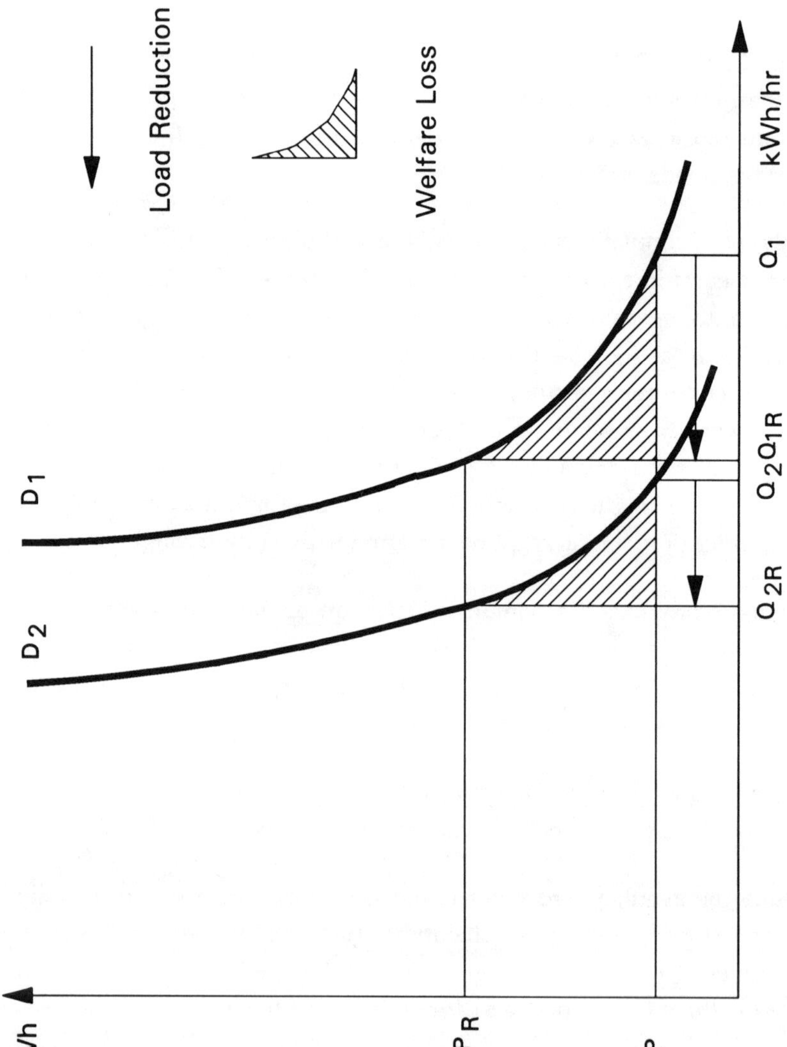

Figure 7. Load and Welfare Changes from Price Rationing

Table 2

LOAD REDUCTION AND WELFARE LOSS;
COMPARING PRICE AND QUANTITY RATIONING

Typical Industrial Customer, Summer Afternoon
Max Demand = 3,200 kW, Avg. Demand = 2,200 kW
RTP Price = $.50/kWh
6 Hour Curtailment

	Load Reduction kWh/Hour	Welfare Cost, $	$/kWh Unserved
Quantity Constraint			
mean	624	4461	1.19
std. deviation	468	11126	1.35
minimum	12	22	0.04
maximum	1450	44248	5.57
Price Constraint			
mean	624	469	0.13
std. deviation	110	78	0.01
minimum	447	338	0.11
maximum	796	601	0.14

Moreover, the range of outage cost across days is much smaller under the pricing scenario. The simulations also demonstrate that pricing programs may provide customer flexibility without sacrificing load reduction benefits to the utility. Notice that the load reduction is much more stable under the pricing programs–ranging from 447 to 496 kWh/hour–than under the quantity constraint program, where the range is from 12 to 1,450 kWh/hour.

CONCLUSIONS

Existing data provide key indications of the likely value of and directions for product differentiation. First, customers have displayed a willingness to participate and to modify loads. Second, reasonable estimates indicate that total outage costs are both high and highly variable. The level indicates that significant savings are possible by taking advantage of the variability. Third, the very limited evidence suggests that partial outage costs are lower per unit of unserved energy than total outage costs. The importance of partial outage costs and the relative lack of evidence indicates a high payoff to research in this area. Finally, simulations based on a reasonable parameterization of the PRISM demand model indicate that programs with price flexibility, such as real-time buy-through prices, are likely to have much higher customer acceptance, and may at the same time provide more stable load reductions than programs with enforced outages.

REFERENCES

D.W. Caves and B. Neenan. "Real-Time Pricing: Will It Work? Experimental Evidence from Niagara Mohawk's Ongoing HIPP Experiment". Selected for Competitive Papers Session, 1990 Southeastern Regional Public Utilities Conference, Public Utilities Report, Inc., August 1990.

D.W. Caves, J.A. Herriges, and R.J. Windle. "Customer Response to Interruptible and Curtailable Rates". Final report to the Electric Power Research Institute, EM-5630, vol. 1-3, March 1988.

D.W. Caves, J.A. Herriges, and R.J. Windle. "Customer Demand for Service Reliability: Existing and Potential Sources of Information". Final report prepared for the Electric Power Research Institute, Research Project 2801-2, May 1989.

M.J. Doane, G. McClelland, W. Schulze, and C.K. Woo. "Industrial Outage Cost Survey: Final Report". Submitted to Niagara Mohawk Power Corporation, May 1990.

Ebasco Business Consulting. "Innovative Rate Design". Final report prepared for the Electric Power Research Institute, EA-3830, January 1987.

RCG/Hagler, Bailly, Inc. "Cost Benefit Analysis of Power System Reliability: Determination of Interruption Costs". Final report prepared for the Electric Power Research Institute, EPRI EL-6791, Project 2878-1, vol. 1-3, April 1990.

F.C. Schweppe, M.C. Caramanis, R.A. Tabors, and R.E. Bohn. *Spot Pricing of Electricity*. Kluwer Academic Publishers, Boston, MA, 1988.

R.A. Tabors, F.C. Schweppe, and M.C. Caramanis. "Utility Experience with Real Time Rates", *IEEE Transactions on Power Systems*, vol. 4, no. 2, pp. 463-471, May 1989.

INTRODUCING MARKET FOCUS INTO RATE DESIGN

by

John H. Chamberlin and Kenneth A. Jensen
Barakat & Chamberlin, Inc.

A brief quotation from a recent report we prepared for EPRI sets the stage for the following discussion:[1]

> "Electric utilities, like all other companies, are in the business of providing value to customers. As competition grows, their customers have increasing options from which to choose. Some customers can build their own electrical capacity. Others can use alternative fuels such as gas to meet their needs. Still others may 'purchase conservation,' participate in third-party shared savings programs, or relocate to another utility's service territory where they view their needs as being better met. . . Traditional planning methods have focused on the revenue-requirements-minimizing mix of reserves needed to provide a uniform, undifferentiated electric service. With growing competition in the energy market, however, factors other than cost (i.e., quality of service, customer responsiveness, customer confidence) have become increasingly important. As a result, it is now essential for utilities to identify the types of services sought by customers as well as to determine which options are financially attractive and technically feasible for the utility."

---

1 John H. Chamberlin, *Integrated Value-Based Planning–An Overview*, prepared for the Electric Power Research Institute, August 1989.

The specific issues that gave rise to the case study I am going to briefly describe centered around the financial and sales implications of proposed rate increases. Would these increases be the "straw that broke the camel's back" for some customers, and would it result in their initiating some action that would hurt the utility's revenues and profits?

This basic question set the stage for addressing other concerns that required attention including appropriate pricing and marketing strategies.

OVERALL APPROACH

The approach we took to this assignment can be characterized quite simply. First, the effects upon customers and markets of the proposed rate increases were examined. Second, where it was determined that these increases would reduce sales, a series of service and pricing options were suggested. Finally, these analyses were integrated into a set of overall strategic recommendations.

Specifically, this required:

- Evaluating current utility marketing efforts
- Understanding the residential, commercial, and industrial customer base in terms of:
  - Sector size and structure
  - Competitive forces affecting various sectors
  - Energy use patterns
  - Technological trends affecting competitive position
- Assessing the nature of competition among energy resources.
- Estimating the energy price and value of service responses of firms and sectors to be able to:
  - Identify customer needs

- Develop appropriate strategic responses to support the continued vitality of critical financial performance parameters

- Target market segments that require marketing assistance to assure retention, expansion, and/or attraction

In turn, this permitted us to:

1. Estimate likely impact of proposed rate increases, based upon:

   - Evaluation of current energy markets, encompassing:

     - Market segments and conditions within these markets critical to pricing decisions.

     - Examining important energy-using sectors and the critical energy-purchasing/locational factors for these sectors.

   - Evaluation of effectiveness of alternative pricing mechanisms.

2. Assess the implications of both short- and long-term alternative pricing strategies to mitigate rate impacts.

3. Recommend market and pricing strategies to maximize the value of utility services and products to its customers.

Briefly stated, the utility required a set of insights–pricing, marketing, and regulatory–that would permit it to respond proactively under a variety of future possibilities.

STUDY METHODOLOGY

The foundation for a comprehensive assessment of the likely utility service area response to rising electric prices and for adequately characterizing appropriate marketing and pricing strategies required the creation of a comprehensive framework for analysis. The Strategic Assessment Methodology (SAM) was an essential study element. The structure of this methodology permits evaluation of a number of possible future scenarios, including both impact analyses such as examining customer response to a given level and pattern of rate increases as well as determining the best segment pricing policy *given* the need to raise overall prices at some level to cover increased costs of production.

The framework for determining customer response in various market segments consisted of basing prices on short-run and long-run price elasticities, perceived value of service, and profitability requirements. Several types of data were used in the analysis, including:

- Utility Marketing and Customer Database: Appropriate commercial, industrial, and residential segments were identified. For each segment, customers were further disaggregated between existing and "new" customers. The new customer group includes those existing customers who are considering replacement of equipment, examining cogeneration possibilities, or looking at other alternatives.

- Historical Usage Data: Aggregate and segment-specific usage data from the 1980s were used to estimate price elasticities, income and economic activity coefficients, and usage responses to seasonal weather patterns. Per customer usage equations were estimated at the aggregate level for both the residential and general service segments. These estimates established a baseline forecast and provided short-run electricity usage elasticity estimates. The historical data also provided estimates of segment usage for competitive or substitutable end-uses by segment.

- Customer Choice and Competitive Technology Information: Historical data was supplemented with data from other sources to estimate long-run price and marketing responses. Long-run usage responses for each segment's set of substitutable end-uses were determined through incorporating detailed information regarding the comparative economics of competing electric and gas technologies (Figure 1). In turn, this technology

TECHNOLOGY COMPARISONS

Sector	Segment	Heating	Cooling	Water Heating	Cooking	Refrig-eration	Process Heating	Pumping	Cogen/ Self-Gen.
Residential	Region 1	C	C, F	C, F	C				F
	Region 2	C	C, F	C, F	C				F
Nonresidential	Large Office	C	C	C, F					C
	Manufacturing	C	C	C, F			C	C	C
	Large Retail	C	C	C, F					C
	Grocery	C	C	C, F		C, F			C
	Restaurant	C	C	C, F	C	C, F			C
	Hotel	C	C	C, F	C				C
	Hospital	C	C	C, F	C				C
	School	C	C	C, F	C				C
	College	C	C	C, F	C				C
	Other	C	C	C					C

Figure 1. End-Use Competition

<u>Legend</u>

C: Current Competing Technology
F: Future Competing Technology

comparison was combined with an assessment of customer financial requirements, such as payback requirements to estimate impact of future price increases and marketing efforts on market share.

- Cost Data: Cost information was developed to determine overall profitability requirements for the residential and general service sectors and annual operating expenses by sector.

All of these inputs were necessary to simulate future customer behavior with the Strategic Assessment Methodology. This 123-equation model was employed in two basic ways:

1. It served as a revenue/profitability accounting system for evaluating overall system and segment-specific responses to various price changes and value of service alternatives.

2. It provided estimates of ideal or best prices subject to profitability requirements. These ideal prices ("Ramsey" prices) are based on the inverse of price elasticities and on value of service attributes in each sector. These prices minimize usage reductions across all segments and are "ideal" from an economic-efficiency standpoint.

The assessment methodology input requirements, equations, and outputs are depicted in Figure 2. The model equations are contained in six categories:

- One profit constraint.

- Two aggregate sector usage equations which serve as "adding-up" constraints.

- 36 segment-specific total usage equations. Per customer usage across the 12 segments is determined for existing and new customers. Only short-run price responses affect usage for existing "non-replacing" customers, while both short-run and long-run price responses affect usage for new customers.

- 24 probability equations.

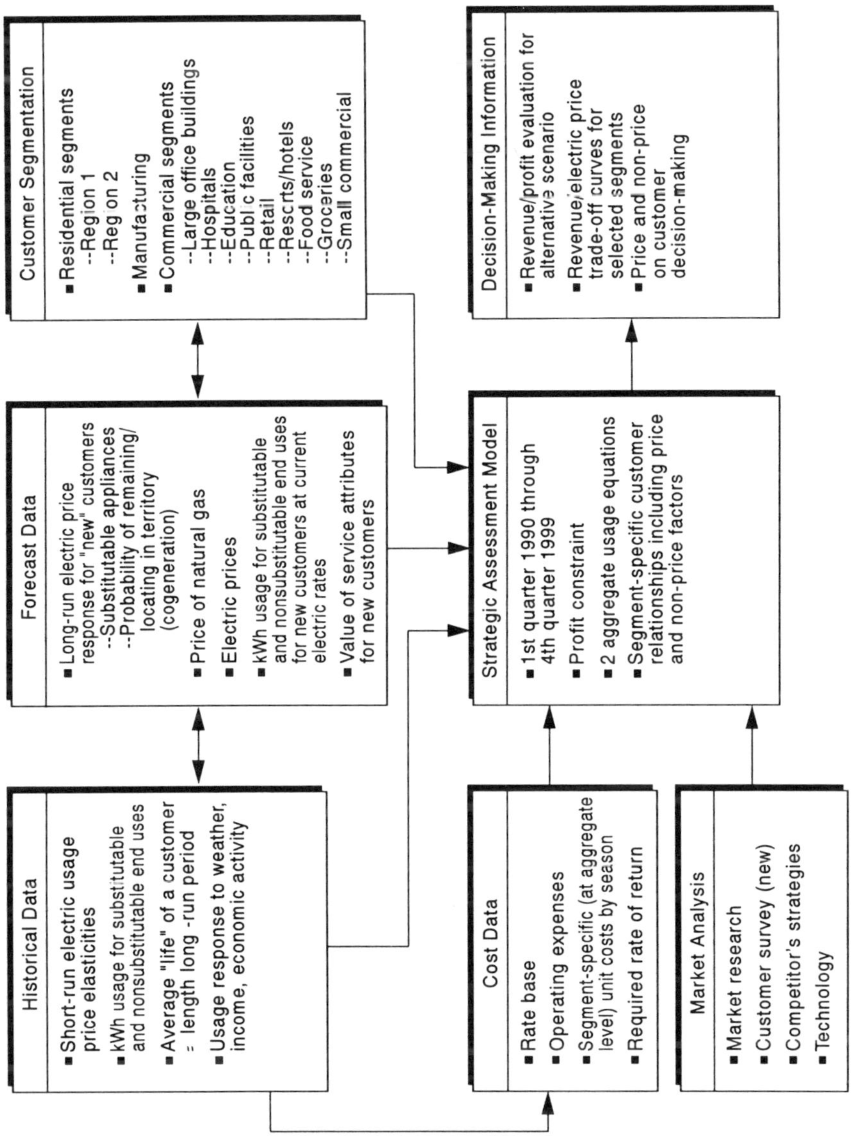

Figure 2. Approach: Strategic Assessment Methodology

- 12 usage "weight" equations. The share of substitutable and nonsubstitutable end-use usage (saturations) for new customers changes over time in response to previous price changes. For example, if the share of substitutable end-uses for a new customer falls from 50% to 45% in response to an electric price increase, this 45% share becomes the base substitutable usage for a new customer in the following time period.

- 36 customer equations. For each segment there are three equations: total customers from the previous time period, existing customers who are not replacing equipment in the current time period, which equal the total number of customers multiplied by one minus "decay" rate, and new customers in the current time period, which equal those existing customers that faced a decision to move off system or replace equipment plus the number of new customers. This last group of equations includes probability terms that contain long-run price and value of service responses which affect the decision to remain, to become a utility customer, or to change old equipment.

- 24 electric price equations. Ideal (Ramsey) prices are determined for new and existing customers in each segment based on short-run and long-run responses. All other things equal, prices are higher for a segment that is price inelastic and places a high value on service.

The approach used in characterizing the impact of changing electric prices on system revenue and other performance parameters was to compare a base case with a case incorporating competitive forces in the service area energy market. By "subtracting" the "competitive" case from the base case, the difference so calculated became a measure of the impact or reduction in performance associated with the explicit introduction of competition. Thus, the absolute levels for either the base case or the competitive response are less meaningful than the difference in values between the two cases.

Response analyses were performed under alternative price, non-price and competitive conditions to identify a range of impacts. Understanding the response levels provides the ability to assess not only the effect of a price change, but to, in turn, develop an appropriate pricing/marketing strategy to counter a potential threat.

Key to defining alternative scenarios for assessing impacts was the development of assumptions in the following areas:

- Electric prices over the next decade
- Natural gas prices over the same period of time
- The electric and gas customer end-use technologies that would be competitive during the 1990s
- Residential, commercial and industrial customer energy equipment decision-making criteria

The blending of these various assumptions permitted the development of a set of scenarios to characterize the near-term future.

The Strategic Assessment Methodology provides for the ability to evaluate separately, and in the aggregate, the influence of a variety of forces on the ultimate financial performance of the utility. Initially, a particular future scenario is defined–consisting of an electric price forecast over the next ten years; a natural gas price for the same period; and an identification of various end-use technologies and their performance characteristics that will "compete" in the end-use markets for load. The methodology incorporates a variety of internal analyses to yield, among other elements, the following outputs for a particular market segment and for the retail market as a whole over the period of analysis:

- Annual customer growth
- Annual electricity sales (kWh) growth
- Average usage levels (kWh per customer) trends
- Changes in electric market share over time
- The number of customers that cogenerate/self generate
- Annual revenues

- For the strategic pricing scenarios, the optimal segment prices that need to be achieved to meet revenue requirements

By comparing alternative scenarios, losses or gains in relation to a particular base case can be evaluated. Response analyses were performed under alternative price, non-price and competitive conditions to identify a range of impacts.

TYPICAL STUDY FINDINGS

Current Markets

Figures 3 and 4 display the current distribution of customer segments and end-use markets within the prototypical utility's service area. For the customer segments displayed above, Table 1 illustrates the differences, often significant, in average and marginal electric prices facing various market segments, an important consideration when examining segment competition. These variations in electric costs and perceived value of service combined with the particular price responsiveness of a given segment, determine the relative attractiveness to a customer of switching from purchased electricity to another fuel such as gas or to consider self-generation.

Figure 5 indicates that amount of the current electric usage estimated to be substitutable, i.e., that portion of total electric consumption considered to be potentially vulnerable to competition from gas. Understanding this potential for substitution sets the stage for estimating the impacts of future price increases on electric market share position in the various customer segments.

The Next Ten Years

A number of scenarios were examined, each composed of a base case and a competitive response.

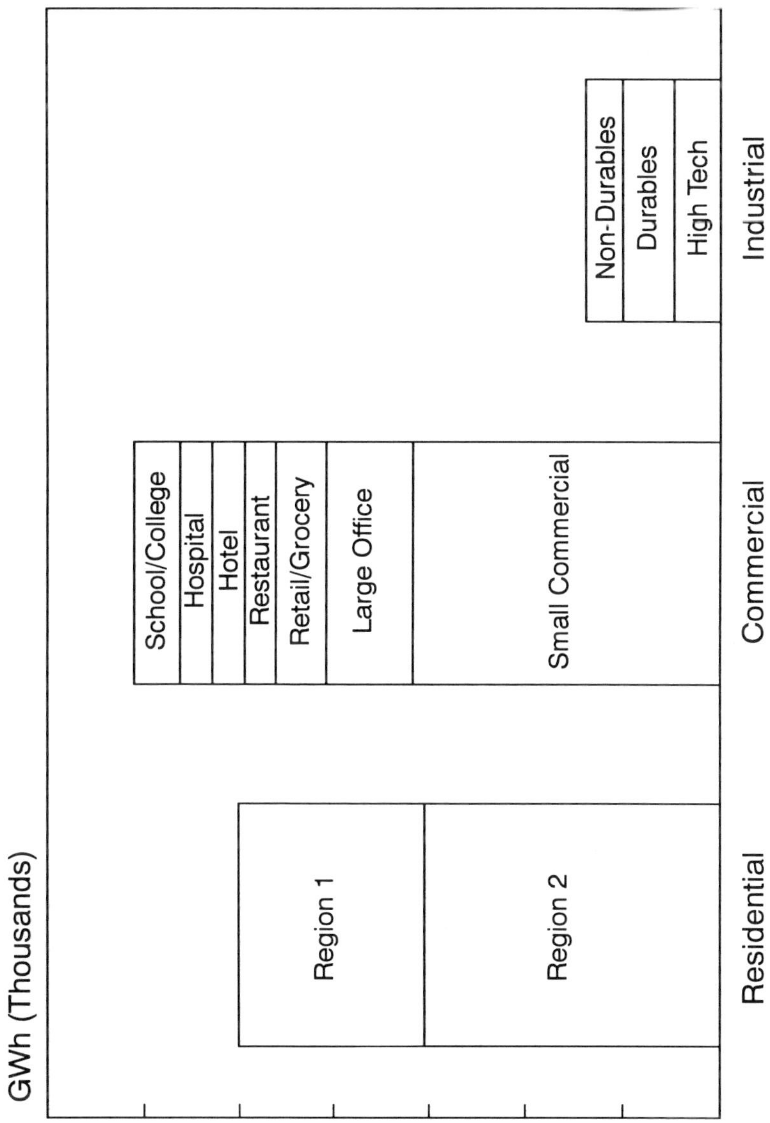

Figure 3. Current Electricity Markets: Customer Segments

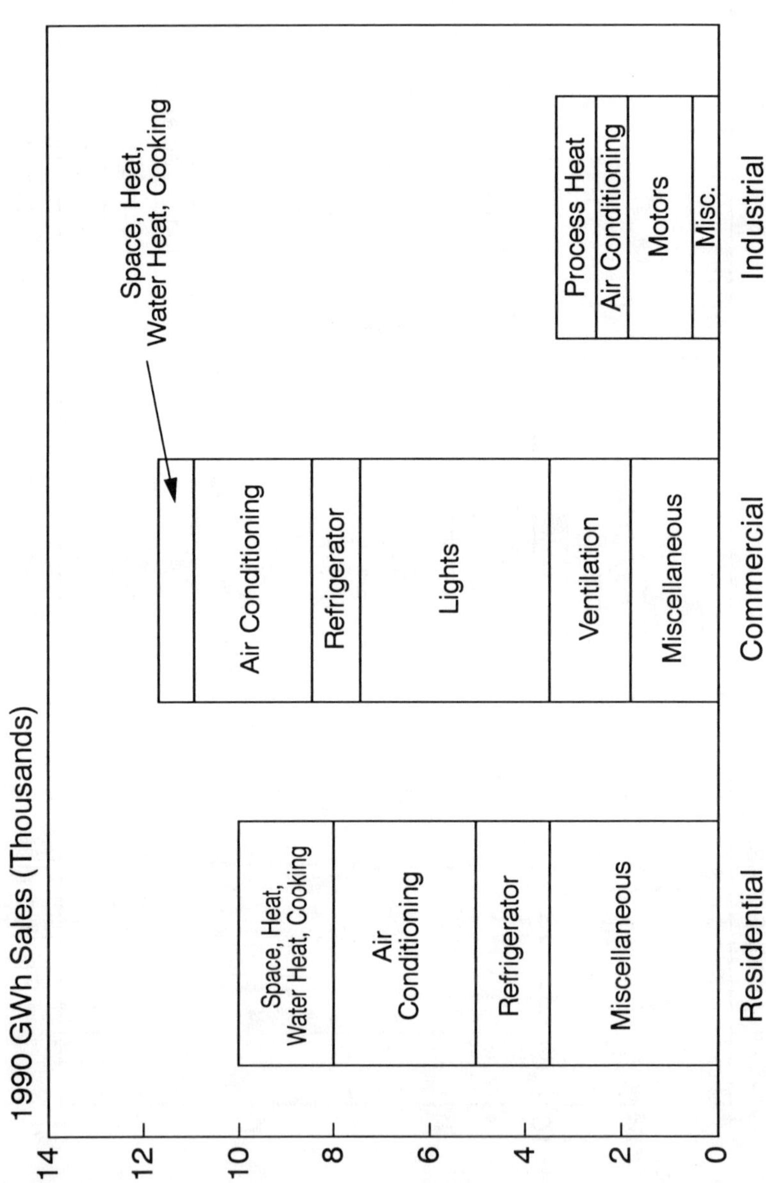

Figure 4. Current Electricity Markets: Major Sectors and End Uses

Table 1

CURRENT ELECTRICITY MARKETS:
MARKET SEGMENT PRICES AND RATES

Segment	Customer Average Price	Customer Marginal Price: Summer Demand ($kW-yr)	Summer Energy ($/kWh)	Winter Demand ($kW-yr	Winter Energy ($kWh)
Residential					
Region 1	12¢	$0	15¢	$0	10¢
Region 2	11¢	$0	12¢	$0	10¢
Commercial					
Large Office	8¢	$17	6¢	$20	5¢
Manufacturing	7¢	"	8¢	"	7¢
Large Retail	9¢	"	6¢	"	5¢
Grocery	8¢	"	6¢	"	5¢
Restaurant	11¢	"	9¢	"	9¢
Hotel/Resort	8¢	"	6¢	"	5¢
Hospital	7¢	"	6¢	"	5¢
School	10¢	"	9¢	"	8¢
College	6¢	"	6¢	"	5¢
Small Commercial	10¢	"	9¢	"	8¢

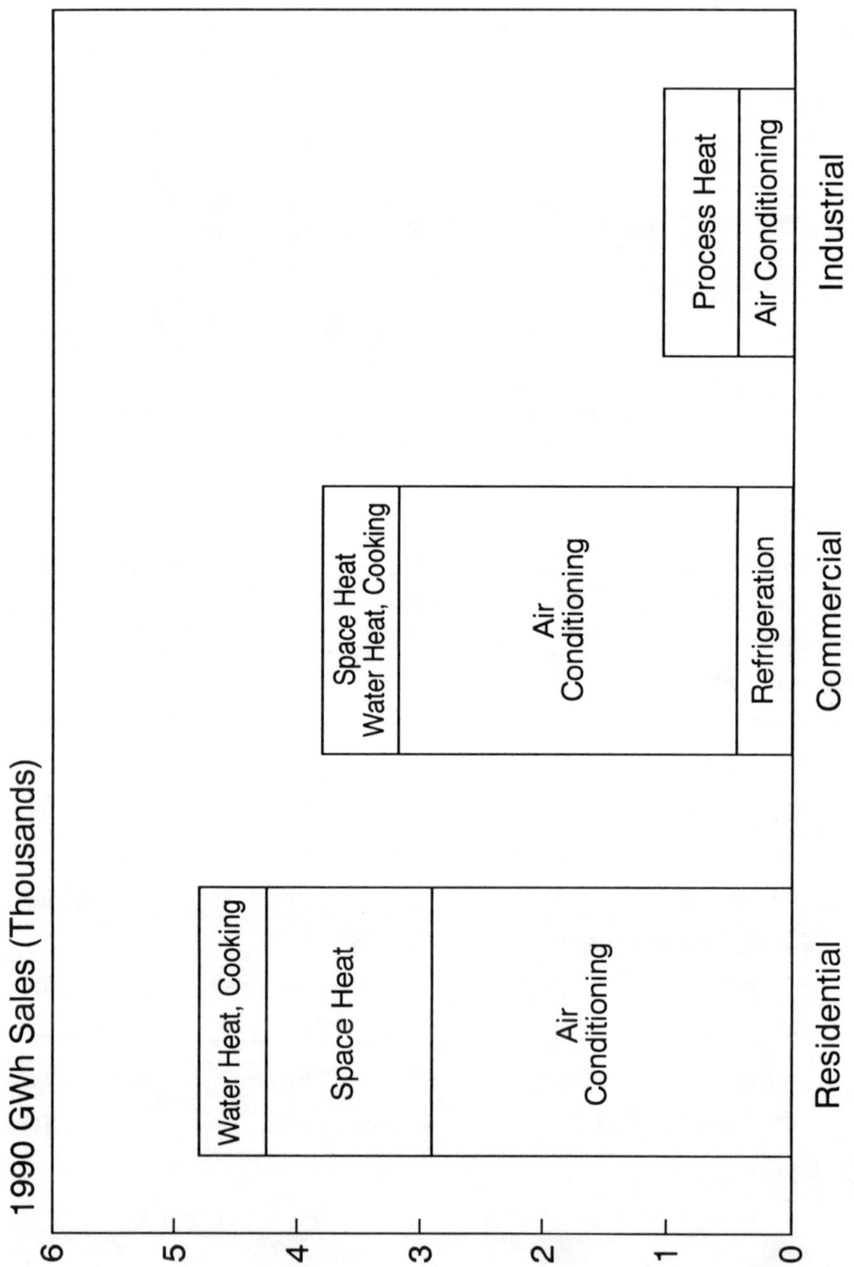

Figure 5. Current Electricity Markets: Substitutable End Uses

During the period of analysis, depending on the scenario under examination, a range of impacts can occur. An example would be the following:

BASE CASE

Basic Assumptions

- Electric price forecast for the analysis period
- No explicit fuel switching
- Electric utilization levels over the forecast period are a function of economic activity and electric price forecasts. Essentially, this base case reflects a traditional rate case projection without consideration of competitive pressures on electricity sales and revenue levels.

RESPONSE CASE

Basic Assumptions

- Same electric price forecast used in Base Case
- Explicit consideration of natural gas price forecast
- The incorporation of detailed analysis at an end-use level of competing technologies and the impact on electric market share in those end-uses where electricity and gas are substitutable
- An assessment of likelihood of cogeneration/self-generation in those market segments where it is feasible
- Incorporation of emerging gas technologies beginning in latter part of the decade

The Response Case represents the results, under the given energy price forecasts, of a series of competitive forces influencing electric consumption and utility revenues.

The comparison between these two scenarios, permits an examination of the likely revenue shortfall–annual and cumulative–associated with the proposed rate case.

The possible responses are displayed in Figures 6 and 7. Figure 6 shows the shortfall in revenue associated with this scenario by 2000.

Figure 7 separates the estimated response to price increases into the impact of currently available technology and the impact of emerging new gas technologies, assumed to be available in the latter part of the analysis period. This display, which shows the cumulative impacts over the forecast period, also compares this basic response to a Customer Perception scenario built around the current customer "feeling" that there will be a growing disparity between electric and gas prices over the next decade.

Figure 8 illustrates the implication of optimal pricing by market segment. It illustrates the results of a comparison between the proposed rate increase and how it was allocated on a segment basis to a set of optimal prices on a segment basis reflecting segment prices that would assure achievement of revenue requirements.

In summary, the underlying methodology has the following features:

- Based on a dynamic Ramsey pricing methodology
- Extends inverse elasticity rule to include both short-run and long-run responses
- Evaluates impacts of proposed rates as well as the design of alternative rate proposals
- Explicitly addresses competition from other fuels at market-segment and end-use levels

The methodology was designed to provide both normative and nonnormative demand, revenue, and profitability assessments. In normative or policy cases, the customer simulation explicitly assumes that the utility undertakes optimal (Ramsey) pricing to set market segment rates. In nonnormative cases, customer response was simulated assuming rates are predetermined over the analysis period, permitting the development of a broad range of pricing and marketing strategies.

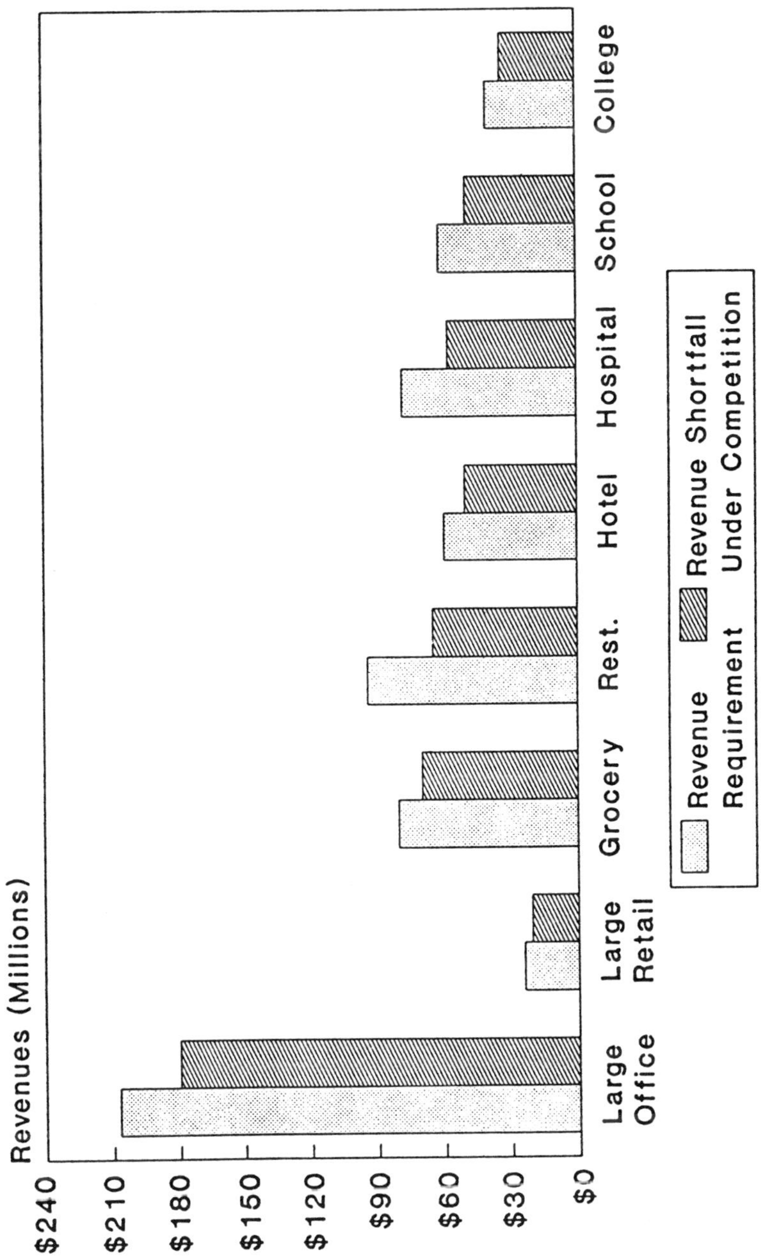

Figure 6. Revenue Shortfall within Commercial Sector in Year 2000

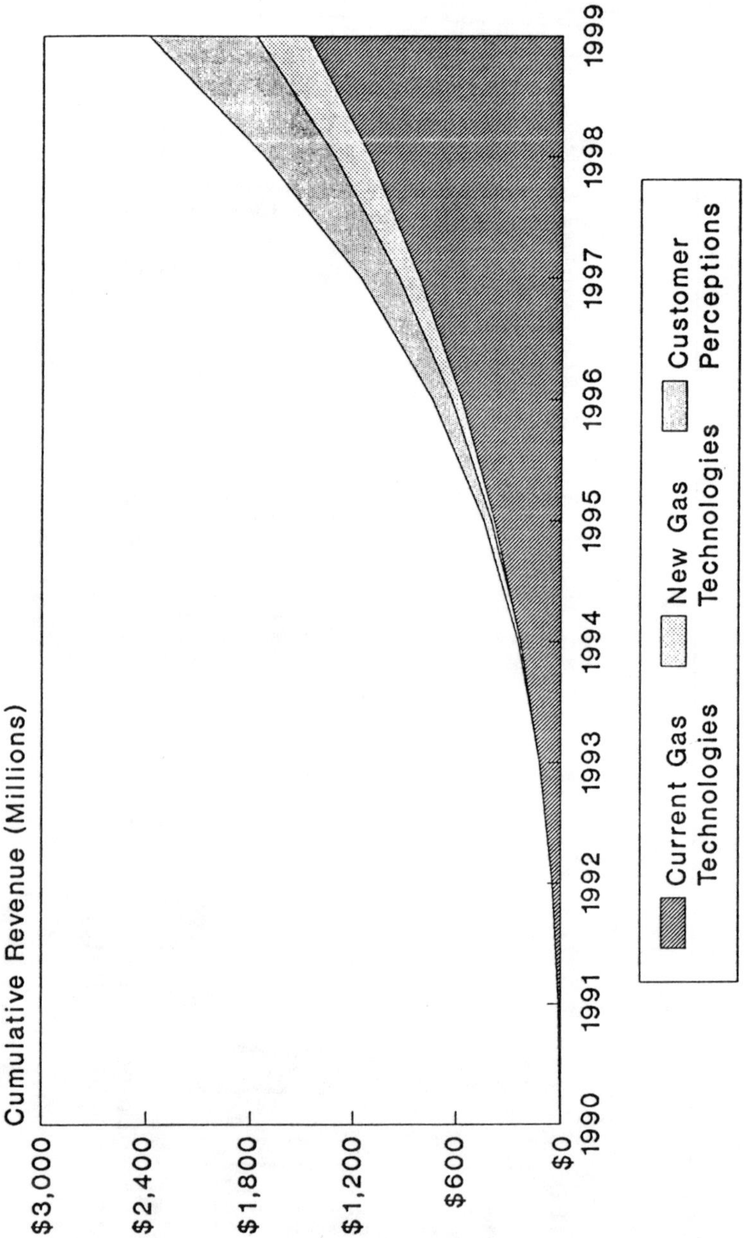

Figure 7. The Next Ten Years: Cumulative Revenue Shortfall Trends

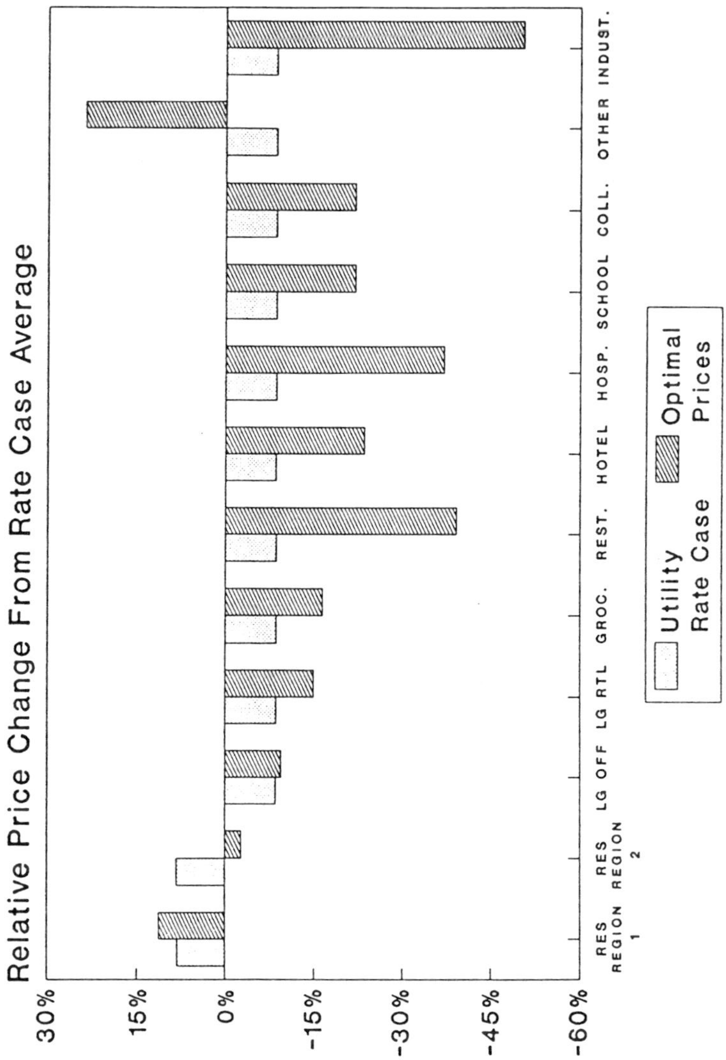

Figure 8. The Next Ten Years: Rate Case Segment Price Increases Versus Optimal Prices

WHAT CAN WE LEARN FROM CUSTOMER SURVEYS?

by

Gregory L. Hamm
Applied Decision Analysis

and

Steven R. Sim
Florida Power & Light (FPL)

INTRODUCTION

EPRI and FPL Interest in PRISM Programs

Priority service programs offer electric customers varying levels of electricity prices in return for varying "levels" of electricity service. Under these programs, customers with flexible energy needs can receive discounts, and customers with premium energy needs can purchase premium service at higher rates. The programs help utilities retain customers by increasing service value and reduce risks by more closely matching the utilities' costs and revenues.

The Electric Power Research Institute's (EPRI) Priority Service Project (PRISM) is a long term effort to study priority service programs. Since the study's initiation, Florida Power and Light (FPL) has served as a utility advisor to this project. Recently, FPL and EPRI cooperated on a series of intensive, qualitative face-to-face interviews with some of FPL's largest commercial/industrial (C/I) customers to determine customers' most important criteria when deciding whether or not to participate in priority service programs. This paper reports on these interviews.

At the time of the interviews, FPL had two C/I load management programs that were implemented in 1988 (C/I Load Control and Interruptible Rates) plus a third program, Curtailable Rates, that had been operating for more than ten years. Under the programs, customers agreed to have their load reduced by FPL to a pre-specified "firm" level of demand. In return the customer received a rate reduction, based on the difference between the firm level and the customer's billing demand and a $/kW value for this reduction specified in the applicable tariff.

Motivations for the Joint Study

The reasons for this joint study were:

- "Theory versus reality" for PRISM project. After making significant theoretical progress on the design of PRISM programs, the project team saw a need to gain practical experience to verify or modify emerging theories; and the project team also saw an opportunity to learn about the design of effective surveys of large C/I customers.

- FPL desire to enhance C/I load management programs. The original target for FPL C/I load management programs was 335 MW by 1995; this goal was moved to 1992 due to an "overnight" jump of 1000 MW in the load forecast. Compression of the program schedules heightened FPL's desire to enhance the marketability of the programs.

SURVEY DESIGN

Major Survey Design Decisions

After identifying the need for more information about customers' preferences regarding priority service rates, the question of whether to gather data from actual experience or through a survey arises. Surveys offer several advantages, these include:

- can gather precisely the information desired;
- can be focused on the particular customer segments of interest; and
- are relatively inexpensive versus experiments, and can therefore be updated frequently and quickly.

The disadvantages of surveys include:

- do not describe real actions -- customers have different information and motivations when making real decisions about programs than when answering hypothetical questions, and
- are of limited duration bound by the customer's patience; therefore, surveys cannot collect the very detailed information available from extended monitoring of loads.

No simple rules guide the choice between using historical or experimental data and using survey data. The guiding factors in this case, as in most, were the unavailability of historical data that closely matched the decisions and customer segments to be considered, the cost of experimentation, and the time available for information gathering. The advantages of surveys in each of these areas led to their use in the FPL study.

The survey contained both qualitative and quantitative questions. The qualitative questions were used to investigate customers' decision processes, concerns, and other important issues affecting their decisions to participate or not participate in priority service programs. Quantitative questions were used to collect more precise and detailed information and to test quantitative question formats.

Several types of quantitative questions that can be used in surveys have been identified in the literature (EPRI, 1989). These include:

- Direct cost. An outage or curtailment is described and the customer is asked to state the cost of the outage or curtailment.
- Contingent valuation. An outage or curtailment is described and the customer is asked to state how much he would pay to avoid

the event (Willingness-to-Pay, WTP) or how much he would have to be paid to accept the event (Willingness-to-Accept, WTA).

- Contingent Ranking Method. Respondents are asked to rank or choose from a list of described outages, curtailments, or interruptible/curtailable rates.

The FPL study used both direct cost and contingent ranking methods. A variation on the direct cost type question, the ratio question, was also tested. In a ratio question, the respondent identifies the percent increase in direct costs caused by a change in a curtailment or program. One particular type of contingent ranking question used was a trade-off type question in which just two options are compared.

Briefly, the survey asked respondents to:

- provide information on business and energy use,
- identify and size energy using functions and end uses,
- describe how they would adapt to limitations,
- directly estimate costs,
- answer ratio questions about costs,
- answer trade-off questions about curtailments,
- describe the process for choosing rates,
- state expectations about current programs and about how changes in program characteristics would change firm levels,
- rank program descriptions, and
- answer trade-off questions about priority service programs.

Quantitative Questions

In the direct cost estimation portion of the interview, respondents were asked to estimate their losses at different levels of electricity service curtailment, 10%, 20%, 40%, and 80% load reduction. Losses suggested to respondents were:

- losses during curtailments such as lost wages, wasted materials, and profits not later recovered;
- losses after the limitation such as restart costs and damage repair;
- losses during any makeup work such as overtime charges; and
- any other losses.

Following the direct cost estimation questions, respondents were asked to answer a number of cost ratio questions. These questions asked respondents to state the percent change in costs caused by a change in a curtailment characteristic. Figure 1 presents a typical cost ratio question.

Most respondents were uncomfortable with making estimates of the actual costs of curtailments. There seemed to be several reasons for this:

- uncertainty of costs associated with events such as lost customers;
- many non-monetary costs such as safety and comfort;
- cost variations among limitations depending on time-of-day, weather, work load, ongoing activities; and
- lack of time and information available at the interview.

Two types of firms could estimate the losses due to limitations more easily. At firms with slack production schedules, the cost of a service limitation was limited to increased production cost or make-up work. Firms with back-up generation often felt that the operating cost of the back-up was the only cost of a limitation.

We have been discussing four hour load curtailments.

- If load curtailment lasted two hours, by what percent would your costs of a load curtailment be reduced? _______ %

- If load curtailment lasted eight hours, by what percent would your costs of a load curtailment be increased? _______ %

Figure 1: Example Cost Ratio Question

Estimating the cost to participate in a priority service program has additional difficulties. First, the customer may have to estimate the timing and number of actual limitations. Second, the customer must estimate capital costs for new controls and wiring required to participate in the program.

Three types of contingent ranking questions are illustrated in Figures 2, 3, and 4.

The tradeoffs illustrated in Figure 2 involved different limitation scenarios. Each question specified the duration, notice, depth, and timing of two limitations. (Depth refers to the amount of load cut, the difference between the billing demand and the firm level when discussing programs.) Values for depth that were appropriate for the individual respondent were filled in at the interview. The respondent answering the question indicated on a scale, found below the descriptions, his or her preference and strength of preference. For example, circling a one indicated a strong preference for Limit A over Limit B and circling a seven indicated the opposite.

In the card ranking exercise, respondents were handed a stack of cards with program descriptions and asked to rank these cards. The descriptions included the maximum frequency, maximum duration, and minimum notice for limitations and specified the firm level, rebate, and buy-through.

Which would you prefer?

CHARACTERISTIC	LIMIT A	LIMIT B
Duration (hours):	4	1
Notice (hours):	4	1
Depth (kW):	_______%	_______%
Timing	Summer Weekday 4-8 pm	Summer Weekday 4-8 pm

1 2 3 4 5 6 7

Strong Left | No Preference | Strong Right

Figure 2: Example of a Curtailment Trade-off

(Buy-through is economically equivalent to a penalty; it is a payment per excess kW made to the utility when load is not reduced to the firm level during a limitation.) Respondents could give cards equal ranking and several only used two ranks, i.e. acceptable and unacceptable. Figure 3 illustrates a typical card, firm level was filled in by the interviewer at the time of the interview.

The final contingent ranking exercise asked the respondent to make trade-offs between alternative priority service programs. Typical questions are illustrated in Figure 4.

Program A		
	Max. Frequency:	15/yr
Max. Duration:	4 hr.	
Min. Notice:	4 hr.	
Buy Through:		$24.00/kW
Rebate:		$3.40/kW
Firm Level:		_______%

Figure 3: Example of a Program Ranking Card

Which would you prefer?

CHARACTERISTIC	PROGRAM A	PROGRAM B
Min. Notice:	4 hr.	4 hr.
Buy Through:	$24.00/kw	$24.00/kw
Rebate:	$3.40/kw	$6.00/kw
Firm Level:	_______%	_______%

1	2	3	4	5	6	7
Strong Left			No Preference			Strong Right

Figure 4: Example of a Program Trade-off

The respondents responded well to all the contingent ranking questions. The questions were found to be thought provoking, possible to answer, and relevant.

Sample

The sample consisted of 18 respondents. Types of firms were:

- two municipal sewer facilities,
- a school district,
- three hospitals,
- four mining and minerals processing firms,
- a newspaper,
- a data processing firm,
- four manufacturing firms, and
- two heavy industrial firms.

The firms had 100 to 2,200 employees and averaged 550 employees. The firms were 85% non-union, which may indicate a good deal of flexibility in scheduling employees activities. The firms operated very intensively, averaging 133 working hours per week with 50% operating 24 hours per day and 7 days per week.

Table 1 lists energy use characteristics of the sample. The respondents use relatively large amounts of energy with average peak demands of 5.2 MW and monthly energy use of 2,800 MWh. Further, electric energy is a significant portion of their operating costs, averaging 8% of costs. Much of their energy goes to a single end-use, the most common of these large end-uses being motors, and the second most common being air conditioning. The "Firm load in PRISM programs" number in Table 1 considers only the ten firms in the sample that participate in one of the FPL programs. Seven of the firms were on the load control rate and three firms were on the curtailable rate. On average, the participants made very deep load reductions; they reduced their loads to just 16% of their peak during curtailments.

Table 1
ENERGY USE CHARACTERISTICS

CHARACTERISTIC	MIN.	MAX.	AVERAGE
Peak demand	0.5 MW	30.5 MW	5.2 MW
Monthly energy	87 MWh	13,000 MWh	2,800 MWh
Electricity as a % of expenses	0.3	15	8
Largest end use as % of peak demand	40	99	71
Firm load in PRISM program (percent)	0	34	16

Two additional energy use characteristics may be of interest: only three firms had energy management systems that might be used to control loads, and seven firms had back-up generation equal to over 60% of peak demand.

RESULTS

Segmentation

The sample size was not large enough to allow for statistical analyses; however, several subjective conclusions were drawn about segments that are good candidates for priority service programs.

First, firms with back-up generation can often reduce loads quickly, at low costs, and with little disruption. Their major costs during a curtailment are fuel costs, costs to monitor the generators, and any additional maintenance costs. The key concern for these firms is generator failure at the time a curtailment is called. If in these very rare situations emergency power from the utility is available, even at very high cost, this concern is limited.

Firms in which electricity costs are a high percentage of total expenses can benefit significantly from discounts and have a keener interest in priority service programs. Finally, firms with low operating rates have the opportunity to recover lost production during off hours. Because their energy needs are more flexible, they are more likely to participate in priority service programs.

The interviews indicated that customers vary widely in their costs of curtailments and the types of programs that they might join. However, the interviews also indicated that most customers joining a program would be willing to reduce loads significantly during curtailments; most would cut their loads by more than 50%.

Program Characteristics

Although there was not sufficient data for quantitative analyses, subjective opinions about the importance of program characteristics were also developed. The attributes judged to be of high importance to customers were:

- duration of the individual curtailment,
- frequency of curtailments,
- rebate paid to participants, and
- notice of coming curtailments (if less than one hour).

The attributes of moderate importance were:

- length of the priority service contract and
- buy through or penalty provisions.

Attributes of lesser importance were:

- notice (if one hour or more) and
- payment method.

Interview Design

One goal of these interviews was to determine useful formats for questions about priority service programs. The following types of questions were answered with relative ease:

- quantitative questions about company characteristics such as number of employees and average operating hours,
- estimates of the relative sizes of end-uses–respondents used rules of thumb relating motor sizes and air conditioning tonnage to kW,
- program and curtailment trade-offs, and
- program ranking questions.

Respondents had more difficulty estimating curtailment costs and identifying their choice of firm level under different priority service programs.

Based on these interviews, several recommendations can be made about interview design and implementation. Foremost, before asking questions about preferences, loads and means of reducing loads should be reviewed. An immediate response to priority service programs will often be more conservative than a more considered response.

As far as possible, the interviewer should provide tools, such as worksheets or computer programs, for calculating load reductions and rebates. If such calculations are difficult or cannot be made, respondents will be very reluctant to express opinions or will tend to choose the status quo.

Because interviews are a supplier/customer contact and accuracy depends on respondent interest, respondents must be kept committed to the interview process. To do this, interviews should avoid unrealistic or threatening questions -- for example, asking how the customer will react to numerous curtailments without explaining why such curtailments would occur or what compensation the customer would receive. When using a trade-off format, interviewers should avoid discussing or trading off programs that are clearly not feasible to the customers or to the utility -- such questions generate doubts about relevancy of the study.

The recommended interview structure follows these steps:

1. Review respondent's business characteristics and energy use
2. Educate respondent about load limitation possibilities
3. Determine feasible load limitations for respondent
4. Estimate potential program payments and
5. Use ranking and tradeoff questions to determine preferences.

USE OF THE INFORMATION

FPL made substantial use of the data collected in these interviews. The subjective evaluation of the importance of program characteristics was used in the following ways:

- Duration. FPL is using a linear programming model to analyze projected future peak day load shapes. The analysis determines the expected duration of control periods by season and by year. This information will be useful in terms of program design and notifying customers of expected curtailment durations.
- Frequency. LOLP analyses of power plant outage projections (planned & forced) and new plant construction schedules are providing input on expected needed annual frequencies of control. This information is also being compared to customer inputs gathered in the study.

- Rebate. No change have been made to-date; however, rebates are evaluated regularly with cost-effectiveness models and with inputs from the surveys.

- Notice (if less than one hour). C/I Load Management practice is now de-emphasizing the absolute need for advance notices of more than one hour, and tariff changes are being attempted to guarantee one-hour notices except in emergency conditions.

- Contract length. Tariff change are being attempted to lower commitment from ten years to five years largely due to customer sentiments such as those expressed in the surveys.

- Buy-through. Allowing buy-through is under investigation.

- Penalty. Tariff changes are now being attempted to lower the strict "no middle ground" language on penalties that is presently in the tariffs.

FPL found that the rapid feedback of information gained in the joint study was of great benefit. All the "High Importance" and "Moderate Importance" program characteristics underwent thorough review based on this customer feedback. In particular, the information regarding customers' desire for advanced notice was of the most interest (and surprise) to FPL.

REFERENCES

EPRI, 1989. "Customer Demand for Service Reliability, A Synthesis of the Outage Costs Literature." EPRI P-6510.

IV. SUPPLY SIDE CONSIDERATIONS

TECHNICAL FOUNDATIONS FOR PRICING SYSTEMS SECURITY

by

Fernando L. Alvarado
The University of Wisconsin - Madison

with contributions from:
Dennis Ray, Yi Hu, Rodney Stevenson and Eileen Cashman
The University of Wisconsin - Madison

INTRODUCTION

This paper establishes technical foundations for the determination of the expected costs resulting from system outages. Outages refer to the inability of the system to supply part or all of the system load, not to equipment outages. The paper uses static system security (system adequacy) concepts to separate regions of normal operation from regions where outages occur.

Security is a function of configuration and operating condition. Security can be expressed as a function of a single variable (such as total load or transfer capability between two areas) or as a constraint on this variable. When the system is secure, most actions have negligible impact on security. However, when security is in jeopardy, many actions can have a significant effect on security. Thus, while at times security can be ignored, at other times security is most influential on decisions about the operation (and operating costs) of a system.

Landgren et al. [14] and Brown [3] established interchange capability as a function of the capacity of certain lines. Prediction of loadability is based on a linearization around a base case operating condition. These linearizations work reasonably well for the active power component, provided the resulting deviations are not too large and loadability is limited only by line flow restrictions. These ideas eventually resulted in the concept of maximum loadability [12], which included generation limits.

Limits on generation capability and/or individual transmission lines are not the only limiting influences on security. Systems are reaching a more fundamental limit: the inability of the network to transmit power because of a "bifurcation" condition. One manifestation of bifurcation is steady state system instability. A second manifestation is voltage collapse [11].

When a single parameter in the system is varied, eventually some system limit is reached. This limit can be a transmission line or transformer overloading limit, a generation capacity limit, or a system collapse condition. The limit based on the collapse condition can be calculated using the Point of Collapse method [1,19] based on the singularity of the system Jacobian matrix [18]. Sauer et al. [17] present a modern view of loadability as the ability of the system to reach a point of collapse. It reconciles dynamic and static viewpoints, relating the stability Jacobian to the Power Flow Jacobian.

The cost of security is statistical [10,20]. This makes the security problem similar in some sense to the system reliability problem [16]. At any time, however, either the system is operational (no outage cost incurred) or it has sustained an outage. A priori quantification of outage costs can only be done as expected values. To characterize an outage fully it is also necessary to predict its duration, extent and location.

In this paper we refer to slow system changes (such as load changes) as different system *conditions*, while rapid changes that alter the system result in different *configurations*. System conditions are assumed to vary independently of configuration, and vice-versa. This is not exactly true: for example, heavily loaded components are more likely to fail. Each configuration has a given probability of occurring. Actual system conditions may be different than those expected hours or a day in advance. Variations in system conditions may be either uncorrelated or correlated. Correlated variations are closer to reality, particularly for peak loads which are often quite weather sensitive. The main model used in the paper uses correlated load variations.

SYSTEM TIME FRAMES

The adequacy of a system only makes sense in the context of a given time scale of interest. Figure 1 illustrates various time frames. Within each time frame it describes the analytical and computational tools that may be used to study the system, the types of control actions that respond within the type frame, and the nature of security in the context of the time frame.

The longest time frame considered is the "planning" time frame. This time frame spans multiple years. The system is "controlled" by commissioning and decommissioning generating plants and transmissions lines. This is the time frame within which power system reliability studies are performed. The concepts of Loss of Load probability, Demand not Served and related ideas are used to decide when is new generation capacity (or new transmission) needed, and of what size. The power flow is the main tool used to study the capability of the integrated generation and transmission network. In this time frame the response of the system is under the control of system planners. Uncertainties in this time frame are uncertainties in load growth and equipment availability. Optimization within this time frame can take the form of traditional minimum expansion cost planning or the form of "least cost planning" (where demand is assumed to be controllable by the planner in addition to supply). Minimum cost is not always the only criterion used. Risk-aversion can result in the selection of an optimal compromise as the best plan for a given set of assumptions about the future. In this regard, refer to the recent paper by Merrill [15]. The time constants associated with this time frame involve the delay times necessary for plant construction and for equipment procurement. The hard constraints in this time frame can be limits on the availability of sites for generation or transmission, or they can also be financial constraints.

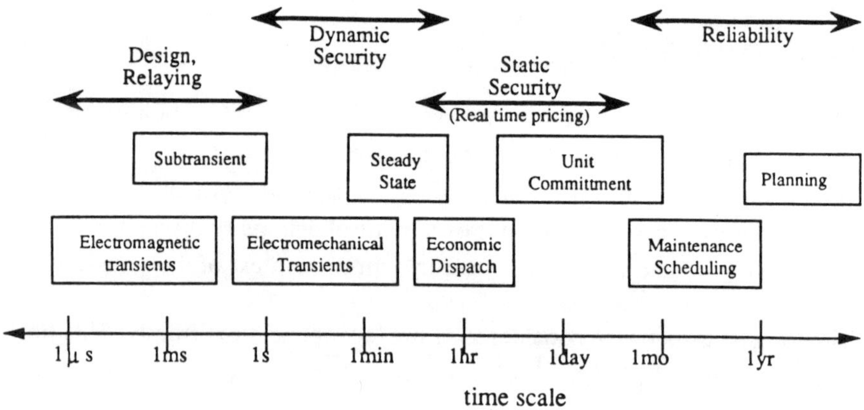

Figure 1. Time Frames of Power System Control and Operation

At the other end of the time spectrum from the planning time frame is the "Electromagnetic Transients" time frame. This time frame spans from a microsecond or so to a few cycles. In this time frame, the entire behavior of the power system is dictated by the electrical properties of the system. Furthermore, the limited speed of propagation of electrical signals plays a key role in determining system behavior. Events do not occur simultaneously at different points in the system. Travelling waves develop. Overvoltages are a serious consideration. Little actual energy is dissipated within this time frame. One of the primary tools for the study of the system during this time frame is the electromagnetic transients program.

In between these two extremes lie several other relevant time frames. During the subtransient period the system behavior is dominated by the electrical characteristics of generators and lines. The subtransient period spans from a few hundred microseconds to several cycles. Phenomena in this time frame are so fast that there is no opportunity to take any substantial control action. Control of system behavior during this time period is dictated entirely by the parameters and the design of the system hardware, as well as the system topology. Because parameters of components cannot usually be altered at will, there is often little that can be done to alter subtransient system behavior. The inertia of the generators and even of the loads makes mechanical dynamics during this period largely irrelevant. It is during this period that pre-set relay settings within the system must operate. Some HVDC and Static VAR controls may be fast enough to have some influence on system behavior during this time period. One of the main tools to study the behavior of the system in this time frame is the short circuit analysis program.

The transient period of response is the period from a few cycles to a few seconds. This is the period within which voltage regulators, exciters and even governor action take place. Some relay actions also take place during this time frame. While there is no opportunity for operator action during this period, it is possible to substantially alter the response of the system and the integrity of the system during this time period by the appropriate design and selection of generator and exciter controls and of HVDC controls. Energy considerations are quite prominent during this period of response, but only as far as transient stability issues are concerned: will the system continue to operate in a synchronous manner? The primary tool for the analysis of the system in this time frame is the transient stability program. Also of value are eigenvalue calculation programs. Measures of dynamic system security make most sense in this time frame.

Beyond the transient time frame is the steady state time frame. This time frame spans from several seconds to a few minutes. This time frame assumes that the system has survived the events of any disturbance and has now settled into an operable (although perhaps quite unacceptable) operating point. The primary controls available during this time frame are voltage settings at the various generators as well as the scheduling of active power demands among generators. The primary tool for the study of the system during this time period is the power flow. Some power plant dynamics and a few stabilizer and tap changer dynamics are often also of importance. For these types of problems a mid-term transient stability program may be of value. It is in this time frame that the notions of steady state security and adequacy make most sense. Whether the system survives an event often depends on the nature of the post-disturbance steady state operating condition.

Beyond the mere steady state time frame is the economic operation time frame. This time frame spans from about one minute to a few hours. In this time frame it is assumed that the system has been steered to a deliberately selected steady state operating point, not to the steady state that merely results after a transient or disturbance. The primary controls available for this time frame include generator powers and voltages, transformer tap positions, in some cases loads, inter-area power interchanges and modulation of HVDC power orders and voltages. Different operating policies and objectives can lead to very different economic operating states. During this time frame energy becomes quite important. The main tools for the study of the system during this time frame are economic dispatch programs and optimum power flows. If true real time prices for a system were to be implemented, this is probably the fastest time frame within which they would make sense. Even here, however, it is doubtful that sufficiently fast response could be achieved to justify real-time pricing in this time frame.

Beyond the economic dispatch time frame is the unit commitment time frame. Economic operation of the system is possible only inasmuch as equipment is available. It is during this slower time frame from fractions of an hour to a couple of days that decisions are made as to what equipment must be available for operations. The security of the system as well as the ability to operate the system economically are critically dependent on the decisions made during this time period. It is during this time frame that transactions among utilities are often negotiated. It is also during this time frame that day-ahead real time prices must be decided.

Beyond the unit commitment time frame is the maintenance scheduling and fuel supply time frame. This is the time frame within which one decides what components of the system can safely be removed for maintenance. It is also during this time frame that fuel supply is often a consideration.

Which brings us back to the planning time frame, spanning from a few months to decades, and the issues of long term reliability.

THE OPERATIONAL LIMIT BOUNDARY

The Operational Limit Boundary (OLB) is a surface in bus (active and reactive) demand space that results in operational limits being attained. It can be used to measure the security of a given operating point (or demand condition) and to determine how power system operators could respond effectively should the security (adequacy) of a given operating point be undesirable.

A simple and direct computation of the expected value of the outage probability of a system is possible if the OLB is available, and if the probability distribution of a system states can be assumed known on the same space where the OLB is defined. This permits the computation not only of the expected outage probability, but also of the incremental outage probability.

The OLB can be computed from the knowledge of:

- Configuration (generators and lines in service),
- Condition (demand levels at each bus),
- Limits (transmission line and generator limits),
- System operating policies.

Figure 2 illustrates how the OLB is established for a given configuration for the case of a system with only two independent demands. The OLB concept generalizes to an arbitrary number of demands. The surfaces shown in

Figure 2 denote demand levels that result in power system problems established by generation and transmission limits or by voltage collapse conditions. For a two-dimensional space, these limit surfaces are lines. For an n dimensional space of demands, these surfaces are manifolds of dimensions $n-1$. The composite OLB is the surface of demand levels that satisfy all of the individual boundary conditions. This composite OLB is the surface on which this paper focuses.

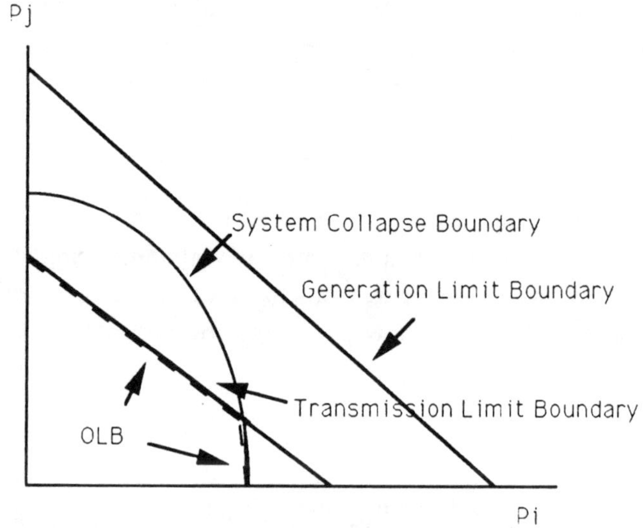

Figure 2. Surfaces that Define the Operational Limit Boundary

It is useful to describe the meaning of this boundary in the context of the time frames from the previous section. The different "portions" that comprise the boundary are not all necessarily from the same time frame. Specifically, line flow limits or transformer limits are usually not hard limits. Exceeding these limits may be possible for short periods. On the other hand, the steady state operational limit boundary is not only a hard limit, but is a limit that can never be attained because a system that approaches this limit may not be able to survive some of the faster time frames such as the transient time frame: any disturbance may result in system failure under conditions when, in theory, a feasible operating point should exist.

To reconcile all these operational boundaries, we assume that effects in time frames faster than the steady state time frame cannot be controlled. They do, however, influence the location of the OLB. Thus, we think that the correct determination of the OLB should incorporate dynamic effects. We are, thus, assuming that the OLB is independent of system operating state. This is, in general, not precisely correct. However, it may be sufficiently close for practical use in static security determination. The mechanism that is used to incorporate dynamic effects into the OLB is the subject of on-going research.

Similarly, we will assume that soft limits become, at some point, hard limits. Thus, we will use hard limits for line flows.

With these two assumptions, we have now established a unified basis for the interpretation of the OLB. However, to account for the uncertainty and variability in the OLB, we intend to extend our work to consider the characterization of the OLB not as a separating line, but more as a separating region. One way of accomplishing this is to define not one but several OLB's: a median OLB along with OLB's at various percentile probabilities of occurring, much as in the case of different configurations. This is not pursued further here, but the example section contains additional ideas in this regard.

The operating policy also affects the location of the OLB. For a given demand condition, power system operators have control over generation levels (active and reactive), unit commitment, and interchange levels with other utilities. Altering any of these variables affects the distance of that operating point from the OLB.

Since operating policies affect the OLB, it is possible to specify different OLBs depending upon the choice of operating policies. The simplest OLB is obtained using predetermined participation factors for all generators. A more realistic OLB can be realized using a policy of economic dispatch. In fact, depending on the assumptions about the time frame within which the system is to operate, different OLB's can be obtained. Time frames were described in the previous section.

In view of these comments on the nature of the OLB, it makes sense to talk about a transition region rather than a line. As an alternative, the OLB can be interpreted as the median point for a "fuzzy" region during which the system makes a transition from operable to unoperable. A probabilistic OLB is perhaps the best way to take into account the dynamic effects of some of the faster time frames, while retaining the steady state analytic framework set forth in this paper.

It is possible to enlarge the size of the feasible operating region by altering the operating policy. For example, it is possible to operate the system in a manner that sacrifices economy but results in a larger secure region. This can be done by selecting less than economically optimal operating conditions. This is security constrained economic dispatch. If such an operating policy is adopted a-priori, it is taken into account in the formation of the OLB. On the other hand, the present paper lays the foundations for permitting security to be taken into account not always as an a-priority constraint, but also as a cost.

DISTANCE TO THE OLB

Euclidean distances from the current operating point to the OLB give a simple indication of the possibility that a security problem might occur. The further the current operating point is from the OLB, the more secure the system is. Figure 3 illustrates the OLB in bus demand space.

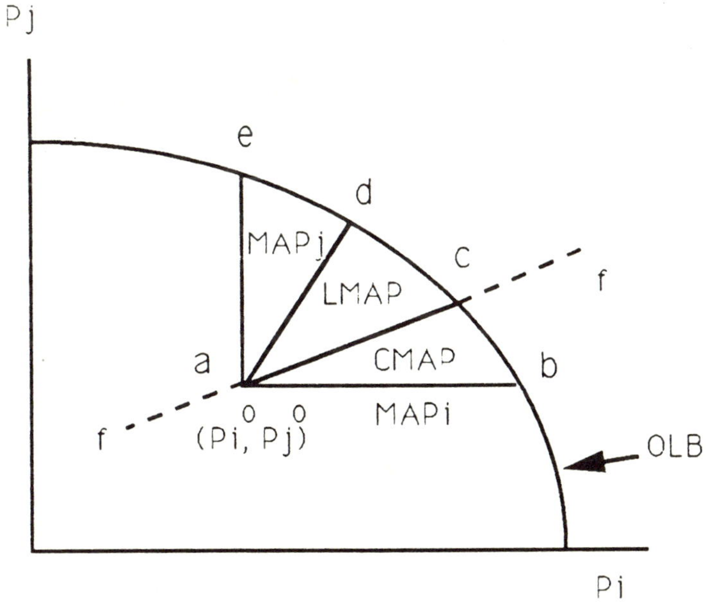

Figure 3. Distance Measures of Proximity to the OLB

Three possible distance measures are:

1. Uncorrelated maximum available power (MAP_i) is the distance from the operating point to the OLB when the demand at bus i is increased. In Figure 3, MAP_i is the distance from a to b, and MAP_j is the distance from a to e.

2. Correlated maximum available power (CMAP) is the magnitude of the vector from the current operating point to the OLB surface along a line of simultaneous demand increases. In Figure 3, if the demands are perfectly correlated, then all of feasible demands lie along a line such as f-f, and the CMAP is the distance from a to c.

3 Lowest maximum available power (LMAP) is the minimum distance to the OLB from the operating point [13]. This distance is found by (1) determining the normal to the OLB that passes through the current operating point, and (2) determining the distance along the normal from the OLB to the current operating point [8,9].

Sensitivity of the distance measures to changes in demand or changes in generation level provides information about how decisions by customers or power system operators affect system security. The normal to the OLB plays an important role in the determination of the sensitivity of distance measures between to changes in operating point (either changes in generation or changes in demand). Figure 4 illustrates vectors normal to the OLB. For example, the cosine of the angle α between the normal to the OLB and the direction of correlated demand increases indicates how correlated changes in demand affect the LMAP distance measure as the system approaches the OLB. The computation of normal vector to the OLB is done using the left eigenvector to the system equations at the point of collapse [8].

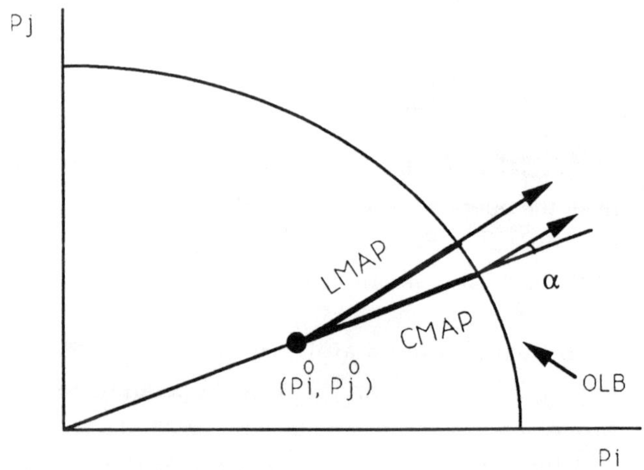

Figure 4. Illustrating Normal Vectors to the OLB

Distance measures have an intuitive interpretation, but do not indicate likelihood, magnitude or economic significance of outages. The probabilistic measures described in the next section provide that information.

The discussion of proximity measures in this section used the OLB for one configuration. A weighted average of distance measures can be used to determine an aggregate measure of security over multiple configurations.

PROBABILISTIC MEASURES

These measures are applicable to operating the pricing policies. Since demand is only known stochastically, there is a joint distribution of bus demands around an operating point which is at the mean of the distribution. Some demand combinations in the joint distribution fall below the OLB and normal operating status occurs. Other combinations fall beyond the OLB resulting in security problems and possible outages. Figure 5 illustrates possible distributions of bus demands.

The probabilistic measures include the following:

1. Probability of normal operating status
2. Expected demand not-served,
3. Expected energy not-served, and
4. Expected outage cost.

The ordering of these measures indicates an increasing amount of information required to make the computation. Measure 1 requires knowledge of the OLB and the joint probability density function of bus demands. Measure 2 requires knowledge of the *extent* of an outage (where extent denotes what buses and fraction of loads are involved in an outage). Measure 3 requires the additional knowledge of the outage *duration*.. Finally, Measure 4 requires the information used in computing measures 1-3 plus a knowledge of the *cost* of the outage to customers and the utility. Knowledge of sensitivity of Measure 4 to load changes is useful for real-time pricing decisions [6,5].

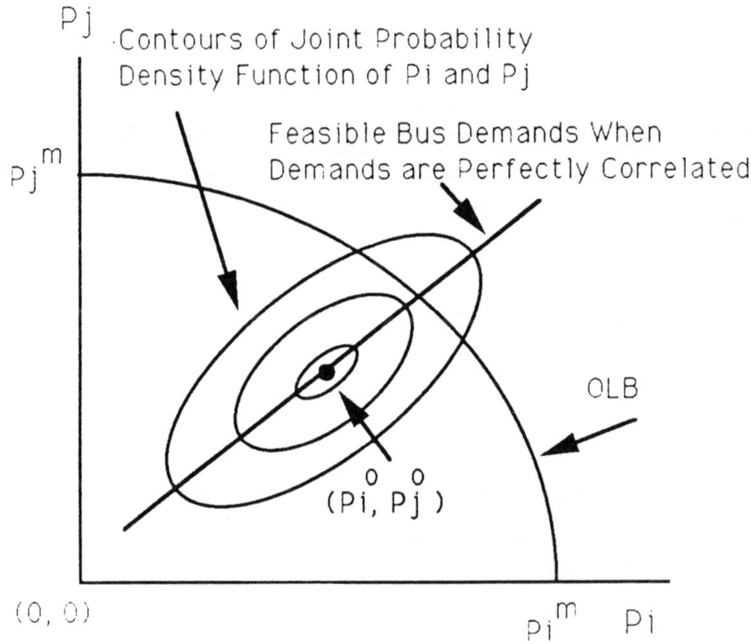

Figure 5. Contours of the Joint Probability
Density Function of Bus Demands

Let P_i equal the active power demand at load bus i. P_i is a random variable defined by:

$$P_i = P_i^0 + u_i$$

where $E(u_i) = 0$. Thus $E(P_i) = P_i^0 \bullet u_i$ is the difference between actual and expected demand for bus i at a specified time of day.

Assuming a two-load bus system, let the joint probability density function be specified by $f(u_i,u_j)$. The OLB is defined by:

$$g(P_i,P_j) = 0$$

which implicitly defines either $P_i = g_i(P_j)$ or $P_j = g_j(P_i)$.

The probability that demands at buses i and j fall within the normal operating region where no outage occurs is given by

$$P^N = \int_{-P_j^0}^{P_j^m - P_j^0} \int_{-P_i^0}^{g_i(P_j^0+u_j)-P_i^0} f(u_i,u_j)\, du_i du_j \qquad (1)$$

Thus, the probability of a normal operating status is the "volume" of f inside the OLB. The outage probability is $1 - P^N$.

This equation can be simplified under the assumption that the deviations of bus demands from expected values are perfectly correlated. Under this assumption, the relationship between the deviations can be described as $c_i u_i = c_j u_j$. Thus, the joint probability density function f can be expressed in terms of the probability density function of any bus demand. In Figure 6 the probability of a normal operating state is given equivalently by areas A, A_i, or A_j.

The point (P_i^B, P_j^B) is the intersection of line F with the OLB. If $f_i(u_i)$ is the probability density function for u_i, then the probability of a normal operating state is given by:

$$P^N = \int_{-P_i^0}^{u_i^B} f_i(u_i) du_i \qquad (2)$$

where $u_i^B = P_i^B - P_i^0$.

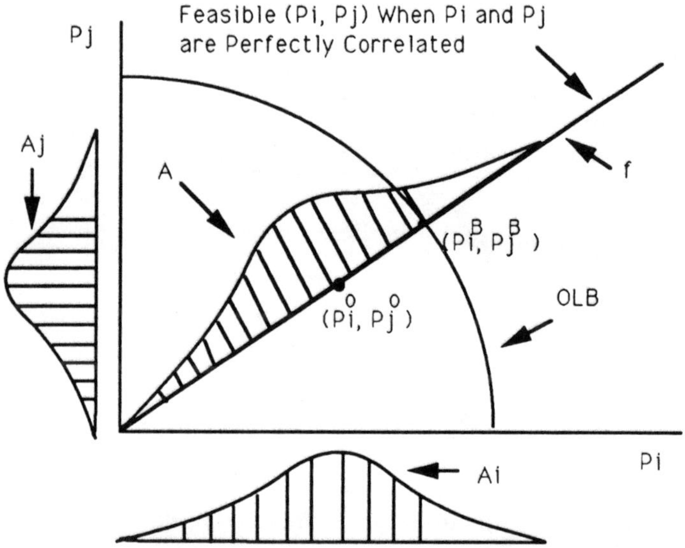

Figure 6: Equivalent Areas of Normal Operating Status

As a consequence, the change in the probability of a normal operating state with respect to a change in expected demand P_i^0 is given by:

$$\frac{\partial P^N}{\partial P_i^0} = f_i(u_i^B)\left[\frac{\partial P_i^B}{\partial P_i^0} - 1\right] \tag{3}$$

where it is assumed that $f_i(-P_i^0) = 0$.

Of interest is the effect on the outage probability of changing the operating policy that determined the location of the OLB. When demands are perfectly correlated, the effect of changes in generation on P^N can be determined from:

$$\frac{\partial P^N}{\partial Pg_k} = f_i(u_i^B)\,\frac{\partial P_i^B}{\partial Pg_i} \tag{4}$$

where Pg_k is the active power generation at bus k. A similar derivative can be determined for reactive power generation. The partial derivatives can be determined from elements of the normal vector to g.

The proximity measures of Expected Demand Not Served (EDNS), Expected Unserved Energy (EUE), and Expected Outage Cost (EOC) quantify the magnitude and economic significance of different levels of security. Their computation requires knowledge of the extent, duration, and cost of an outage. For a simple illustration of concepts, this paper assumes that the extent and duration of an outage (if it occurs) can be pre-determined and are fixed known quantities. The work can then be extended to cases that requires more complex characterization of both extent and outage.

With regard to cost computation, Crew and Kleindorfer [7] suggest that cost is composed of lost customer benefit plus the cost of interrupting customers (a "rationing" cost), less the operating cost savings because generation is reduced during an outage. Outage costs have a variable component that depends upon the amount of unserved energy. Caves et al. [4] note that studies of the functional relationship between outage costs and unserved energy have produced wide-ranging results.

For a more detailed view of the mathematics of computation for these probabilistic measures, refer to [2].

The equations given in Section 5 for the proximity measures apply to one configuration with its associated OLB. Probability weighting for different configurations yield probabilistic measures over multiple configurations.

NUMERICAL EXAMPLE

This section presents the results of determining proximity measures to a given OLB. Demands are assumed to be perfectly correlated.

Definitions and ideas are illustrated through a five-bus, two-machine system illustrated in Figure 7. The example is the same as used in [2]. The base case operating conditions listed in Tables 1 and 2 give two operating points: one operating point is considered as a "normal" operating point. The second operating point is deliberately close to the system OLB, and is considered an extreme operating point. The OLB is computed based entirely on static considerations (no transient stability effects). In reality, a method for ensuring a more conservative OLB to account for dynamic effect is desirable. One possible way to accomplish this is to seek an OLB that does not make the smallest eigenvalue exactly zero but falls below a certain value. This or other modifications to the OLB method to take into account system dynamics are not considered here.

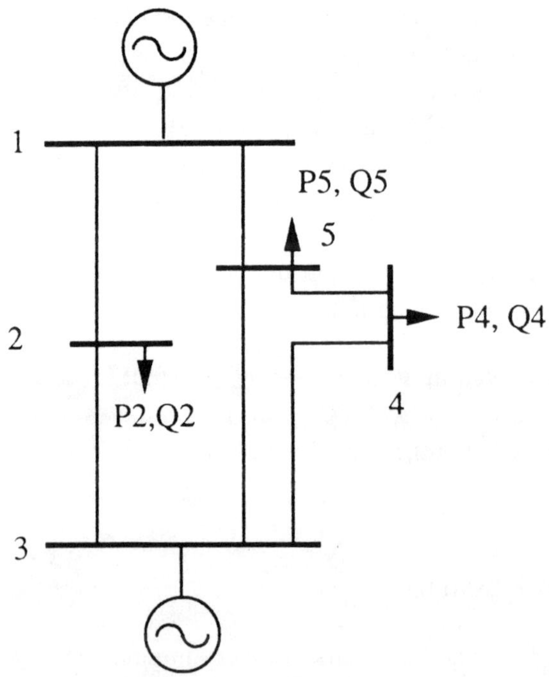

Figure 7. Sample 5 Bus System

Table 1

BASE OPERATING CONDITIONS

Bus	V	P+jQ	$P_g + jQ_g$
1	1.04 ∠ (rad)	0	2.5687 + j0.8863
2	0.9502∠– 0.1665	1.4 + j0.6	0
3	1.02∠ – 0.1304	0	1.1 + j1.0342
4	0.9019∠ – 0.2594	0.7 + j0.3	0
5	0.9475∠ – 0.1768	1.4 + j0.4	0

Table 2

EXTREME OPERATING CONDITIONS
These conditions may be outside the OLB
if dynamic effects are considered

Bus	V	P+jQ	$P_g + jQ_g$
1	1.04 ∠ (rad)	0	6.5427 + j2/5090
2	0.8557∠– 0.5207	3 + j0.6	0
3	1.02∠ – 0.4892	0	1.1 + j2.4533
4	0.8390∠ – 0.6043	0.7 + j0.3	0
5	0.8496∠ – 0.4841	3 + j0.4	0

Under each operating condition, there are loads at buses 2, 4 and 5. P_2 and P_5 can vary arbitrarily within the Operational Limit Boundary, but reactive powers are fixed. The computed OLB is illustrated by a solid line in Figure 8. MAPs illustrate how much additional active power the system can supply to bus 2 and bus 5. This OLB is obtained from the system without constraints or system dynamic effects. Once constraints are imposed on the system, the OLB changes, along with the associated MAPs. Any given operating point may no longer be in the secure region. This means constraints may force system outages.

Figure 8 illustrates the computed OLB for the 5 bus system. In addition, it shows the effect of placing limits on active generation power on the OLB boundary. Figure 9 illustrates the original OLB plus the OLBs that result if different line outage cases are considered. Both operating points are within the original OLB, but only the "normal" operating point is within all three boundaries (and only marginally so). Figure 10 illustrates the effect of two different values of line flow limits on line 1-2 on the OLB. Again, the "normal" operating point is inside both limits, but the "extreme" operating point is not.

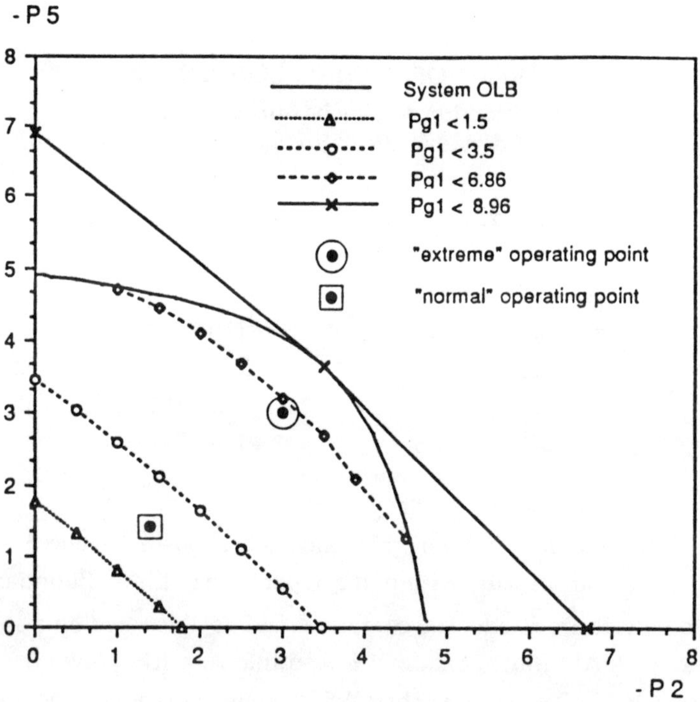

Figure 8. Actual OLB for 5 Bus System
Indicating the effect of limits on active generation power limits on the OLB

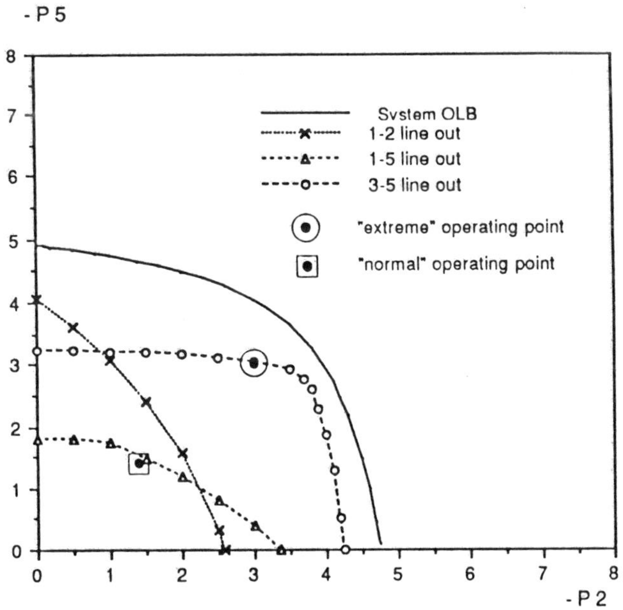

Figure 9. Effect of Configurations (Line Outages) on OLB

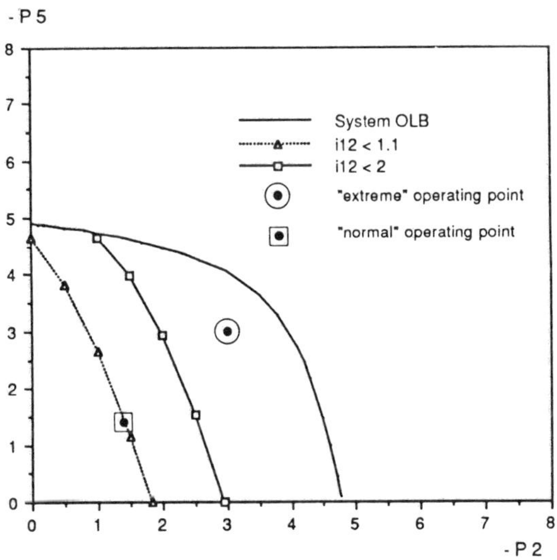

Figure 10. Effect of Line Flow Limits on OLB

The various MAP measures for the system OLB at different operating point are given in Table 3. The sensitivities of these MAP measures both to demand at a bus and to generation rescheduling are listed in Table 4. Under normal operating conditions, the effect on security is negligible.

Table 5 summarizes the probabilistic measures of proximity to the OLB. The probability density functions for the u_i at operating points (3,3) and (1.4,1.4) are N(0,0.683) and N(0,1) respectively. The extent of the outage is assumed to be total demand (that is, system collapse), and the presumed outage duration is 15 minutes. The outage cost is assumed to be $10 per kWh of unserved energy. The probability of an outage, $1 - P^N$, is reported in Table 5. The results show that when the expected demands are close to the OLB, there is a high probability of collapse with its associated effect on EDNS, EUE and EOC.

Table 6 summarizes the sensitivity of the probabilistic measures to a change in injected power at various buses. Increasing demand at buses 2 and 5 increase outage probability, EDNS, EUE and EOC. Altering the operating policy by increasing active power generation at bus 3 improves all the security measures.

Table 3

DISTANCE MEASURES OF SYSTEM OLB

Distance Measure	Operating at (1.4,1.4)	Operating at (3,3)
MAP_2	3.1132	0.9649
MAP_5	3.2392	1.0363
CMAP	3.0703	0.8075
LMAP	3.0674	0.8062

Table 4

SENSITIVITY OF DISTANCE MEASURES AT (3,3)

P_i	$\frac{\partial MAP_2}{\partial P_i}$	$\frac{\partial MAP_5}{\partial P_i}$	$\frac{\partial MAP}{\partial P_i}$	$\frac{\partial MAP_5}{\partial P_i}$
P_2^0	-1.0000	-0.6078	-1.8585	-1.1490
Pg_3	0.6819	0.6822	0.6486	0.6484
P_5^0	-0.5299	-1.0000	-1.1151	-1.9150

Table 5

PROBABILISTIC MEASURES OF PROXIMITY TO THE OLB

Operating Point	$1 - P^N$	EDNS MW	EUE MWh	EOC 1000 $
(3.0,3.0)	28.39%	258	64.5	645
(1.4,1.4)	≈ 0%	≈ 0	≈ 0	≈ 0

Table 6

SENSITIVITY OF PROBABILISTIC MEASURES
TO CHANGES IN INJECTED POWER,
to be weighted by the probability of occurrence of the configuration

P_i	$-\frac{\partial P^N}{\partial P_i}$	$\frac{\partial EDNS}{\partial P_i}$	$\partial EUE/\partial P_i)$	$\partial EOC/\partial P_i$
pu			KWh/KW	$/KW
P_2^0	0.1859	1.7418	0.4355	4.355
Pg_3	-0.1628	-1.2767	-0.3192	-3.192
P_2^0	0.1530	1.4838	0.3710	3.710

CONCLUSIONS

The concept of Point of Collapse can be used to find "distances" to ultimate operational limits in demand space. Distance and probability measures of proximity to operational limits provide useful information for the calculation of total and incremental values for expected demand not served and expected outage costs. This approach to power system security determination is capable of considering all technical limitations to power transmission imposed by the system: transmission line and transformer capacity, generator and prime mover limitations, and system collapse conditions, all within a unified framework. The notion of different time frames was used to unify diverse measures of security into a single measure. This framework is computationally efficient and is able to take into account any kind of system model or operational limit.

ACKNOWLEDGEMENT

Support from the National Science Foundation under contract ECS-8907391 is acknowledged. Also acknowledged is support from the Electric Power Research Institute under contract RP-4000-14 under the supervision of Dr. Rambabu Adapa. Thanks are due to Ian Dobson, Chris DeMarco, and Laurence Kirsch for valuable suggestions.

REFERENCES

1. F.L. Alvarado and T.H. Jung. "Direct Detection of Voltage Collapse Conditioning". In EPRI Report EL-6183, Proceedings of Conference held in Potosi, MO, September 1988, pp. 5.23-5.38, January 1989.

2. F.L. Alvarado, Y. Hu, D. Ray, R. Stevenson and E. Cashman. "Engineering Foundations for the Determination of Security Costs". Report ECE-90-6, Department of Electrical and Computer Engineering, The University of Wisconsin, Madison, September 1990.

3. H.E. Brown. "Interchange Capability and Contingency Evaluations by a Z-matrix Method". *IEEE Trans on Power Appl. & Syst.*, vol. PAS-91, pp. 1827-1832, May 1972.

4. D.W. Caves, J.A. Herriges and R.J. Windle. "Customer Demand for Service Reliability, A Synthesis of the Outage Costs Literature". Palo Alto, CA: Electric Power Research Institute, P-2801, September 1989.

5. D.W. Caves and B. Neenan. "Real-Time Pricing: Will It Work?" Atlanta, GA. 1990 SE Reg. Pub. Utilities Conference, August 1990.

6. B. Chapman and T. Tramutola. "Real-Time Pricing: DSM at its Best?" Boston, MA.: ECNE National Conference on DS Management, November 16-17, 1989.

7. M.A. Crew and P.R. Kleindorfer. *Public Utility Economics*. New York: St. Martin's Press, 1979.

8. I. Dobson. "Observations on the Geometry of Saddle Node Bifurcations and Voltage Collapse in Electric Power Systems". ECE Report ECE-90-5. Submitted for publication.

9. I. Dobson, Y. Hu, F. Alvarado and L. Lu. "Direct Calculation of Minimum Distance in Parameter Space to Voltage Collapse". In preparation.

10. T.E. DyLiacco. "The Adaptive Reliability Problem." *IEEE Trans on Power Apparatus and Systems*, vol. PAS-86, pp. 517-531, 1967.

11. EPRI. "Bulk Power System Voltage Phenomena-Voltage Stability and Security". Proc. of Conf. held in Potosi, MO, Sept. 1988. Report EL-6183, Jan. 1989.

12. L.L. Garver, P.R. Van Horne and K.A. Wirgau. "Load Supplying Capability of Generation-Transmission Network". *IEEE Trans on Power Apparatus and Systems*, vol. PAS-98, No. 3, pp. 957-961, 1979.

13. T.H. Jung, K.J. Kim and F.L. Alvarado. "A Marginal Analysis of Voltage Stability with Load Variations". Graz, Austria: Proceedings of the 10th PSCC, August 1990.

14. G.L. Landgren, T.L. Terhune and R.K. Angel. "Transmission Interchange Capability". IEEE Trans on Power Apparatus and Systems, vol. PAS-91, pp. 2405-2410, June 1972.

15. H.M. Merrill. "Risk and Uncertainty in Power System Planning." Graz, Austria: 10th PSCC Conference, August 19-24, 1990.

16. M.V.F. Pereira, L.M.V. Pinto, M. Mazumdar and S.I. Yengar. "Development of a Composite System Reliability Evaluation Program". EPRI Report EL-6926, vol. 1 & 2, August 1990.

17. P.W. Sauer, J. Evans and M.A. Pai. "Maximum Unconstrained Loadability of Power Systems". New Orleans, LA: 1990 ISCAS Conference, May 1990.

18. A. Tiranuchit and R. Thomas. "A Posturing Strategy Against Voltage Instabilities in Electric Power Systems". *IEEE Trans on Power Apparatus and Systems*, pp. 83-87, February 1988.

19. T. VanCutsem. "A Methods to Compute Reactive Power Margins with Respect to Voltage Collapse". Atlanta, GA: IEEE/PES Winter Mtg., February 1990.

20. F.F. Wu and Y-K Tsai. "Probabilistic Dynamic Security Assessment of Power Systems: Part I–Basic Model". *IEEE Trans. on Circ. & Syst*, vol. CAS-30, pp. 148-159, March 1983.

OPTIMIZING DEMAND SIDE CONTRIBUTIONS TO POWER SYSTEM SECURITY

by

R. John Kaye
University of New South Wales, Sydney, Australia;

Felix F. Wu
University of California, Berkeley;

Pravin P. Varaiya
University of California, Berkeley

INTRODUCTION

It has been widely recognized that both economic and environmental benefits can be obtained from influencing demand side actions so that they are better coordinated with the rest of the industry. The focus of attention of industry regulators and utility planners and operators is thus broadening to include demand side options. Industry decision making is becoming more decentralized, with consumers and increasing numbers of non-utility generators becoming more participants.

In this paper, we consider the consequences of this change in industry structure on power system security. We propose a scheme for maintaining optimal security at least social cost by exploiting the cheapest options for contribution to security responses, many of which will come from the demand side of the industry.

Power system security refers to the ability of the system to sustain a significant disturbance and to then continue to supply the demand for electrical energy. The unexpected disturbances, referred to as *contingencies* include the failure of large generators, the loss of transmission capacity and sudden increases in demand for electrical energy.

An insecure power system is one which could not withstand one or more possible disturbances. It is thus at risk of losing synchronism and experiencing a subsequent blackout. The social and economic disruption that can be associated with such events is well documented [1]. Research and development activities in the technical aspects of assessing and maintaining power system security have been well documented in the literature (see, for example, the bibliography in [3]).

Traditionally, power system security has been the responsibility of supply utilities, which maintain their own response capabilities for each disturbance that is believed to be both possible and threatening. The size and nature of spare resources that are held in readiness for rapid response to emergency events is often determined using a list of credible contingencies. The configuration of the transmission system and the amount of spinning reserve is then chosen so that the system can survive each contingency.

However, the economic, political and technical circumstances of the electricity supply industry are changing. The use of potential demand side responses to system emergencies is now not only feasible because of changes in communication technology but it is also economically desirable because of the high fixed and variable costs of supply side plant. For example, there are now many situations where the cost to a utility of purchasing an interruptible load contract from a large consumer is less than the costs of maintaining the equivalent amount of supply side spinning reserve [4].

In this paper, we describe a proposal in which utilities purchase from demand side participants (i.e., consumers, cogenerators and third party suppliers of electrical energy) their capacity to respond to security events. This approach generalizes existing concepts of interruptible load. By establishing the appropriate purchase price for potential (contingent) demand side responses, the utility can minimize the total cost involved in security control, including the costs of avoiding system blackout.

The research reported in this paper extends the work of Schweppe et al, [10] who first proposed the use of pricing to maintain system security [4, pp. 214-222]. Using the approach of our earlier work [5], we have developed a probabilistic framework for describing the socially optimal level of security which properly allocates the burden of maintaining system security to participants. The security/economy trade-off is thus resolved.

The mathematical development and proof of the results presented in this paper can be found in [2]. In the present paper we concentrate on presenting the theoretical framework and describing the main results.

SECURITY IN A DECENTRALIZED POWER SYSTEM ENVIRONMENT

Traditionally, the utility exercised complete control over all generation, transmission and distribution resources. Consumers were considered as an exogenous demand for electrical energy which could not be affected by supply side actions. This situation is illustrated in Figure 1. Under this arrangement, the main operating objectives of utilities were to supply the demand for electrical energy at the lowest possible cost which was consistent with maintaining adequate security. Production costs were minimized using economic dispatch of generators and security levels were maintained by carrying a significant level of operating (spinning) reserves. Thus, security was solely the concern of the utility and its maintenance was achieved using utility owned equipment.

In modern power systems, changes in economics and technology have made it increasingly important to consider the possibility of using demand side responses to minimize system costs. The demand side participants are the consumers, cogenerators and other non-utility generators. The latter includes consumer-owned backup supply generators which are used to enhance consumer reliability such as uninterruptible power supplies (UPS).

Modifying the actions of demand side participants has become a significant option in power system control. Such modifications include voluntary reductions in demand and increases in output from non-utility generators. Arrangements between utilities and demand side participants for exploiting these demand side options include:

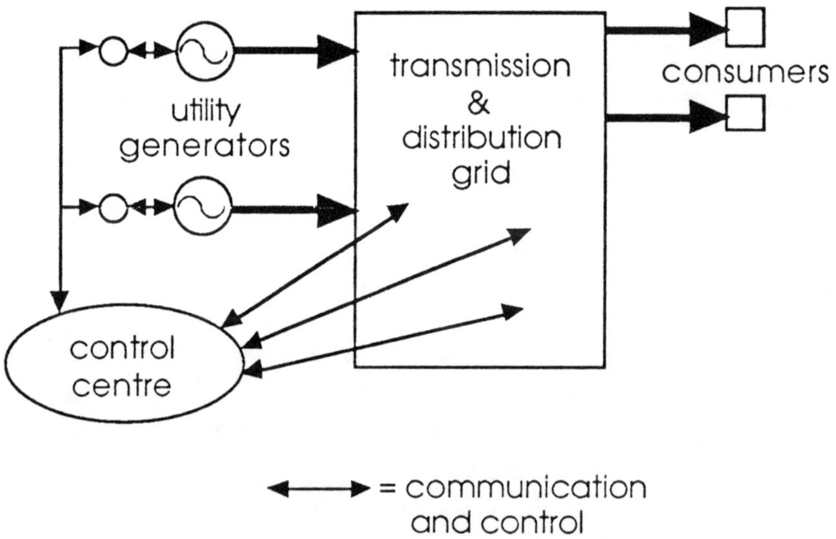

Figure 1. Operation of Traditional Power Systems

The utility has complete control over the generators and the grid and no attempt is made to coordinate the actions of the consumers.

- Dynamic pricing [5] in which the price varies according to the supply-demand balance. The price rises when a reduction in consumer demand (or an increase in the outputs of non-utility generators) would benefit the system [6].
- Contractual arrangements [4] in which demand side participants agree to reduce their demand by specific amounts upon request from the utility, and
- Direct utility control of demand side equipment. One example is utility dispatch of non-utility generation.

Each of these arrangements requires some form of real time communication between the utility and the demand side participant. This situation is illustrated in Figure 2.

In a decentralized power system, the operating objectives of the utility remain substantially unaltered: to supply the demand for electrical energy as cheaply as is consistent with maintaining adequate levels of security. Also, because of changing demand side economics and end-use technologies the appropriate level of security should be reassessed.

The operating objectives of the other participants are mostly concerned with maximizing their own (operating) profits. They are thus not directly concerned with maintaining system security, although, of course, a loss of system stability would cause interruptions to their own supply. It is thus necessary to give demand side participants appropriate incentives to contribute to system security.

As with supply side equipment, there are two aspects to demand side contributions to maintaining system security: preparedness and actuation. The time scales involved in responding to a contingency event imply that responses must be prepared before the event. Just as maintaining appropriate levels of supply side spinning reserve requires significant preparation, demand side responses to contingencies will also require a degree of change to the normal operating state. Examples of preparedness on the demand side include:

- reconfiguration of plant operating schedules so that rapid changes can easily be made,
- changes in staffing levels,
- choice of levels of storage of, for example, backup generation fuel stocks or intermediate products, and
- purchase of new capital items of equipment or modifications to existing items.

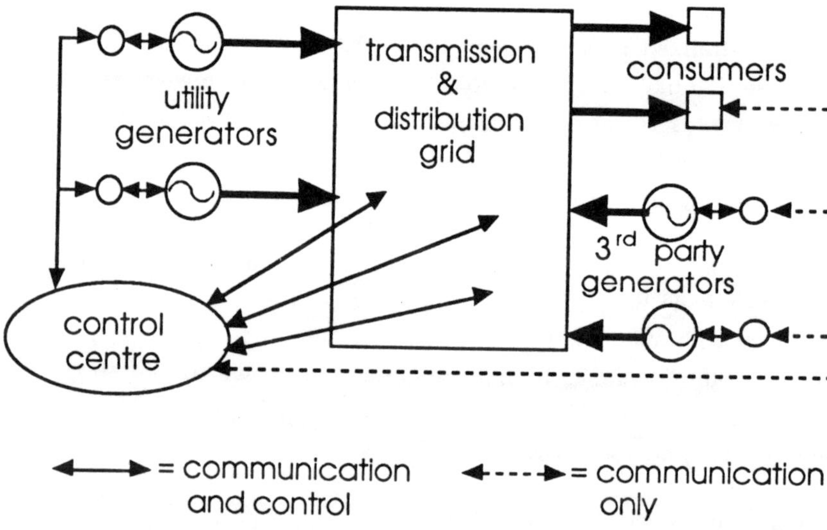

Figure 2. Operation of a Decentralized Power System

The utility maintains control over its own resources but also coordinates the actions of the demand side resources. This involves communication between the utility and the demand side participants.

Having prepared for a given set of responses, the second aspect of demand side participant response to system security is the actual contingent response, which is referred to as *actuation.* This involves rapid changes to the plant to achieve either a reduction in consumption or an increase in generation.

Achieving a sensible mix of preparedness and actuation for security control between and amongst supply and demand side participants requires the resolution of three main issues:

- Determining the appropriate level of system security that should be maintained. This can be measured by the probability of system collapse (similar to the planning concept of loss of load probability) or the expected time to system collapse [7].
- Determining the optimal levels of contribution (preparedness and actuation) for each participant; and
- Designing arrangements such as incentives so that participants make optimal contributions.

The least cost solution to these questions can be found by taking a social view of the industry in which costs on the supply and demand sides of the industry are considered on an equal basis. Thus, demand side and supply side actions are compared on an equal basis. To achieve this, the utility and each demand side participant should be considered as participants in the industry and the objective should be to minimize the sum of the costs of all participants [6].

In the current context, the costs for each participant can be divided between the cost of preparedness and the cost of actuation. The social cost of system collapse must also be considered.

For a given participant, the cost of preparedness is the cost of supplying the ability to respond to contingencies. It is, thus, the cost associated with the change of state in normal operations to achieve the level of preparedness. For example, this might include the loss of efficiency or increased fuel costs associated with reconfiguring the plant to enable a rapid response to a request for a change in consumption. Preparedness costs are incurred independently of the actual occurrence of any contingencies.

The actuation costs of a participant are those costs incurred as a result of responding to a contingency. Thus, they include increased fuel costs and the cost of any reduction in end-use satisfaction such as would result from the loss of production at an industrial facility. Actuation costs are only incurred in the event of a contingency occurring.

If the system fails to survive a contingent event, then all participants in the industry are adversely affected. Consumers lose supply and generators are unable to sell their electrical energy into the grid. Blackouts are also associated with considerable social disruption [1], which suggests that the societal cost of system collapse might be greater than the sum of the losses to the industry participants.

A SECURITY ASSESSMENT AND CONTROL FRAMEWORK

It is useful to construct a theoretical framework to analyze the above notions of contribution to security and the associated costs.

Let Ω be the set of all possible power system contingencies. Examples of contingencies $\omega \in \Omega$ include the loss of a major transmission line, a sudden increase in the demand for electrical energy and the unexpected outage of a large generating unit. Each contingency $\omega \in \Omega$ can be ascribed a certain probability of occurring.

Define K to be the set of participants. Thus, each participant $k \in K$ is either the supply utility, a consumer, a cogenerator or a third party supplier of electrical energy.

For each participant $k \in K$, define its *actuation* to be:

z_k = additional power that k actually supplies during a contingency.

This additional supply of power would be either an increase in generation or a reduction in load. In general, the actuation would be a function of the nature of the contingency, that is,

$$z_k = z_k(w) \tag{1}$$

Further, define for each participant $k \in K$ its *preparedness* to be:

P_k = additional power that participant k is prepared to supply during any contingent event.

The preparedness places a limit on any actuation. This is expressed as the constraint

$$0 \leq z_k \leq P_k \ . \tag{2}$$

The level of preparedness P_k would be determined during normal operation, before any contingency has occured.

The above parameters define a two stage decision model for each participant, as shown in Figure 3. When the system is operating normally, each participant makes its usual set of operating decisions and, as part of these decisions, determines its level of preparedness to respond to any contingency. In the event of a system contingency occurring, the response of each participant will be determined by its preparedness and the nature of the contingency. We have not yet specified the nature of emergency communication between the participants and the system which will determine the actuations.

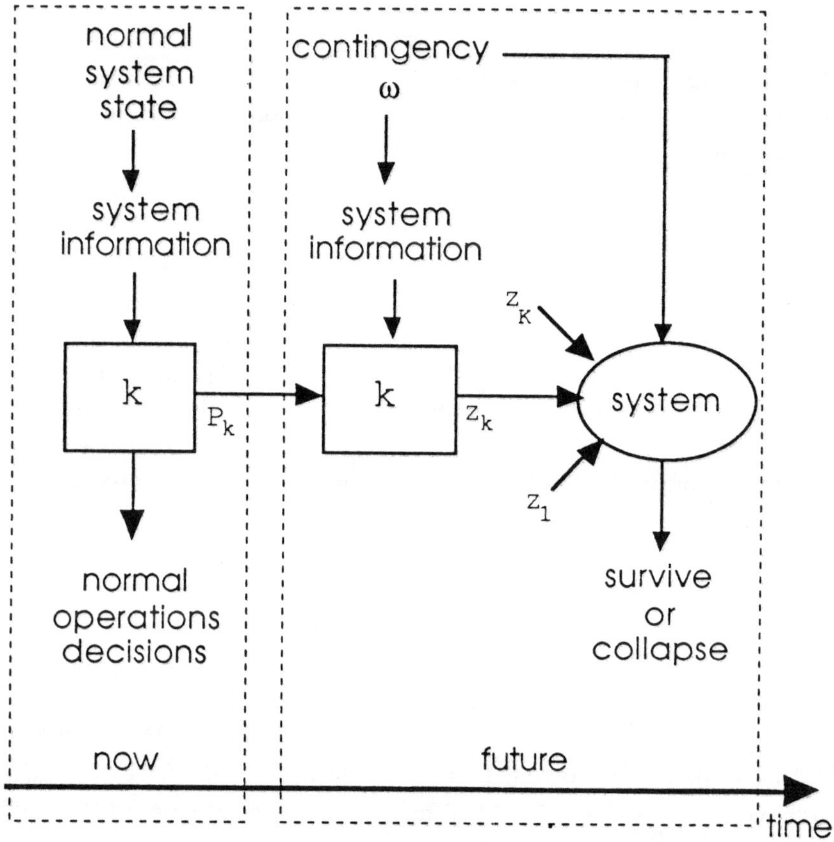

Figure 3. Two Stage Model of the Participant Decision Process

Participant k determines its preparedness level P_k which places a limit on its future ability to respond to contingencies. In the event of a contingency, the participant is sent information from the system and responds with the appropriate actuation, z_k. The ability of the system to survive a given contingency depends on the actuation responses of all the participants.

Consider the situation where each participant $k \in K$ has determined its level of preparedness, P_k. Then the range of possible actuations, which we term the *reachable response region,* is the set

$$Z = \{z_k : 0 \le z_k \le P_k \ \text{ for all } \ k \in K\} \ . \qquad (3)$$

This set is illustrated in Figure 4 and represents the range of possible re-dispatch options available in the event of a contingency. Note that Z is a function of $\{P_k : k \in K\}$.

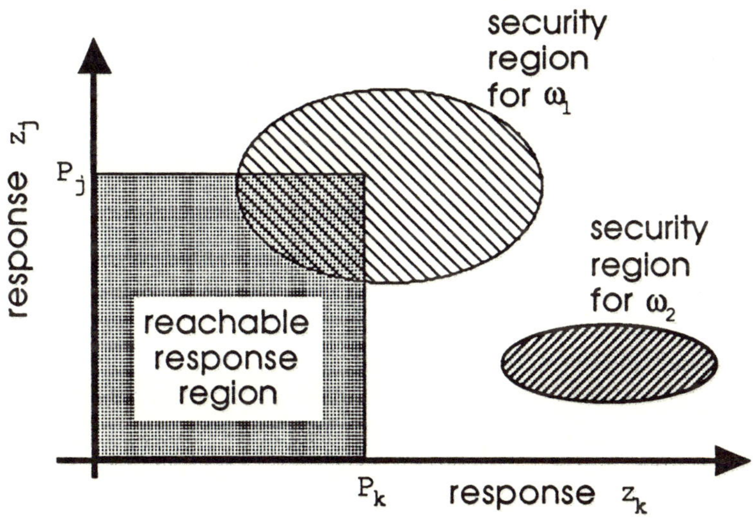

Figure 4. Schematic of the Determination of System Survivability

The system can survive for a particular contingency ω if there is at least one re-dispatch option within the reachable response region that is also in the security region for that contingency (see [8,9] for details). Thus, in the example in this Figure, the system can survive contingency ω_1, but will collapse if contingency ω_2 occurs.

Whether a contingency is survivable depends on the system's ability to settle, after re-dispatch of supply and demand side resources, into a new operating condition which does not cause equipment overload or abnormal voltages. Thus, for each contingency $\omega \in \Omega$ and for each set of participant preparedness, $\{P_k : k \in K\}$, it is possible to determine whether there are levels of actuation within the reachable response region, $\{z_k : 0 \leq z_k \leq P_k$ for all $k \in K\}$, such that the system survives the contingency ω. The exact determination can be performed using load flow [8] and transient stability analysis [9]. It is thus possible to classify each pair of sets of preparedness $\{P_k : k \in K\}$ and contingencies ω as either survivable or not survivable. It is assumed that if there exists some levels of actuations within the reachable response region such that re-dispatch using those levels will cause the system to survive, then those re-dispatch actions occur and the system does survive. The least cost approach to security control would allocate security contributions to those participants who can perform them most cheaply. Thus, for example, consumers who can rapidly reduce their loads at short or no notice without incurring great expense would be called on to contribute preparedness. Allocating efficiently between participants requires minimizing the sum of all participants costs. Thus, it is desired to achieve levels of preparedness $\{P_k : k \in K\}$ that minimize the total system costs, which can be written as:

$$S = \sum_{\substack{\text{all participants} \\ k \in K}} \left[\begin{pmatrix} \text{preparedness} \\ \text{costs} \end{pmatrix} + \text{expected} \begin{pmatrix} \text{actuation} \\ \text{costs} \end{pmatrix} \right] + \text{expected} \begin{pmatrix} \text{system} \\ \text{collapse} \\ \text{costs} \end{pmatrix} \tag{4}$$

The expectation in equation (5) weights[1] the actual costs that would be incurred with each contingency $\omega \in \Omega$ with the probability that ω will occur.

---

[1] For any function of ω, $f(\omega)$, expected$[f] = \sum_{\omega \in \Omega} f(\omega) \Pr\{\omega\}$

The preparedness costs will increase with increasing levels of participant preparedness, as greater inconvenience is incurred in the normal system operating condition.

Actuation costs are only incurred if a contingency occurs. Larger levels of participant preparedness allow for larger levels of actuation so that the expected actuation costs will tend to increase with levels of participant preparedness.

On the other hand, the number of contingencies which can be survived can be increased by obtaining greater levels of participant preparedness. Hence, the probability of system collapse will be reduced. The expectation of the system collapse costs equals the product of the probability of the system collapsing and the social costs if it does. Hence, expected collapse costs will reduce[2] with increasing levels of preparedness.

Thus, choosing optimal levels of participant preparedness requires

- resolving the trade-off between increasing preparedness costs and reducing the probability of system collapse (see Figure 5), and
- allocating preparedness to those who can perform the duty at least cost.

USING SPOT PRICING TO OBTAIN OPTIMAL SECURITY

The results of the minimization of the total system costs, S, in equation (4) would indicate how much preparedness each participant should maintain in order to optimize the systems security at least total cost. It does not,

---

2 Strictly speaking, all that can be asserted is that expected collapse costs will *not increase*.

One possible mechanism would be to centrally allocate preparedness amongst participants. Such central control is usually unsuccessful. A socially optimal outcome would require that some central body maintain complete knowledge of the cost structures of each participant. This is usually impractical and attempts at centralized allocation usually result in inefficiencies.

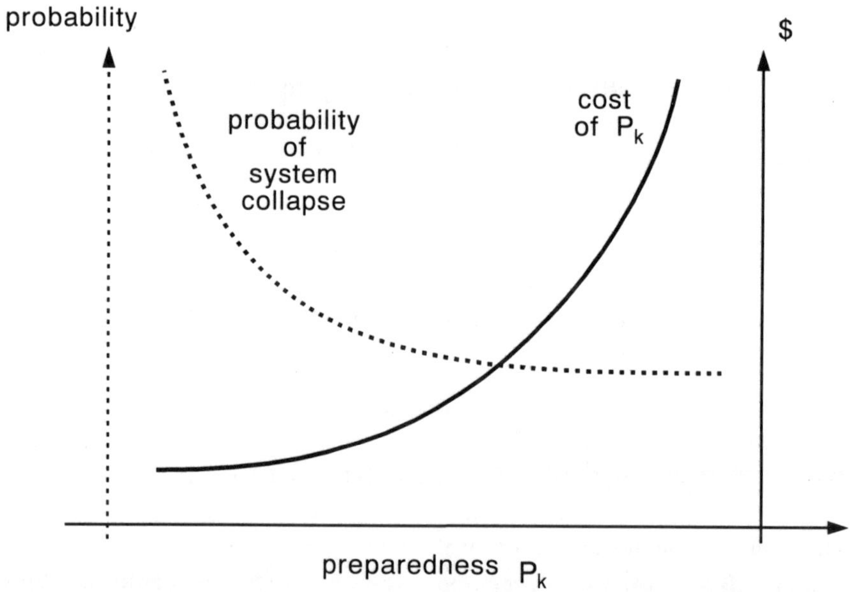

Figure 5. The Trade-off Between the Cost of Preparedness and the Probability of System Collapse (Illustrative Only)

Another approach is to extend the notions of spot pricing [5,6] to include emergency response. In effect, this involves reducing the period between updating spot prices to the time scales of security events. However, the key to achieving appropriate preparedness amongst participants is the availability of good quality probabilistic forecasts of future values[3] of spot price. These forecasts must include the low probability, high price events associated with each possible contingency.

A participant $k \in K$ would respond to probabilistic forecasts of future spot prices by choosing a level of preparedness P_k which would minimize its present costs plus its expected future costs, that is:

$$I_k(P_k) = \begin{pmatrix} \text{cost of} \\ \text{preparedness } P_k \end{pmatrix} + \text{expected}\left[\begin{pmatrix} \text{actuation} \\ \text{cost} \end{pmatrix} - \begin{pmatrix} \text{income from} \\ \text{contingent} \\ \text{spot price} \end{pmatrix}\right] \tag{5}$$

In equation (5), the expectation is calculated using the probabilistic forecast of future spot prices. Participant k would thus be making a trade-off between the cost of preparing to respond and the income that would be earned by responding to the high spot prices associated with contingencies.

It can be shown that if probabilistic forecasts of future prices were based on the range of possible future short run marginal costs (SRMC) [6], then participants' preparedness chosen so as to minimize their own costs (equation 5) would also minimize social costs (equation 4). To achieve this outcome, the forecast must include high values of SRMC during contingency events which would, in part, be determined by value of unserved energy [6]. Thus, probabilistic price forecasts can act as coordinating signals which elicit socially optimal preparedness from individual participants.

---

[3] A *probabilistic forecast* is one in which each possible outcome is enumerated and assigned a probability of occurring.

Further, in theory, socially optimal actuation would also result from participant responses to SRMC-based spot prices during contingencies.

However, such schemes raise a number of practical difficulties. Contingencies are rare events and thus there would not be much experience on which to base the component of price forecasts which relates to contingency events. Further, in the absence of detailed knowledge of the cost structures of each participant, the level of preparedness in response to a given forecast would not be known by the forecaster. Thus, price forecasting would be happening in an "open loop" environment: there would be no feedback of the effects of different forecasts on the levels of preparedness. It would, thus, be unlikely to achieve optimal, or even satisfactory levels of system security.

Another unresolved issue with spot pricing based schemes relates to demand side communication and control requirements. The success of such schemes depends on the ability of participants to respond rapidly to sudden increases in prices. This would almost certainly require the use of automated price response mechanism. Some participants with plant that might offer cost effective opportunities for response might not yet possess the required level of sophisticated equipment to perform such calculations in the time available.

TRADING DEMAND SIDE RESPONSE CAPABILITIES TO OBTAIN OPTIMAL SECURITY

One way to avoid some of the problems with the spot pricing approach is to establish a market for preparedness. There are a number of possible schemes for forming a market, one of which is described in this section.

It is convenient to postulate the existence of a system authority which has responsibility for maintaining system security. This would most likely be the utility and will be referred to as such.

Each participant would determine its own level of preparedness in response to the price set by the utility. However, in the event of a contingency the utility would determine each participant's actuation. Demand side participants would thus surrender control of their plants in the event of a contingency.

During times of normal operation, the utility would offer to pay each participant in return for preparedness. Thus, the utility regularly announces:

- a purchase price for each unit (MW or MWh) of preparedness, and
- a probabilistic forecast of the level of actuation. This forecast would be parameterized by the level of preparedness.

Each participant $k \in K$ would be issued with a price for preparedness, λ_k which means that if it offered a level of preparedness P_k it would be paid the product of price and quantity, $\lambda_k P_k$. The participant would also be issued with a probabilistic forecast of the level of actuation that the utility would take. The participant would be told how this forecast would change with different levels of preparedness. Thus, referring to this forecast as Π_k,

$$\Pi_k(z_k \mid P_k) = \text{Probability}\left[\begin{pmatrix}\text{response}\\ z_k \text{ taken}\end{pmatrix} \mid \begin{pmatrix}\text{offered level of}\\ \text{preparedness } P_k\end{pmatrix}\right]. \tag{6}$$

The individual participant k would then respond to λ_k and Π_k by choosing a level of preparedness that would maximize its own profits which can be written as:

$$J_k(P_k) = \begin{pmatrix}\text{income from}\\ \text{sale of}\\ \text{preparedness } P_k\end{pmatrix} - \begin{pmatrix}\text{cost of}\\ \text{preparedness } P_k\end{pmatrix} - \text{expected}\begin{pmatrix}\text{actuation}\\ \text{cost of } z_k\end{pmatrix} \tag{7}$$

The first term in equation (7) is the product $\lambda_k P_k$. The expectation in equation (7) is based on the forecast Π_k. While a participant's income from sale of preparedness will rise with increasing levels of preparedness, the cost and expected actuation cost will also tend to rise. The participant's decision results from a trade-off between these costs and the income.

When a contingency occurs the system then chooses a level of actuation, z_k, from each participant $k \in K$ within the constraint

$$0 \le z_k \le P_k \quad . \tag{8}$$

These levels of actuation could be pre-scheduled for each possible contingency $w \in W$, based on the levels of available preparedness, $\{P_k : k \in K\}$. The objective would be to save the system if it is possible to do so.

The utility's objective is then to set λ_k, the price for P_k, and Π_k, the forecast of actuation z_k, so that each participant responds by choosing a level of preparedness P_k which is socially optimal (i.e., minimizes the total system costs as in equation (4). Under this arrangement, price for preparedness and forecast of actuation are the coordinating signals. The main result of [2] establishes that this is indeed possible. It suggests that if the price λ_k paid for a unit of preparedness is set equal to the incremental effect of P_k on expected contingency costs, that is

$$\lambda_k = \frac{\partial}{\partial P_k}\left(\text{expected} \begin{pmatrix} \text{system} \\ \text{collapse} \\ \text{costs} \end{pmatrix} + \sum_{\substack{\text{all participants} \\ k \in K}} \text{expected} \begin{pmatrix} \text{actuation} \\ \text{costs} \end{pmatrix} \right) \tag{9}$$

and if each participant is given an "honest" probabilistic forecast Π_k of the actuation that will be taken from it, then participant k will choose the socially optimal level of preparedness P_k.

Thus, by pricing preparedness as its marginal social value and by issuing forecasts of actuation that are based on the best available information, the utility can allocate security support preparedness in an efficient manner and minimize the industry costs of maintaining security.

An advantage of this approach is that during normal operating conditions, the price setter is aware of individual levels of preparedness. Thus, in a situation where it is felt that there is a shortage of contingency response capability, the price for preparedness would increase. This would lead to an increase in the total level of preparedness. There is thus a strong feed-back signal for price setting.

CONCLUSIONS

In this paper, a probabilistic framework for power systems security in a decentralized environment has been described. A technique for encouraging economically efficient levels of demand side participation in system spinning reserves has been developed. The objective is to make available the cheapest options for system response to contingencies.

The main result establishes guidelines for setting efficient prices for demand side participant contributions to system security.

The proposed approach exhibits the following characteristics:

- Decision making is decentralized in order to optimally exploit local information.
- Supply and demand side are treated on an equal basis in terms of both comparisons of costs and potential actions to support the system.
- The objective is to create an environment in which utilities, other producers and consumers can cooperate in maintaining system security.
- The security/economy trade-off is directly addressed.

The implementation of the proposed approach would rely heavily on the development of an adequate communication, computing and control (3C) system for:

- transmitting prices and forecasts of actuation from the utility to the demand side participants,
- participants' calculation of their own optimal preparedness in response to these prices and forecasts,
- participants communicating their levels of preparedness to the utility and the calculation and logging of appropriate billing adjustments, and
- utility control of demand side participant planning the event of a contingency.

The latter could be an onerous 3C task due to the speed requirements on both communication and computing. The determination of the actual 3C requirements for such schemes is, at present, an open question [11].

LIST OF KEY SYMBOLS

K = the set of participants

k = a participant (supply utility or demand side participant)

λ_k = price offered to participant k for each unit of its preparedness

P_k = participant k's preparedness, that is, the additional power that participant k is prepared to supply during a contingent event.

Π_k = probabilistic forecast of actuation taken from participant k (see equation 6)

W = the set of possible contingencies.

ω = a contingency

z_k = participant k's actuation, that is, the additional power that k actually supplies during a contingency.

ACKNOWLEDGEMENTS

The research reported in this paper was supported by the National Science Foundation under grant ECS-8715132, and was performed while the first author was on Special Study Leave from the University of New South Wales. The support of both organizations is gratefully acknowledged.

This work has greatly benefited from the influence of many years of conversations with Hugh Outhred at the University of New South Wales and Hugh Bannister at Intelligent Energy Systems Pty Ltd. The comments of both Ross Baldick, now at Lawrence Berkeley Laboratories and Tom Gedra at the University of California at Berkeley on earlier versions of this work were also very helpful.

REFERENCES

1. J. Corwin, W. Miles. *Impact Assessment of the 1977 New York City Blackout*, U.S. Department of Energy, July 1978.

2. R.J. Kaye, F.F. Wu, P.P. Varaiya. "Pricing for system security", to be presented at the 1992 IEEE Power Engineering Society Winter Meeting.

3. F.F. Wu. "Real-time network security monitoring, assessment and optimization". *Electric Power and Energy Systems*, April 1988, vol. 10, pp. 83-100.

4. D.W. Daves, P. Hanser, J.A. Herriges, R.J. Windle. "Load impact of interruptible and curtailable rate programs: evidence from ten utilities". *IEEE Trans. Power Systems*, November 1988, vol. PWRS-3, pp. 1757-1763.

5. R.D. Tabors, F.C. Schweppe, M.C. Caramanis. "Utility experience with real time rates". *IEEE Trans. Power Systems,* May 1989, vol. PWRS-4, pp. 463-471.

6. R.J. Kaye, H.R. Outhred. "A theory of electricity tariff design for optimal operation and investment". *IEEE Trans. Power Systems,* May 1989, vol. PWRS-4, pp. 606-613.

7. F.F. Wu and Y-K. Tsai. "Probabilistic dynamic security assessment of power systems Part I: Basic Model". *IEEE Trans. Circuits and Systems,* March 1983, vol. CAS-30.

8. F.F. Wu and S. Kumagai. "Steady-state security regions of power systems". *IEEE Trans. Circuits and Systems,* November 1982, vol. CAS-29, pp. 703-711.

9. R.J. Kaye and F.F. Wu. "Dynamic security regions of power systems". *IEEE Trans. Circuits and Systems,* September 1982, vol. CAS-29, pp. 612-623.

10. F.C. Schweppe, M.C. Caramanis, R.D. Tabors and R.E. Bohn. *Spot Pricing of Electricity.* Kluwer Academic Publishers, 1988.

11. P. Varaiya, et al. "An integrated communication-computing-control (3C) system for electric power systems". Tempe, Arizona: NSF Workshop on University Research for Electric Power Systems Engineering, August 8-11, 1987.

DESIGN AND MANAGEMENT OF CURTAILABLE ELECTRICITY SERVICE TO REDUCE ANNUAL PEAKS*

by

Shmuel S. Oren
University of California Berkeley

and

Stephen A. Smith
Santa Clara University

INTRODUCTION

Interruptible and curtailable service contracts for electricity have gained popularity over the last decade as an efficient method for reducing utilities' operating cost and mitigating capacity shortages. Discounts are offered to customers (usually industrial) who allow part of their load to be curtailed at the utility's discretion. The contracts typically specify the warning time, the customer's firm power level, the maximum duration and the maximum frequency of the curtailments. In some cases, customers can choose the terms of their contract from a menu that specifies the discounts associated with various available sets of options.

The models and analysis described in this paper were developed as part of a case study conducted at New England Electric System (NEES) which currently offers a curtailable service called CIS (Cooperative Interruptible Service) to its large industrial and commercial customers. The case study was jointly sponsored by NEES and the Electric Power Research Institute (EPRI). Some related background details concerning NEES are outlined in Section 1. A more complete description and rationale for the program is contained in a working paper by Wharton (1988).

This case study considered two key issues for curtailable/interruptible service:

- How should the existing contracts be used in the best possible way to reduce the utility's peak loads?
- What is the incremental value of additional interruptible service contracts and what options should be offered?

The specific objective function chosen for this study is minimization of the utility's annual peak load. This was motivated by the needs of NEES that stem from the cost allocation rules of the New England Power Pool (NEPOOL) to which NEES belongs. In general, reducing the annual peak load is an important objective for all electric utilities, since capacity requirements and reserve margin requirements are strongly related to annual peak load. The methods developed here can also be applied to increase the available reserve margin or to reduce the peak real time price or spot price that the utility experiences during the year.

The economics literature dealing with design and pricing of interruptible/ curtailable service contracts for electricity has addressed these issues from the point of view of product differentiation with respect to the attribute of service reliability. Some early work on the efficient rationing of electric power and the differentiation and pricing of service reliability in the electric power industry is due to Crew and Kleindorfer (1978), Fisinger (1980), Marchand (1974), Telson (1975), Tschirhart and Jen (1979) and Vickery (1971). More recent work has focused on the design and pricing of priority service and the alternative implementations which include inter-

priority service and the alternative implementations which include interruptible and curtailable service contracts. This work is contained in the articles and reports by Chao et al. (1986), (1987) (1989), Oren and Doucet (1990) Smith (1989) Viswanathan and Tse (1989).

The work presented in this paper differs from previous research in several respects. First, much of the earlier work on priority service and rationing is based on supply uncertainties, while here the focus is on the reduction of demand fluctuations. Second, while most of the previous work does not address the operational aspects of implementing a priority service program, a main focus of this paper is the operational dispatching of service curtailments. From this perspective, curtailable service contracts are viewed as a supply resource rather than a component of service reliability. Consequently, the management and design of the contracts becomes a problem of allocation and acquisition of a scarce resource to meet uncertain demand. A key objective of this research was to develop operational tools and decision aids for

- the system dispatcher, who decides whether interruptions should be called for on a particular day
- the rate design manager, who decides what menu of service options and prices to offer for future contracts.

An important consideration in this development has been the availability of information and the ease of use of the operational tools.

The first part of this report describes a methodology used for dispatching the customer load reductions available from a given set of interruptible service contracts. The methodology is evaluated using simulation based on the historical load data from NEES. The second part of the paper explores the desirable mix of service contracts and their relative pricing, so as to achieve a reduction in annual peak at the least social cost. Although the analysis is performed in the context of NEES's load patterns and service offerings, its results and insights should apply to other interruptible and curtailable service programs, which are currently offered in some form by most electric utilities. As noted previously, other electric utilities may replace annual peak demand with other metrics to be optimized over the year, such as peak real time price or reserve margin.

Background on NEES

New England Electric Service (NEES) offers a voluntary interruptible service program, known as Cooperative Interruptible Service (CIS) for its major industrial and commercial customers. CIS subscribers specify a firm power level or load, which must be at least 10 percent below their annual peak demand. Upon notification by NEES, subject to a specified warning time, each subscriber agrees to reduce his load below his firm power level for the next day. The period of load curtailment lasts throughout the normal business hours of the day, which constitute the peak period. Such calls to subscribers can be made at most 30 times per year under the current service offerings.

The primary purpose of CIS is to provide a means for reducing NEES's largest daily peak loads. Peak loads are a key factor in determining supply costs for all electric utilities. For the region served by NEPOOL, the New England Power Pool, which is the central supplier and dispatcher of power for NEES, peak loads also increase the of risk power shortages, when generation capacity is tight in this region, as it was during the period of the study. NEES pays a yearly demand charge to NEPOOL based on its annual peak load; thus peak load reduction results in a direct costs savings on this demand charge. Reduction in the largest daily peak demands also decreases the risk of power shortfalls, both for NEES's customers, and for NEPOOL as a whole. Because its warning time requirement is 12 to 16 hours, CIS cannot respond directly to unexpected supply shortfalls such as the failure of a generating unit, which must be handled by other procedures.

The pattern of daily peak demands at NEES is highly variable, as shown in Figure 1. There are two seasonal peaks: a Winter or heating peak that includes December, January and February; and a Summer or air conditioning peak, which includes June, July and August. There is virtually no chance of an annual peak in the other six months of the year. In addition to seasonal changes, weekend and holiday demands fall roughly 25% below the

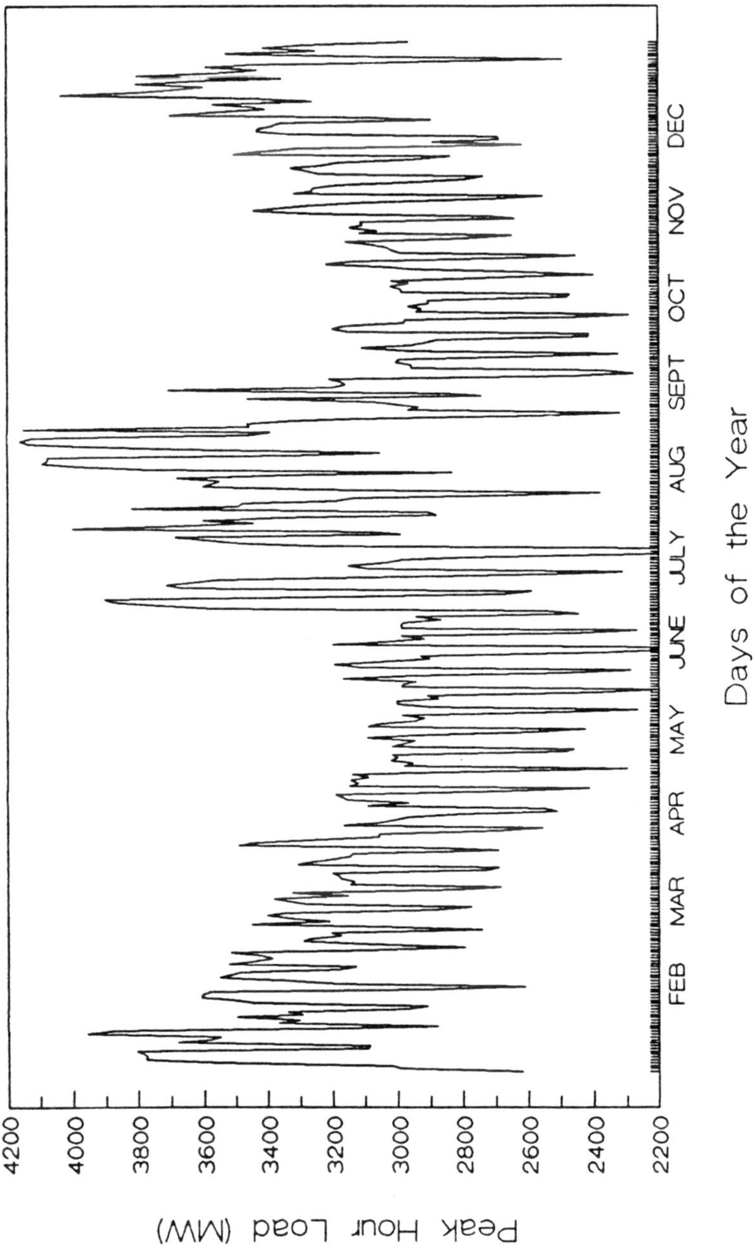

Figure 1. Daily Peak Load

weekday demand in each season, which produces the periodic oscillations in the figure. Again, there is essentially no chance of an annual peak on a weekend or holiday. Within the peak seasonal months, there is considerable variation from one week to the next, which is largely due to the weather. A prolonged hot spell generally results in successively increasing demands for air conditioning as structures gradually heat up. Prolonged cold spells produce similar results in Winter. Thus, the accuracy of the daily peak demand forecasts is similar to the accuracy of the daily temperature forecasts for the service region.

NEES currently has roughly 100 MW of interruptible load subscribed to CIS, which, in principal, should allow its annual peak to be reduced by 100 MW. The decision of whether to call for an interruption is made sequentially each day, and it relies on three imperfect forecasts:

- the forecast of the annual peak
- the forecast of the daily peak for the next day
- the forecast of the number of future daily peaks that will be larger than the next day's forecasted peak.

Errors in any of these forecasts can cause interruptions to be allocated suboptimally. NEES was particularly interested in obtaining a dispatching methodology that could be characterized by a simple heuristic, which could be implemented in a spreadsheet program to be used by the system dispatcher.

PLANNING AND DISPATCHING A SINGLE BLOCK OF INTERRUPTIBLE LOAD

This section describes the solution for the case in which all the interruptible load is dispatched as one block, which is the current situation at NEES. We develop a planning methodology that addresses the question: For a given amount of interruptible load L, how many interruptions are needed for the year and what customer credits should be offered? Given that the total interruptible load is L, we need only be concerned with a band L below the annual peak, since that is the largest possible reduction in the annual peak. The planning model is designed so that the probability of missing a peak within L of the annual peak is no larger than some specified value. We determine the number of interruptions k such that when they are dispatched optimally, the desired confidence level is achieved.

The dispatching model serves as a decision support tool for the system dispatcher who must decide a day in advance whether to call for an interruption. Given k remaining interruptions at any point in time, the best dispatching policy is to attempt to curtail the k highest remaining peaks. At any given time, the utility knows the seasonal distribution of daily peaks, the number of interruptions yet remaining for each class of customers, the number of peak demand days yet remaining, the estimated yearly peak and the daily peak forecast for the next day. The dispatching methodology calculates a threshold such that an interruption is called for if the daily forecast exceeds the threshold. The threshold is updated dynamically each day, as the input information changes.

The dispatching problem is, in principle, a stochastic dynamic programming problem, where the state space includes the number of remaining interruptions and the number of peak demand days remaining. Since, at any point in time, the forecasted future cost depends on the highest peak (after curtailment) observed so far, the state space must also include the highest observed peak. This value is affected by the entire dispatching history. The resulting large state space combined with the uncertainties involved have made the dynamic programming approach intractable. Instead, we use an "open loop" approximation with a rolling horizon. This determines a threshold H for the next day's interruption decision under the assumption that the same threshold will be used throughout the remainder of the contract period. The threshold is computed by balancing the tradeoffs between (1) the probability of α missing a peak due to forecast error; (2) the probability β of running out of interruptions prematurely. While lowering H will reduce the probability of missing an important peak, it increases the probability of exhausting the allotted interruptions prematurely.

The derivation of the threshold level and the relationship between k, α and β discussed above, requires specification of the two probability distributions

$$P\{\text{yearly peak} = x \mid \text{forecasted to be } \mu\} = \phi\left(\frac{x-\mu}{\sigma}\right)\frac{1}{\sigma} \tag{2-1}$$

$$P\{\text{daily peak forecast} = F \mid \text{actual peak value} = x\} = \phi\left(\frac{F-\mu}{\sigma_1}\right)\frac{1}{\sigma_1} \tag{2-2}$$

$$\text{where } \phi(z) = \frac{e^{-z^2/2}}{\sqrt{2\pi}}.$$

The probability densities (2-1) and (2-2) are assumed to be Normal with zero means and to be stationary, in that they are independent of the seasonal time in the year.

Historical data was available at NEES on one-day-ahead forecast errors for the daily peaks. Figure 2 shows a histogram of the daily forecast errors for 1988 for the top 64 daily peaks, representing the typical days on which key interruption decisions will be made. The Normal distribution (2-2) is convenient for analytical purposes, and based on the p-value of the Chi-square statistic for the data in Figure 2, the Normal distribution hypothesis would not be rejected at the confidence level of 10 percent and the mean of the daily peak forecast errors is not significantly different from 0 for this data. The unbiased estimate of the standard deviation σ_1 is 179 MW.

Historical data was not available on the errors in forecasting annual peaks and, in any case, its sample size would be insufficient for statistical analysis. For convenience, the Normal distribution (2-1) was assumed for the annual peak forecast error. Based on discussions with the NEES dispatching personnel, σ the standard deviation of the annual peak forecast error was subjectively estimated to be 100 MW. The total forecast error, which is the sum of the forecast error and the error in estimating the annual peak, thus has a standard deviation given by

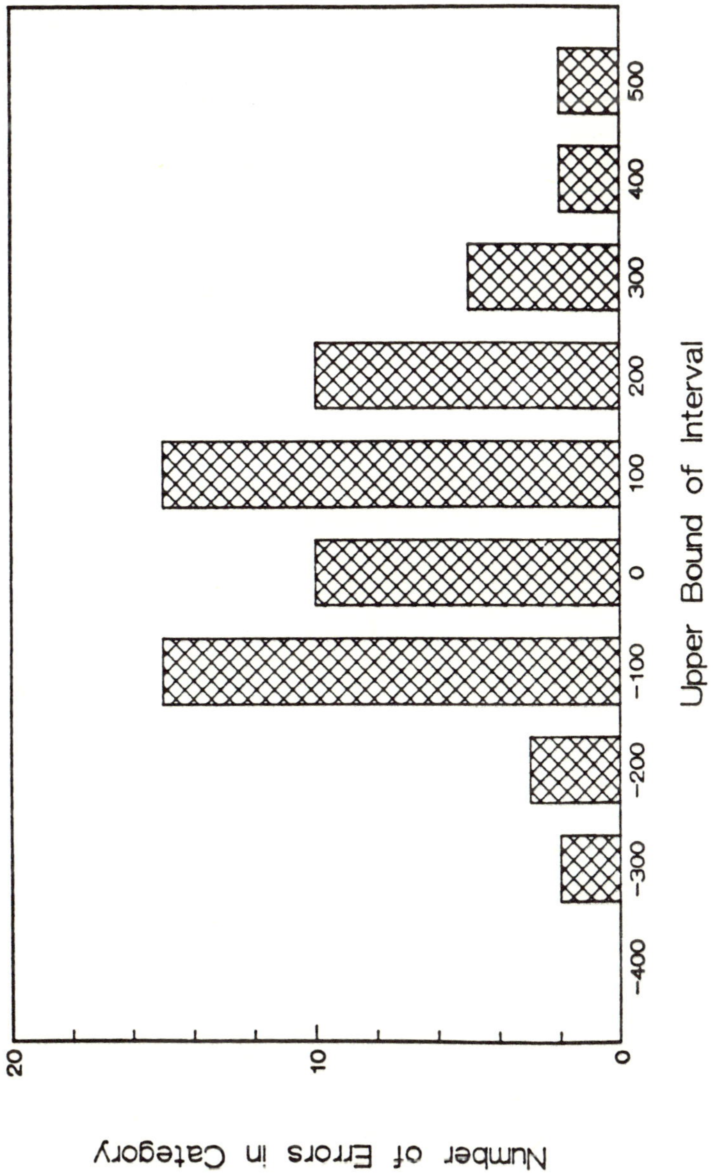

Figure 2. Distribution of Forecast Errors in Top Peaks

$$\sigma_2 = \sqrt{\sigma^2 + \sigma_1^2}. \tag{2-3}$$

[This value is 205 Megawatts in the case of the NEES data.]

To capture seasonal fluctuations, a weight factor w_t was determined for each day t of the year, defined as

$$w_t = P\{\text{day } t \text{ is a peak demand day}\}. \tag{2-4}$$

with $$W_T = \sum_{t=T}^{365} w_t = E[\text{ number of peak demand days remaining at day T}]. \tag{2-5}$$

A "peak day" is classified as such by the system dispatcher. These days can viewed as the set of possible candidates for interruptions. The relative frequency of "peak demand days" was determined for each month, based on data from the three year period 1986-1988. Weekends and holidays were assigned a weight of zero. Days with nonzero weights are assigned equal w_t values within each month determined so that the sum of the w_t in each month equals the expected number of peak demand days in that month based on historical data. This provides us with an estimate of the probabilities in (2-4) for all nonholiday weekdays.

The probability distribution for loads on peak demand days relative to the annual peak is defined by

F(D) = Expected fraction of peak demand days within D of the yearly peak.

The distribution F(D) was calculated empirically, based on the data for peak demand days for the period 1986-88. The data, illustrated in Figure 3, was approximated by a piecewise linear function, as indicated. It is assumed that the fraction F(D) is also stationary, and thus is independent of t.

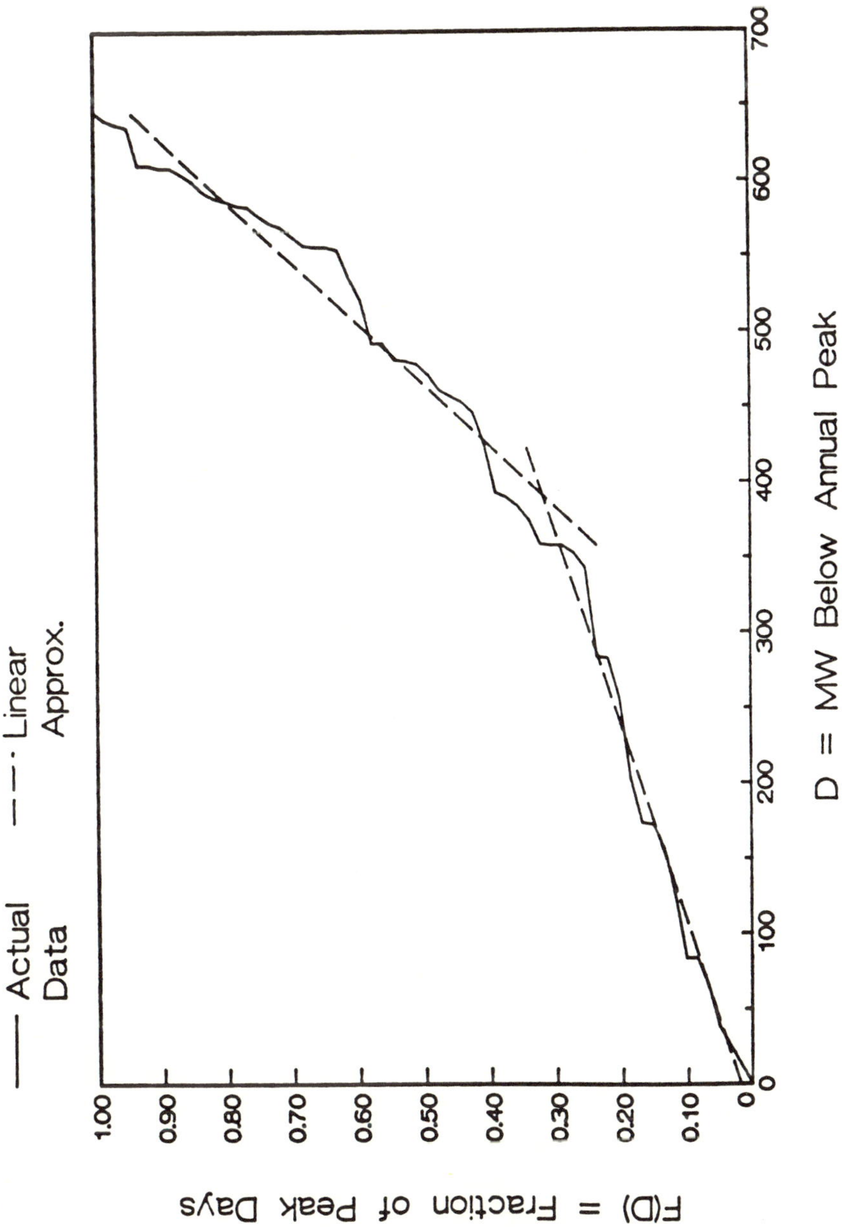

Figure 3. Fraction of Peak Days Within D of the Annual Peak

Given the independence assumption, we have that

$$P\{\text{the peak on day t falls within D of the yearly peak}\} = F(D)w_t,$$

and (2-6)

$$W_T F(D) = E[\ \#\ \text{remaining peak days falling within D of the yearly peak}].$$

Planning Problem Solution

Given the distributions above, a derivation is given in Appendix A that specifies k, the number of interruptions required, as a function of the total interruptible load and the number of peak days in the contract period. For planning, the formula for k requires the selection of the probability α that a peak that should have been curtailed is missed due to forecast error. The exact formula for the planning relationship k cannot be solved in closed form, but is shown graphically in Figure 4. This figure shows the function

$$k = k(y, W_T), \tag{2-7}$$

where $y = z_\alpha + L/\sigma_2$ and $\Phi(z_\alpha) = 1 - \alpha$ determines z_α, for given confidence level α. For example, α=10% yields $z_\alpha = 1.28$ and for 100 MW of interruptible load and $W_T = 60$, we have $y = 1.28+100/\sigma_2 = 1.76$ and thus $k = k(y,W_T) = 33$ interruptions from Figure 4. It can be seen from Figure 4 that increasing the interruptible load L will increase k the number of interruptions required. Similarly, decreasing α, the probability of missing one of the desired peaks, increases z_α which increases k.

Dispatching Problem Solution

The dispatching decision at time T for given k is to choose an optimal threshold H. This decision is independent of L and α. The dispatching threshold H is determined by

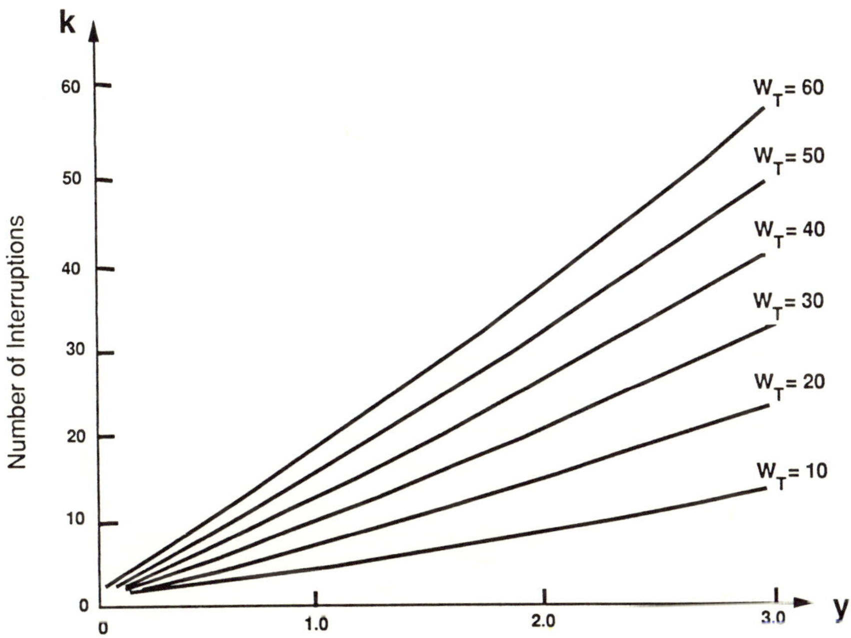

Figure 4. Number of Required Interruptions

$$H = \mu - y\sigma_2 , \tag{2-8}$$

where y is determined by looking up k on the vertical axis of Figure 4 and then using the appropriate W_T curve to obtain $y = y(k,W_T)$. Given a load L, it follows from the inverse of (2-7) that the probability α of missing a peak L megawatts below the annual peak satisfies

$$z = y(k,W_T) - L/\sigma_2, \qquad \text{with } \alpha = 1 - \Phi(z_\alpha) . \tag{2-9}$$

Thus, given k and T, the z_α and the corresponding probability α are adjusted depending on the interruptible load L.

Implementation of the Dispatching Model

The dispatching methodology discussed above was implemented in a spreadsheet, illustrated in Figure 5, for use by the NEES system dispatcher. The user entries on the spreadsheet are shown in boxes and were coded as unprotected cells. The calculation portion of the spreadsheet is not shown. To begin the spreadsheet program operation, the user specifies the initial settings shown in the first square for Yearly Peak Forecast, Standard Deviation (of Forecast Error) and Total Interruptible Load. The user also enters the number of interruptions permitted (30 in this case) and then sequentially enters the Daily Forecast for each day. The spreadsheet calculates an updated Threshold each day, based on (2-8), with y determined as described in Appendix A. The W_T values are reduced each day by the individual daily weight w_t. The number of interruptions k is reduced as interruptions occur, based on the 0,1 values in the Int? column.

To test the methodology, the spreadsheet was applied retroactively to the 1988 data in a simulated day to day fashion. The results, as one might expect, depend crucially on how close the annual peak forecast μ is to the actual annual peak. For the data tested, the actual annual peak was 4280 MW. The simulation is illustrated in Figure 6, for initial annual peak estimates of 4100 MW, 4300 MW and 4500 MW, respectively. The 4100 initial estimate caused too many peaks in December and January to be

1989 Application of Threshold Model

Yearly Peak Forecast	4200	MW
Standard Deviation	205	MW
Interruptible Load	100	MW

25 Interr. Used to Date

	Month	Day	Day of Week	wt	60 WT	30 k	Daily Frcst	Thresh	Rec Int	Act Int	Yrly Peak Estim
Jan	1	1	7	0.000	60	30	2500	3776	0		4200
	1	2	1	0.000	60	30	2500	3776	0		4200
	1	3	2	0.261	60	30	3033	3775	0		4200
	1	4	3	0.261	59	30	4038	3774	1	1	4200
	1	5	4	0.261	59	29	3743	3783	1	1	4200
	1	6	5	0.261	59	28	3765	3793	0		4200
	1	7	6	0.000	59	28	2934	3793	0		4200
	1	8	7	0.000	59	28	2500	3793	0		4200
	1	9	1	0.261	59	28	2500	3792	0		4200
	1	10	2	0.261	58	28	3407	3791	0		4200
	1	11	3	0.261	58	28	2748	3789	0		4200
	1	12	4	0.261	58	28	3462	3788	0		4200
	1	13	5	0.261	58	28	3655	3787	0		4200
	1	14	6	0.000	58	28	3168	3787	0		4200

Figure 5. Spreadsheet Implementation

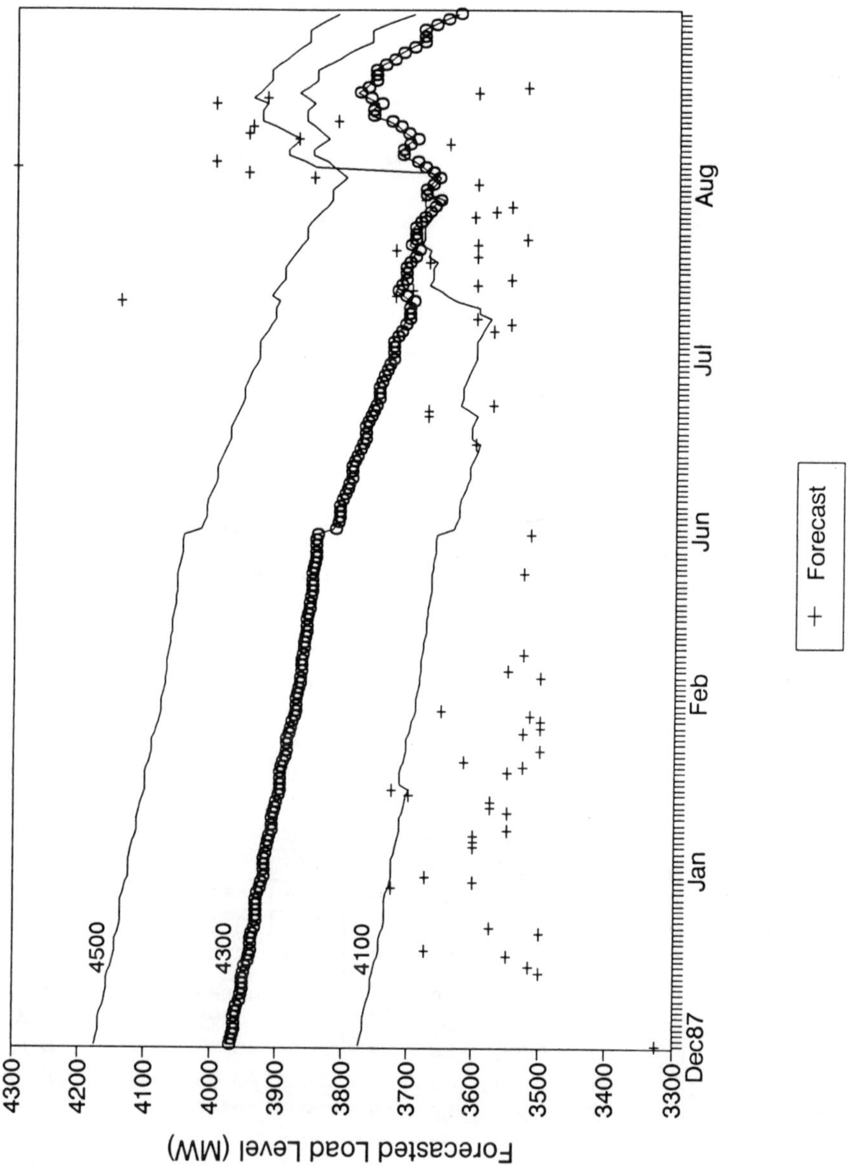

Figure 6. 1988 Daily Forecasts and Threshold Patterns for Three Annual Peak Forecasts

interrupted, as indicated. When peaks higher than 4100 MW were observed, the forecasted annual peak was updated to the largest observed value, which caused the large jump in August. Smaller upward jumps occur in other cases, when the ratio k/W_T is reduced due to a rapid decrease in the remaining interruptions. This "self-correcting" characteristic of the threshold calculation prevents the remaining interruptions from being exhausted before the end of the year. For the 4100 MW forecast case, it also caused some of the large peaks occurring in later August to be missed because the number of remaining interruptions was too small.

Retroactive Simulation on 1989 Data

The model's impact was also evaluated based on a retroactive simulation using 1989 load and interruption data. This simulation seems appropriate for evaluation because the model was developed on 1988 data, in addition to using 1987 and 1986 data for seasonal trends. Since the interruption decisions in 1989 were made without the benefit of the model, this simulation provides an objective measure of the model's value-added in that year. In order to assess the value-added benefits once the model is in operation, one must also forecast which interruptions would be called for without the model.

During 1990, the system dispatcher used the spreadsheet model to calculate the threshold for recommending interruptions. However, no interruptions were recommended, and thus no savings can be attributed to the use of the model for 1990. The reason for this result is that the severe recession in New England, coupled with relatively mild winter weather in early 1990 reduced NEES's daily peak loads 20% to 30% below 1989 levels. Thus, while the operability of the spreadsheet model has been established, its actual impact cannot be felt until the New England economy improves. However, based on the simulations discussed below, the spreadsheet model could result in several million dollars in annual savings under load conditions similar to those in 1989.

The simulation results are illustrated in Figures 7a, 7b and 7c. In Figure 7a, the threshold fluctuation throughout the year is compared to the one-day-ahead forecasts. All forecast points lying above the line would have resulted in interruptions. These can be compared with the interruptions that were actually called based on the recommendations of NEPOOL, which are shown using the actual peak loads for those days. No pool interruptions were called for on NEES's two highest peak days of the year, which were July 26, 27 with peaks of 4030 MW and 4127 MW, respectively.

There was no recorded *a priori* forecast of the maximum annual peak for 1989. A sensitivity analysis with respect to this parameter, obtained by running the simulation for annual peak forecasts of 4000 and 4400, is illustrated in Figure 7b. Although the 4400 forecast resulted in fewer interruptions initially, the top two days were still interrupted. For the 4000 MW forecast, more interruptions were used initially, but the threshold adjusts throughout the year, so that not all interruptions were exhausted. In fact, the two thresholds approach each other in December. For all three annual peak forecasts, the thresholds rise steeply in December, because the unusually large number of high peaks in December caused the remaining interruptions to be used up rapidly. The self correcting property of the threshold allows it to adjust for initial forecast errors as the year progresses.

Greater load reduction can be achieved if there is additional interruptible load, but this generally requires more interruptions to be used and also increases the importance of forecast accuracy. To illustrate this case, the simulation was carried out for an interruptible load of 200 MW. In this case, it is necessary to interrupt the top nine peaks in 1989 to achieve a 200 MW reduction in annual peak load. In the 1989 data, NEPOOL interruptions coincided with four of these top nine peak days, but would not have reduced the NEES annual peak at all, since the top two days were not interrupted. The spreadsheet model interrupted the top six days, but missed the seventh. The spreadsheet model's recommendations resulted in a peak reduction of 174 MW out of a possible 200 MW. Since more daily peaks must

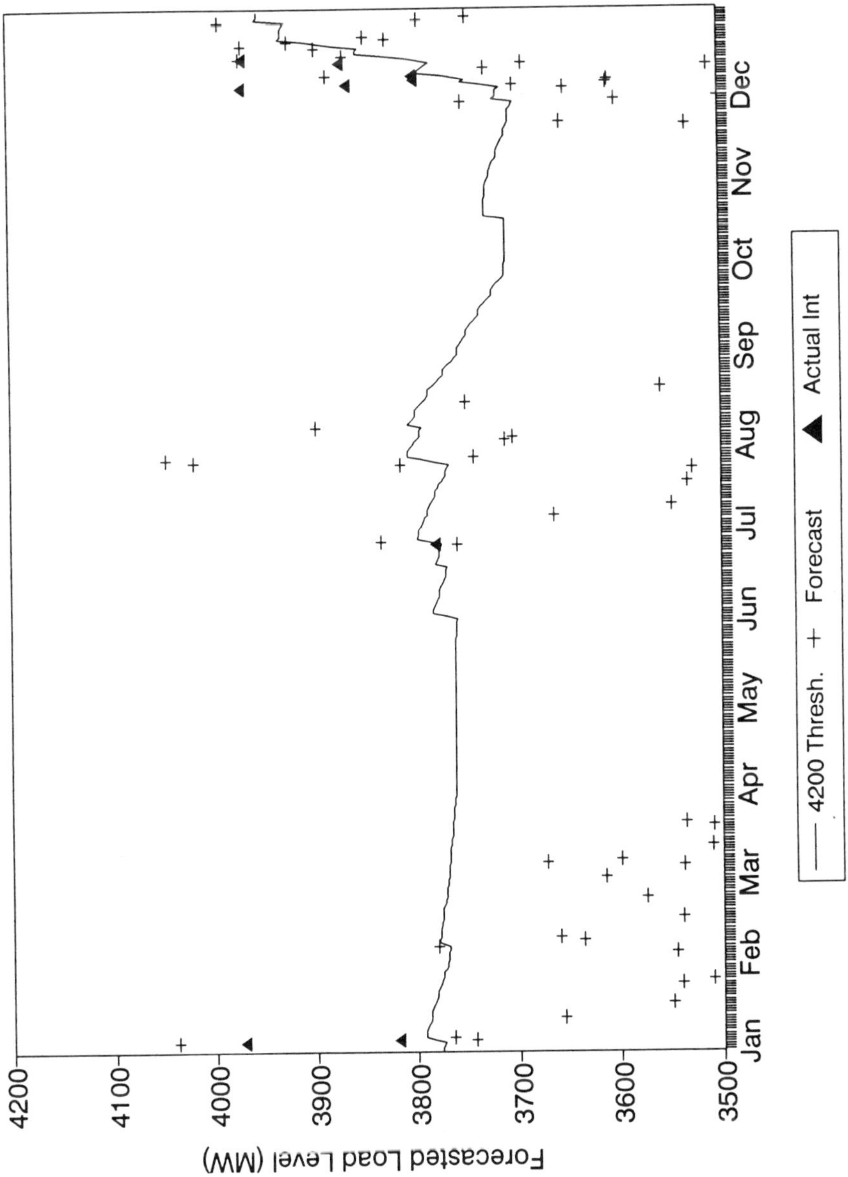

Figure 7a. 1989 Threshold and Daily Forecast
100 MW Interruptible Load, 4200 Initial Annual Peak Forecast

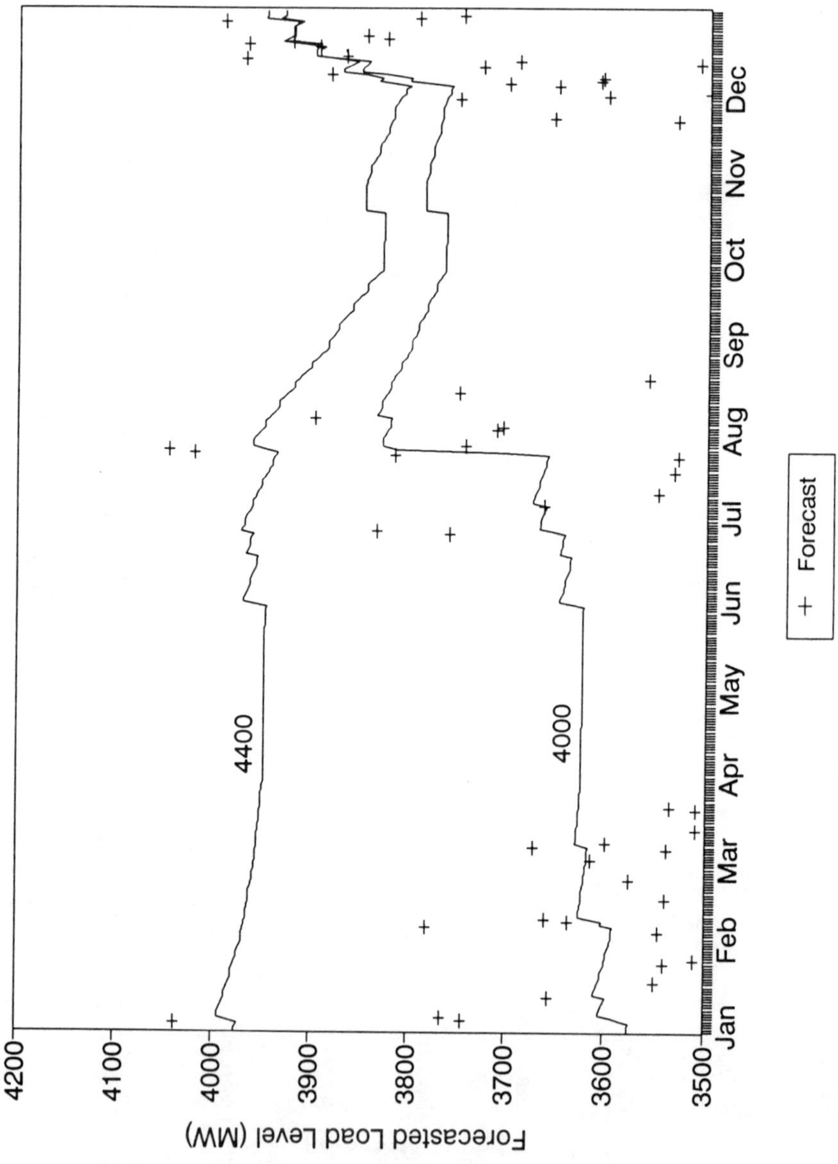

Figure 7b. 1989 Thresholds and Annual Peak Forecast
100 MW Interruptible Load, 4000 and 4400 Initial Annual Peak Forecast

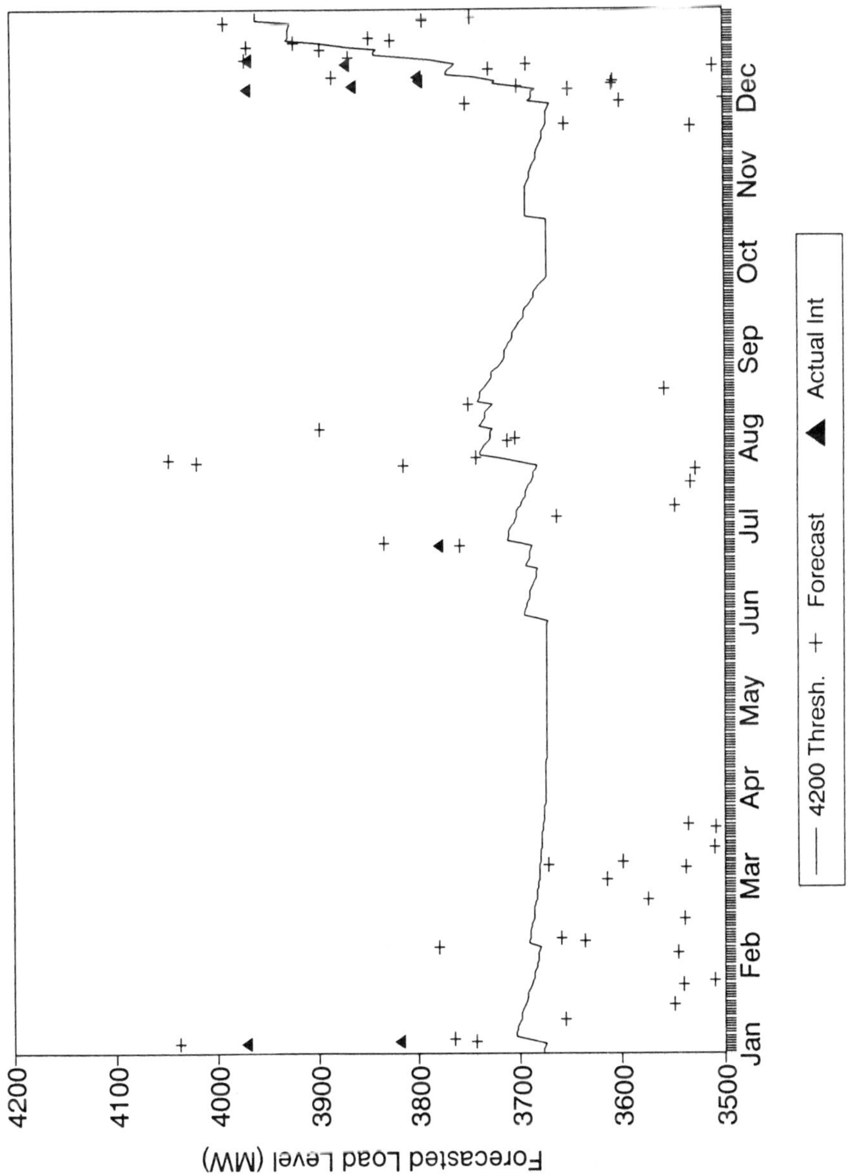

Figure 7c. 1989 Threshold and Daily Forecast
200 MW Interruptible Load, 4200 Initial Annual Peak Forecast

be interrupted when the interruptible load is greater, it becomes less likely that the pool recommendations will achieve the best possible results.

DESIGNING AND DISPATCHING MULTIPLE BLOCK CONTRACTS

In this section, we extend the results presented so far to interruptible loads that are segmented into multiple blocks, which are curtailed in a prescribed priority order as needed. The analytical development assumes that the amount of load curtailed is a continuous variable, ranging from zero to the total interruptible load L. We also show how this is implemented for the case of discrete blocks. The index ℓ is defined in such a way that $\ell = 0$ is the first increment curtailed, and $\ell = L$ is the last. For a fixed value of α, a curtailment policy is equivalent to a set of thresholds $\{h_\alpha(\ell,L)\}$, which are monotonically increasing in ℓ, for any given value of α. The load increment ℓ is curtailed on day t if and only if the forecast $F_t \geq h_\alpha(\ell,L)$. With a single block of size L, as in Section 2, whenever the first increment $\ell = 0$ is to be curtailed, the entire block will be curtailed. Thus $h_\alpha(0,L) = H_\alpha(L)$.

For analytical convenience, we derive planning and dispatching policies only for the case in which the same α value is used for all load increments ℓ. This leads to a simple form for the threshold policy, but is optimal only under certain circumstances. A sufficient condition is that the marginal net benefit of each KW of annual peak reduction is constant in the range $[A_0 - L, A_0]$, where L is the total interruptible load. In other situations, it is possible that the optimal L could vary with ℓ, but we have not analyzed this case.

Given the forecasting error distributions used in this paper and fixed α for all load increments, we have

Lemma 3.1. The thresholds $h_\alpha(\ell,L) = H(L-\ell) = H_\alpha(L) + \ell$. (3-1)

Proof: Focusing on the load increment ℓ, α corresponds to the probability that an actual peak of $A_0-(L-\ell)$ is not curtailed, where A_0 is the actual annual peak. Given α, the curtailments of load increment ℓ should be the same as if we had a single block of size $L-\ell$ and curtailed according to the policy in Section 2. It is shown in Appendix A that curtailment occurs if and only if the sum of the forecast errors $E_t + E_0$ is such that $A_0 - (L-\ell) + E_t + E_0 \leq H_\alpha(L-\ell)$. Thus it follows that

$$\alpha = P\{A_0 - (L-\ell) + E_t + E_0 \leq H_\alpha(L-\ell)\} = P\{A_0 - (L-\ell) + E_t + E_0 \leq h_\alpha(\ell,L)\},$$

while $H_\alpha(L-\ell) = H_\alpha(L) + \ell$ follows from (A-3). QED.

Lemma 3.1 simplifies the form of the optimal policy considerably, because it says in effect that the thresholds $\{h_\alpha(\ell,L)\}$ are implemented by curtailing down to the threshold $h_\alpha(0,L) = H_\alpha(L)$. That is, for any forecast such that $F_t > H_\alpha(L)$, the curtailed load should be the difference $\ell = F_t - H_\alpha(L)$.

The policy for each load increment ℓ is the same as if the total interruptible load were equal to $L - \ell$. Thus, the function $k = k_\beta(H_\alpha(L-\ell),T)$ defined in (A-12) gives the number of interruptions k such that β is the probability of running out of interruptions prematurely when the threshold $H_\alpha(L-\alpha) = h_\alpha(\alpha,L)$ is used for the remainder of the contract at time T. As discussed in the Appendix, the relationship $\beta = \alpha/2$ approximates the optimal tradeoff between missing a peak and exhausting the available interruptions reduces (A-12) to (A-19), which holds for all values of ℓ. To minimize the probability that an actual peak $A_0(L-\ell)$ is not curtailed, we use the relationship $k = k(y(\ell))$ in (A-19), which is plotted in Figure 4, where

$$y(\ell) = z_\alpha + (L-\ell)/\sigma_2 \quad . \tag{3-2}$$

This solves both the planning and dispatching problems in a manner analogous to the one block case with interruptible load $L - \ell$.

We have that $k(\ell) = k(y(\ell), W_T)$ is the number of times that load increment ℓ should be curtailed with W_T peak days remaining. For dispatching any load increment ℓ with given k and W_T, we determine a corresponding y value from Figure 4 and then dispatch it according to the threshold value

$$H = \mu - y\sigma_2 \ . \tag{3-3}$$

In the planning case, $k(\ell)$ can be chosen so that is constant across all ℓ using (3-2). For the dispatching case (3-3), this is true at the beginning of the contract year, but is true in expectation only thereafter. That is, after some curtailments have occurred, the α value for the remainder of the contract year would differ from its initial values (as in the one block case), and would differ for different load increments.

Using Discrete Multiple Blocks

Multiple discrete blocks can be used in practice by selecting any staircase function that uniformly bounds the curve $k(\ell)$ from above, as illustrated for two blocks in Figure 8. In this case, the interruptible load is segmented into two blocks of L_1 and L_2 units, where the subscripts denote order of interruption. Then $k(0)$ interruptions are required of the low priority L_1 units, while $k(L_1) < k(0)$ interruptions are required for the higher priority L_2 units. For any given set of discrete blocks, an analogous procedure can be used to determine the number of interruptions required for each service priority block.

Figure 9 illustrates the appropriate procedure for dispatching multiple blocks. For the two blocks shown, L_2 is the load with higher priority (fewer curtailments per year), which has k_2 interruptions remaining, and L_1 is the lower priority load, which has k_1 interruptions remaining. For a given T value, we select the appropriate W_T curve and determine the two intersections with the horizontal lines drawn from k_1 and k_2. The y value for each block is determined by its right most edge. In general, the

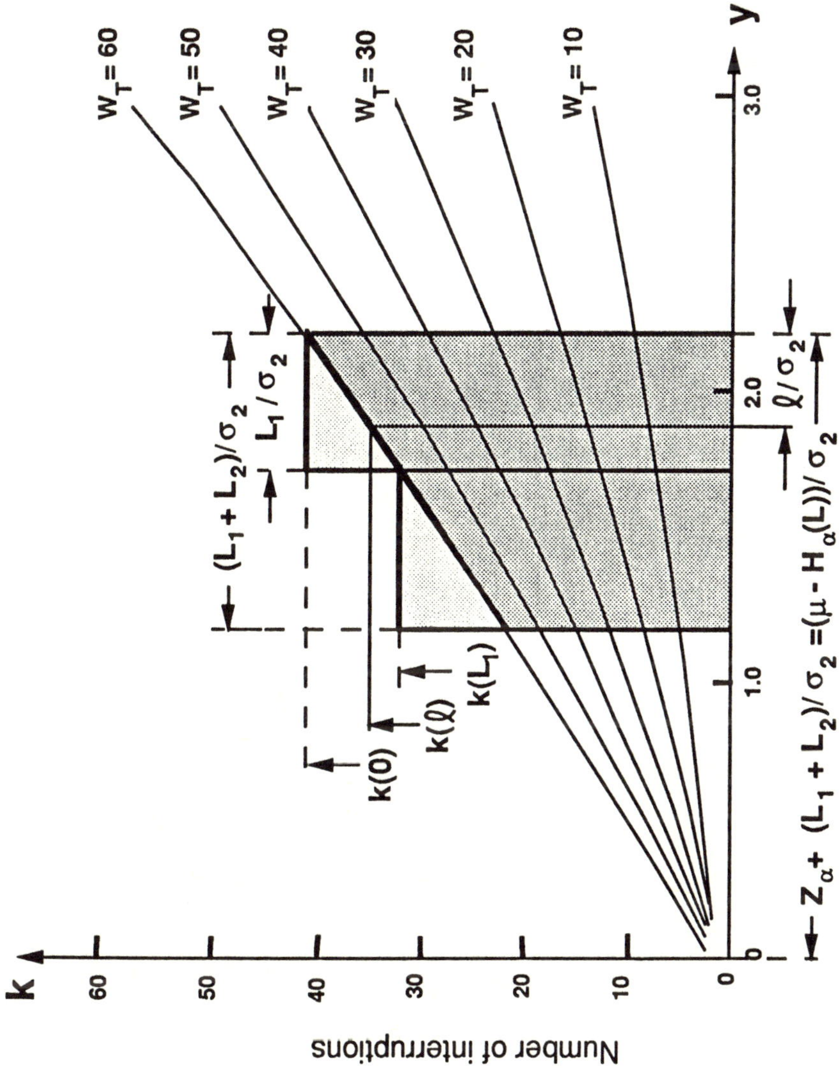

Figure 8. Number of Interruptions for Multiple Blocks

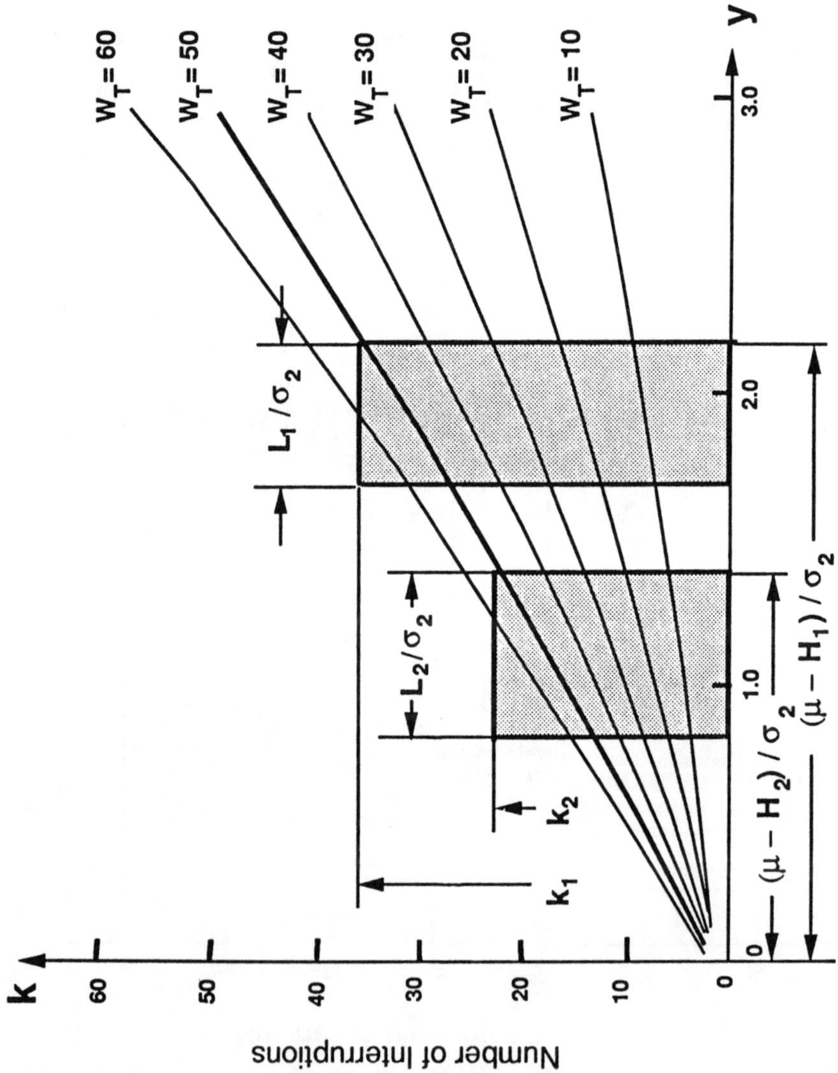

Figure 9. Determining the Thresholds in Multiblock Dispatching

value y_i determines the threshold H_i for each block i from the relationship

$$H_i = \mu - y_i \sigma_2 \,, \tag{3-4}$$

where the same procedure is used for any number of blocks.

At the start of the contract year, all the thresholds will satisfy

$$H_i = h_\alpha(\ell_i, L) \text{ where } \ell_i = \sum_{\{j \text{ interrupted before } i\}} L_j \quad . \tag{3-5}$$

As interruptions are used, some priority levels will become "out of balance." However, when a priority level has been interrupted too often, its threshold will be set disproportionately high based on (3-4), so that the imbalances will tend to correct themselves as the contract year progresses.

Determining a Price Schedule

In this section, we analyze the relative pricing of service priorities. We assume that the total interruption losses for each customer load type are linear in the number of interruptions per year, with the cost per interruption varying over the customer population. The distribution of interruption costs defines a demand function

$v(x)$ = the value such that at least x units of load have a cost per interruption which is $\leq v(x)$.

= credit per interruption which will elicit x units of interruptible load.

The electric utility must know the function $v(x)$ for the customer population, but need not know the interruption cost of any particular load unit in order to design the tariff. Economic efficiency dictates that a lower priority block should consist of load units of lesser interruption cost than a higher priority block. Pricing should induce customers to assign load units to service priorities in this manner, while the contracts for the blocks must also be consistent with the design considerations discussed in the previous section.

These goals can be achieved by a nonlinear credit schedule, in which the credit given to each customer is linear in the subscribed load and the credit per load unit is an increasing concave function of the allowable number of interruptions, illustrated in Figure 10. Since the function $k(\ell)$ specifies the number of required interruptions with ℓ or more curtailed units of load, its inverse $\ell(k)$ denotes the load ℓ that must be available for curtailment during the k most severe interruptions. This can be induced by setting the *incremental* credit $c(k)$ per load unit for the kth interruption so that

$$c(k) = v(\ell(k)) \quad \text{for} \quad k \geq k(L), \quad \text{and} \quad c(k) = v(L) \quad \text{for} \quad k \leq k(L). \tag{3-6}$$

With (3-6), the number of interruptions k selected for each load unit (k) is such that the incremental credit equals the incremental interruption loss, and thus is incentive compatible. Further, since $v(\ell)$ is decreasing in ℓ, the marginal credits are positive and decreasing, thus establishing concavity. Finally, since $\ell(k)$ was used to determine the credit level for k interruptions, the number of subscriptions in each category will be consistent with (A-19) and (3-2).

Discrete Block Pricing

For discrete blocks, the above pricing approach would set the credit per interruption in each block to the value corresponding to the most costly load unit in that block. As shown in Figure 11, the first block (low priority) with L_1 units will be interrupted k_1 times while the second block (high priority) with L_2 units will be interrupted k_2 times. The incremental credit should be $v(L_1 + L_2)$ for the first k_2 interruptions and $v(L_1)$ for the incremental $k_1 - k_2$ interruptions. The total credit has a concave piecewise linear shape with the vertices corresponding to the offered contracts. This contract structure will induce the L_1 units with the lowest interruption losses to select the low priority contract and L_2 units with the next higher interruption losses to select the high priority contract. Generalizing to the

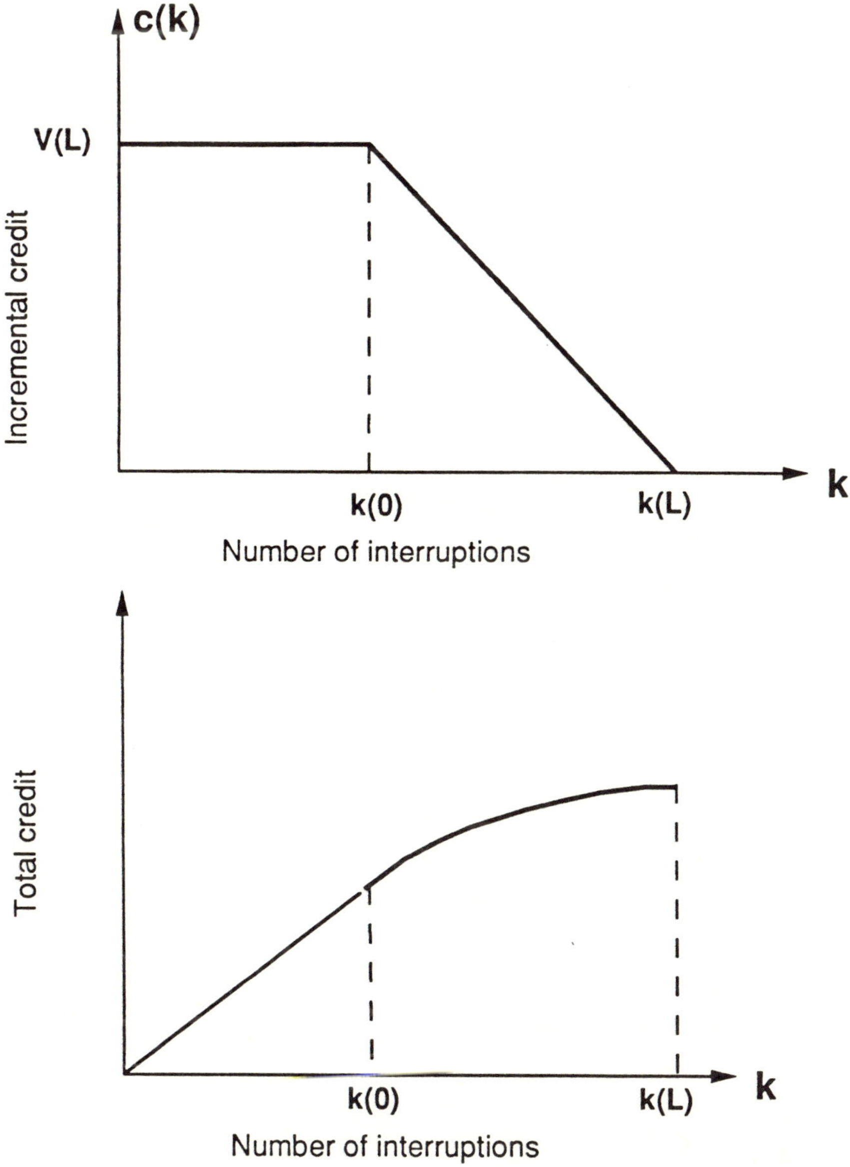

Figure 10. Credit Structure for Continuous Dispatching

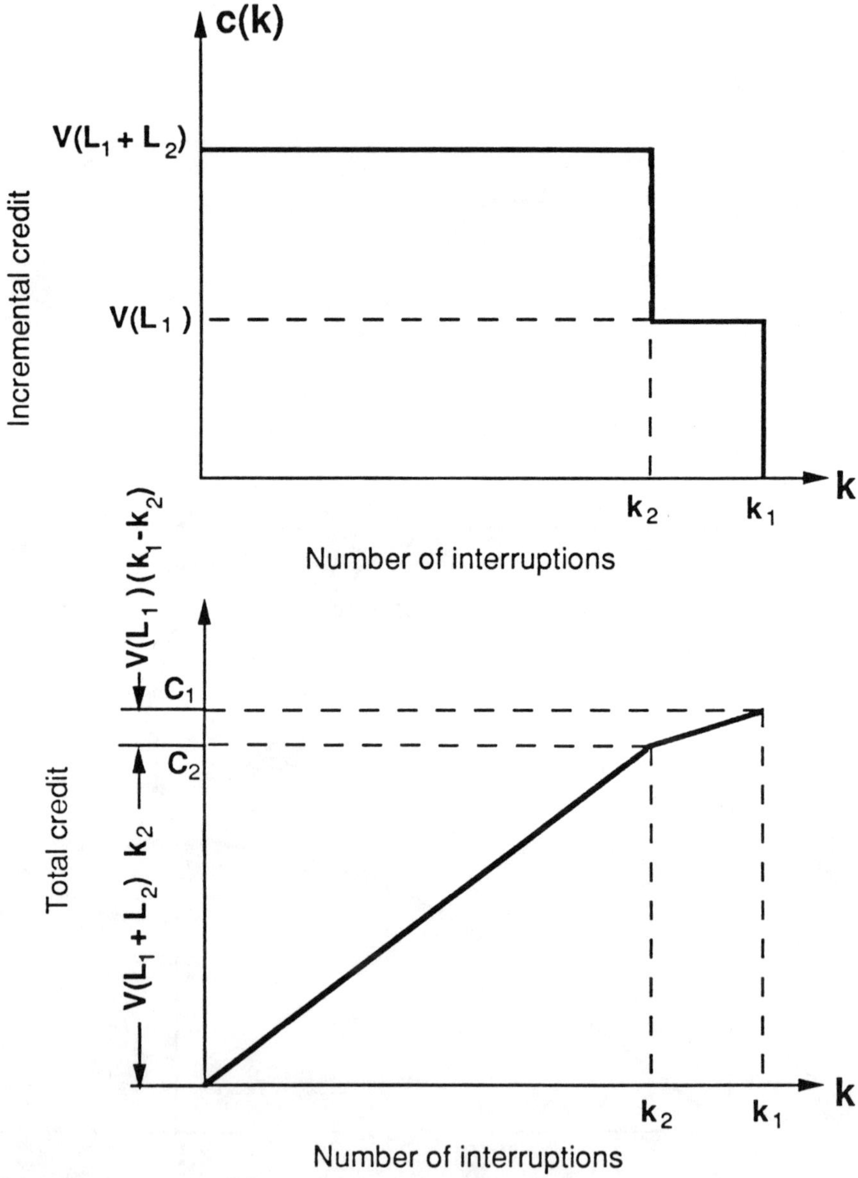

Figure 11. Credit Structure for Two Blocks

case of n blocks with respective loads of $L_1, ..., L_n$ and number of interruptions $k_1 \geq k_2 \geq ... k_n$ will result in a menu of contracts with

$$C_n = k_n v(\sum_{j=1}^{n} L_n)$$

and

$$C_i = C_{i+1} + (k_i - k_{i+1})\, v(\sum_{j=1}^{i} L_j)\ , \quad \text{for } i = 1,...,n-1.$$

where credit C_i is offered for k_i interruptions.

In the one block case, the utility must pay for each incremental interruption an amount that equals the highest loss incurred by any unit of load sustaining that interruption. Thus, the credits paid by the utility substantially exceed the cumulative interruption losses sustained by customers as illustrated in Figure 12. This "overpayment" in turn reduces the utility's incentive to enlist interruptible load, which reduces the social efficiency of the system. Multiple discrete blocks can significantly reduce the "overpayment" and thus provide incentives to increase social surplus. Figure 13 illustrates the saving for each of the $k_1 - k_2$ interruptions in which the high priority L_2 units are not curtailed in the two block case. The area A_1 represents the saved social cost of the spared curtailments, while the area $A_1 + A_2$ represents the savings to the utility based on the original credit for the one block dispatch. The utility achieves an additional savings A_3 due to the fact that the incremental $k_1 - k_2$ interruptions can be compensated at a lower rate. Thus, the total social savings due to blocking is $(k_1 - k_2)A_1$ while the credit savings to the utility is $(k_1\ k_2)(A_1 + A_2 + A_3)$. These savings clearly increase with the number of blocks.

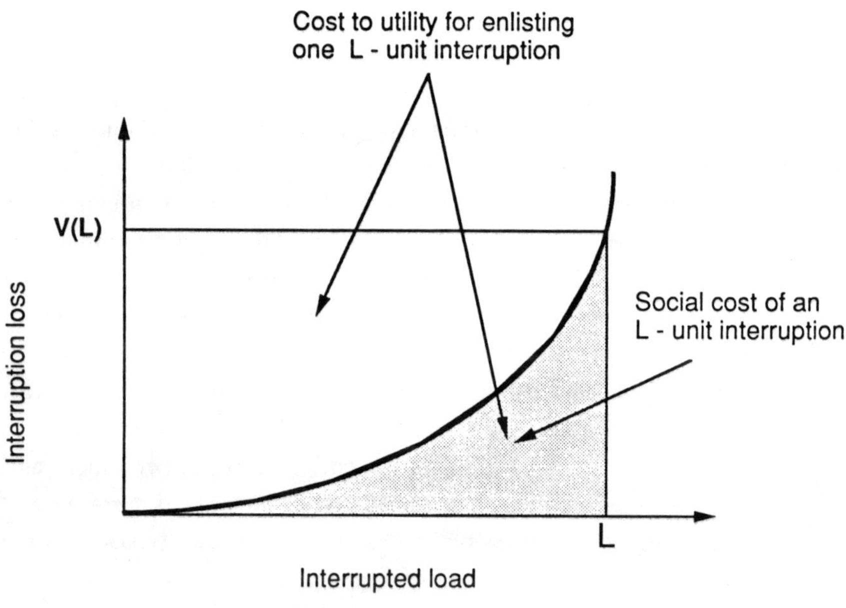

Figure 12. Cost to Utility vs. Social Cost per Interruptions

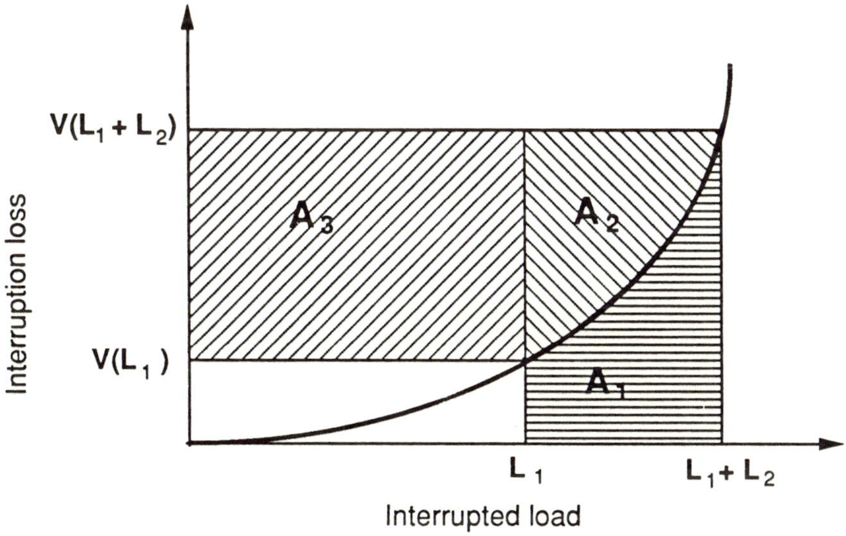

Figure 13. Savings Due to Blocking of the Interruptible Load

CONCLUSION

This analysis in this case study accomplished two main objectives. First, an operational tool was developed for dispatching a single block of interruptible load. This solved a practical problem faced by the New England Electric System. The spreadsheet solution described in this report was used operationally by the System Dispatcher to help select days in which to interrupt CIS customers. Our second objective was to develop insights and practical tools to aid the electric utility in the expansion of its interruptible service program. We developed a methodology for evaluating the costs and benefits of new service options for curtailable service and determining its most efficient features.

The planning methodology was useful in demonstrating to NEES that, given their current subscribers and demand patterns, there is limited benefit in enlisting more interruptions per year from existing CIS subscribers. Instead, the focus should be on enlisting new CIS subscribers, or additional load from current subscribers, by offering service options with fewer interruptions per year to induce additional subscription. Our analysis also showed how the number of required interruptions increases, as the amount of interruptible load increases in the single block case. As interruptible load is added, segmenting the load into blocks that are dispatched according to a priority order becomes more economically efficient and requires lower credit payments from the utility.

We have also shown in this paper how our dispatching algorithm can be extended to the multiple block case, but this generalization has not been implemented currently. For the multiple block case, we have presented a methodology for pricing a menu of service options with different numbers of interruptions during the contract period. The pricing methodology requires knowledge only of the distribution of interruption losses in the population and is based on some simplifying assumptions. The resulting menu of service options induces self-selection by customers. That is, service priorities are selected for load units in a way that produces a socially efficient resource allocation and the desired contract mix for the utility in the multiblock case.

ACKNOWLEDGEMENTS

The authors are grateful to both EPRI and NEES for sponsoring this project. We particularly wish to thank Joseph Wharton, David Gillespie and Paul Liddell of NEES for their time and patience in educating us about NEES's pricing, dispatching and supply systems; and also our EPRI project managers, Hung-po Chao and Riaz Siddiqi, and our colleague, Robert Wilson, who have provided additional valuable insights in the course of this research. Professor Oren's research was also partially supported by NSF Grant IRI-8902813 and by a California Energy Studies grant. The authors are fully responsibility for the opinions expressed in this report and any remaining errors.

REFERENCES

Chao, Hung-po and Robert B. Wilson. "Priority Service: Pricing, Investment and Market Organization." *American Economic Review*, vol. 77, no. 5, , pp. 899-916, 1976.

Chao, Hung-Po, Shmuel S. Oren, Stephen A. Smith and Robert B. Wilson. "Multilevel Demand Subscription Pricing for Electric Power." *Energy Economics*, pp. 199-217, 1986.

------------------. "Selected Papers on Priority Service Methods." *EPRI Report P-5350*. Electric Power Research Institute (August, 1987).

------------------. "Priority Service: Market Structure and Competition." *The Energy Journal*, vol 9, pp. 77-103, 1989.

Crew, M.A., P.R. Kleindorfer. "Reliability and Public Utility Pricing." *The American Economic Review*, vol. 68, no. 1, pp. 31-40, 1978.

Feller, W. *An Introduction to Probability Theory and its Applications*. vol. 1, John Wiley and Sons, New York, 1957.

Fisinger, J. "Peak Load Pricing and Rationing Policies." *Journal of Economics*, vol 40. no. 2, pp. 169-182, 1980.

Marchand, Maurice G. "Pricing Power Supplied on an Interruptible Basis." *European Economic Review*, vol 5, pp.263-274, 1974.

Oren, Shmuel, Joseph A. Doucet. "Interruption Insurance for Generation and Distribution of Electric Power." *Journal of Regulatory Economics*, vol. 2, pp. 5-19, 1990.

Oren, Shmuel and Stephen A. Smith. "Design and Management of Curtailable Electricity Service to Reduce Annual Peaks." *Operations Research*, vol. 40, no. 2, 213-228, 1992.

Smith, Stephen A. "Efficient Menu Structure for Pricing Interruptible Electric Power Service." *Journal of Regulatory Economics*, vol 1, no. 3, pp. 203-224, 1989.

Telson, M. "The Economics of Alternative Levels of Reliability for Electric Power Generation Systems." *Bell Journal of Economics*, vol. 6 (Autumn), pp. 679-694, 1975.

Tschirhart, J. and F. Jen. "Behavior of a Monopoly Offering Interruptible Service." *Bell Journal of Economics*, vol. 10 (Spring), pp 244-258, 1979.

Viswanathan, N. and E. Tse. "Monopolistic Provision of Congested Service with Incentive Based Allocation of Priorities." *International Economic Review*, no. 1 pp. 153-174, 1989.

Vickery, W. "Responsive Pricing of Public Utility Services." *Bell Journal of Economics and Management Science*, vol 2. pp. 337-346, 1971.

Wharton J. B. "Customer Response and Appropriate Credits for Interruptible Rates: NEES Cooperative Interruptible Service Program." Working Paper, New England Power Service Company, 1988.

Wilson, Robert B. "Efficient and Competitive Rationing." *Econometrica*, vol. 57, no. 1, pp. 1-40, 1989.

Wilson, Robert B. "Ramsey Pricing of Priority Service." *Journal of Regulatory Economics*, vol 1, no. 3, pp.189-202, 1989.

APPENDIX A

The models derived in this appendix are used to develop the relationships illustrated in Figure 4. Suppose that our goal is to interrupt a peak if it falls within L of the annual peak A_0. Let us consider a threshold policy in which an interruption is called for if the daily forecast exceeds the threshold H. For any given H, there is some probability that a peak which is actually $A_0 - L$ will be missed due to forecast error, namely

$$\alpha = P\{\text{the forecast } < H \text{ on a day with peak } A_0 - L\}$$

Since the forecast is increasing in the actual peak size, this is the worst case, for all peaks in the range $[A_0 - L, A_0]$. In general, α could also depend on the time of the year T, but we have assumed that annual peak forecast errors are stationary throughout the year.

Conversely, for given α and L, we can determine a threshold $H_\alpha(L)$ such that a peak of size $A_0 - L$ is missed with probability α based on (2-1) and (2-2). In general, the forecast on a day with peak $A_0 - L$ satisfies

$$F_t = A_0 - L + E_t + E_0 \ , \qquad \text{(A-1)}$$

where F_t = daily forecast on day t

E_t = error in the daily forecast for day t

E_0 = error in forecasting the annual peak.

Now define the random variable $Z_t = A_0 + E_t + E_0$. If we assume that E_0 and E_t are independent, it follows from the additive property of Normal distributions that

$$P\{Z_t \leq z\} = \Phi\left(\frac{z-m}{\sigma_2}\right), \qquad \text{(A-2)}$$

where $\sigma_2 = \sqrt{\sigma^2 + \sigma_1^2}$, based on the distributions defined in Section 2.

The probability α that the peak $A_0 - L$ is missed equals the probability that the forecast on that day is less than H. Thus, for the threshold $H_\alpha(L)$, we must have $\alpha = P\{Z_t - L \leq H_\alpha(L)\}$ from (A-1). Since Z_t is normally distributed, we can obtain a corresponding z_α value from a Normal table and obtain $H_\alpha(L)$ from

$$H_\alpha(L) = \mu - L - z_\alpha \sigma_2 \ . \qquad \text{(A-3)}$$

In addition to missing a peak due to forecast error, it could also be missed if the remaining interruptions are exhausted before it occurred. Thus, it is important to consider the probability

$\beta = \beta(H,k,W_T) = P\{$ k interruptions are used up, given threshold H and W_T peak days remaining$\}$.

For any day t and given H, an interruption occurs if and only if $F_t \geq H$. To consider the probability that this occurs, we need to consider all peaks that may trigger an interruption. Let D_t be the random variable corresponding to the difference between the peak on day t and the annual peak A_0. Using the random variables E_t and E_0 discussed above, the threshold H is exceeded by the forecast on day t if and only if

$$A_0 - D_t + E_t + E_0 \geq H \quad \text{or} \quad D_t \leq Z_t - H, \tag{A-4}$$

using the random variable Z_t defined above.

For any value D, let us define an indicator random variable

$$x_t(D) = \begin{cases} 1 & \text{if day } t \text{ falls within } D \text{ of the yearly peak} \\ 0 & \text{otherwise, with} \end{cases}$$

$$P\{x_t(D)=1\} = F(D)w_t \ , \tag{A-5}$$

based on (2-5). The probability that the forecast on day t is greater than H is

$$P\{x_t(Z_t - H) = 1\} = w_t \int_H^\infty F(z-H)\, \phi\left(\frac{z-\mu}{\sigma_2}\right) \frac{dz}{\sigma_2}$$

$$= w_t \int_0^\infty F(\sigma_2 z)\, \phi(z-y) = w_t I(y) \ , \tag{A-6}$$

where $y = (\mu - H)/\sigma_2$.

The function I(y) is the expected fraction of days whose forecasts are within y standard deviations of μ, the forecasted annual peak, or equivalently, the expected fraction of peak days whose *forecasts* are above the threshold H. The variable $x_t(Z_t\text{-}H)$ is a Bernoulli random variable with

$$E[x_t(Z_t - H)] = w_t I(y) \quad \text{and} \quad Var[x_t(Z_t - H)] = w_t I(y) - w_t^2 I^2(y). \quad \text{(A-7)}$$

Given the current day is T, the number of remaining days whose forecast exceeds H is the random variable

$$S_T(H) = \sum_{t=T}^{365} x_t(Z_t - H). \quad \text{(A-8)}$$

It can be shown that the sum $S_T(H)$ satisfies the Central Limit Theorem. This follows from the fact that it is a sum of independent random variables which are uniformly bounded in absolute value [see Feller(1957), pp.238-9]. Thus we have the approximate relationship

$$P\{S_T(H) \leq k\} \approx \Phi\left(\frac{k - W_T I(y)}{s(y,T)}\right), \quad \text{(A-9)}$$

where $y = (\mu - H)/\sigma_2$

$W_T I(y)$ = E[number of remaining forecasts greater than H]

$s(y,T) = \sqrt{W_T I(y) - I^2(y)\sigma_T^2}$ = standard deviation of the number of remaining forecasts greater than H

and $W_T = \sum_{t=T}^{365} w_t$ and $\sigma_T^2 = \sum_{t=T}^{365} w_t^2$.

Since $\beta(H,k,T)$ is the probability that the remaining interruptions are exhausted, it is clear, given there are k interruptions remaining on day T, that

$$1 - \beta(H,k,T) = P\{S_t(H) \leq k\}. \quad \text{(A-10)}$$

Conversely, for given β, H and T, we can determine the number of interruptions $k_\beta(H,T)$ that are required. Using β, we obtain a value z_β from a standard Normal table, which based on (A-10), must satisfy

$$z_{\beta} = \frac{k - W_T I(y)}{s(y,T)} . \tag{A-11}$$

We then solve (A-11) to obtain a formula for $k_{\beta}(H,T)$

$$k = k_{\beta}(H,T) = W_T I(y) + z_{\beta} s(y,T). \tag{A-12}$$

In (A-12), y is the number of standard deviations that H is away from the forecasted annual peak μ, i.e., $y = (\mu - H)/\sigma_2$. Given that the interruptible load is L, we can use (A-3) to substitute for H, which yields

$$y = z_{\alpha} + L/\sigma_2 . \tag{A-13}$$

Solving the Dispatching Problem

For the dispatching problem with given k, the goal of the dispatching methodology reduces to one of attempting to interrupt the k highest remaining daily forecasts in the year. This can be seen intuitively because the optimal use of the k interruptions is to interrupt the k highest peaks. Since the errors in daily forecasts are time independent, this implies that the highest k forecasts are the most likely candidates for the k highest peaks. It is clear that the dispatching solution should depend on k and T, but not on L. Therefore, we solve the case $L = 0$.

For known k, (A-12) and (A-13) provide two equations for the three unknowns y, z_{α} and z_{β}. Thus, one additional relationship is required to obtain an optimal value of y, which leads to an optimal threshold H for the dispatching problem. The solution is completed by determining a relationship between z_{α} and z_{β} that balances the probability of missing a peak due to forecasting error and missing a peak due to running out of remaining interruptions.

Let β equal the probability of running out of interruptions and α equal the probability that the annual peak A_0 is missed due to forecast error. Then the probability that the annual peak is missed can be expressed as

$$P\{\text{missing annual peak}\} = \beta P\{\text{peak occurs after running out} \mid \text{run out}\} +$$

$$(1-\beta)P\{\text{forecast on peak day} < H \mid \text{given that don't run out}\}.$$

As a first order approximation, we assume independence permits the conditioning to be ignored in the two conditional probabilities above. We also take the expected value case in which the interruptions are used at exactly their average rate during the remainder of the year. This implies that β is the probability that the annual peak occurs after the interruptions are exhausted, given that they are exhausted. Thus, substituting these assumptions we have

$$P\{\text{miss annual peak}\} = (1-\beta)\,\alpha + \beta\beta = \alpha - \alpha\beta + \beta^2 \,. \tag{A-14}$$

We then wish to minimize this expression with respect to the ratio $\alpha/\beta = r$. The probability can be rewritten as

$$\alpha - r\alpha^2 + r^2\alpha^2 \cdot \tag{A-15}$$

It can be verified from the first and second order necessary conditions that this expression has a unique minimum at $r = 1/2$, i.e. $\alpha/\beta = 1/2$, for any fixed value of α. Thus we have established a second relationship based on (A-15)

$$\beta = \alpha/2. \tag{A-16}$$

Using (A-16) with a standard Normal distribution table determines a trajectory of possible (z_α, z_β) pairs. Applying linear regression to the points shown gives the approximate relationship

$$z_\beta = 0.8022\, z_\alpha + 0.6272, \tag{A-17}$$

which provides an excellent fit, with an R^2 value of 0.997.

Substituting (A-17) into (A-11), we obtain

$$0.8022\, z_{\alpha} + 0.6272 = \frac{k - W_T I(y)}{s(y,T)}. \tag{A-18}$$

For the dispatching problem, we consider the case $L = 0$ so that (A-13) reduces to $y = z_{\alpha}$, which when substituted into (A-18) reduces to

$$k = W_T I(y) + s(y,T)[0.8022y + 0.6272]. \tag{A-19}$$

This implicit relationship can be used to obtain a tabular solution for y and thus the threshold H by substituting in various values of y and T and calculating the corresponding k. This function is shown graphically in Figure 4. To solve the dispatching problem for a given k, T, we determine $y = z_{\alpha}$ from Figure 4. Then the corresponding dispatching threshold H is

$$H = \mu - y\sigma_2 , \tag{A-20}$$

which is equivalent to $H_{\alpha}(0)$ in (A-3).

Solving the Planning Problem

For the planning problem, we wish to determine the appropriate number of interruptions to allocate for the year. For a given interruptible load L, the planning problem objective is to determine how many interruptions are required so that the probability of missing a peak within L of the annual peak is α, given that they are dispatched in the manner discussed above.

The solution of the planning problem begins with the same relationship (A-19), which describes the solution of the dispatching problem. However, in this case, k is not specified, but any choice of y determines a dispatching threshold H from (A-20). To compute the probability that the dispatching threshold misses a peak that falls within L of the annual peak, we determine what z value is implied by the threshold H, by setting it equal to the righthand side of (A-3) to obtain

$$\mu - L - z_{\alpha} s_2 = H = \mu - y\sigma_2 . \tag{A-21}$$

That is, the probability that a peak within L of the annual peak is missed by a threshold $H = \mu - y\sigma_2$ is $\alpha = 1 - \Phi(z_\alpha)$, where z is determined from a Normal table. Thus to solve the planning problem for a given L and probability α, we set $y = z_\alpha + L/\sigma_2$ and obtain the appropriate k from (A-17).

In the spreadsheet implementation of the dispatching threshold, it was necessary to obtain approximate linear relationships for $I(y)$ and $s(y,T)$ to simplify (A-17). Using the numerical integration and applying regression to the results gave

$I(y)$ ª $0.0089 + 0.2306y$, where $y = (\mu - H - L)/\sigma_2$ (A-22)

$s(y,T)$ ª $\sqrt{W_T}\,\{0.2875 + 0.1464y\}$. (A-23)

The regression for $s(y,T)$ used the T value corresponding to $W_T = 30$. The R^2 values in these regressions were both larger than 0.99.

Substituting in (A-22) and (A-23), (A-19) becomes a quadratic function to be solved for H. Using the quadratic formula, and selecting the positive root for y, we have

$$y = \frac{-B + \sqrt{B^2 - 4AC}}{2A}\,. \qquad \text{(A-24)}$$

where $A = 0.1174$, $B = 0.2306\sqrt{W_T} + 0.3224$,
$C = 0.1803 + \sqrt{W_T}\,[0.00887\,k/W_T\,]$.

This formula was used for the spreadsheet in Figure 6.

V. ROLE OF ENABLING TECHNOLOGIES

UTILITY AND CUSTOMER COMMUNICATION, COMPUTING AND CONTROL (UC-3C) TECHNOLOGIES

by

C. Blumstein and A.H. Rosenfeld
University of California, Berkeley

and

H. Akbari
Lawrence Livermore Laboratory

INTRODUCTION

The reason for giving a talk about utility/customer communication, computing, and control at this conference on new service opportunities for electric utilities lies in the nature of the services being considered. Essentially, these services involve the provision of information about the value of attributes of electricity supply (e.g., the value of reliability, security, or time-of-use). In order for the provision of this information to be a service, it must be communicated to customers in a timely fashion, the customers must be able to decide what to do about the information (computing), and they must do it (control). Also, to settle accounts, it will be necessary to communicate the results of the customers' actions back to the utility.

Thus, this talk is about the means of communicating, deciding about (computing), and acting on (control) information. Its purpose is to describe the outlines of a system that could perform these functions in the future, to discuss ways of getting from here to there, and to point out that, in the process of getting from here to there, we may well find opportunities for the provision of new utility services that go well beyond those being considered at this meeting.

A VISION OF THE FUTURE

Within the next few decades the transmission and distribution networks that deliver electric power to our homes and factories will be paralleled by communications networks and electric meters will be replaced by computers. This new information technology will transform the industry in three ways: (1) existing operations will become more automated, (2) the generation, transmission, and distribution plant will be used more efficiently, and (3) a range of additional new services will be offered. Existing operations that will be automated include meter reading, connection and disconnection, capacitor switching, feeder switching, fault location, and theft detection. This automation will reduce costs and increase reliability. Plant will be used more efficiently by shifting load from peak to off-peak and by using resources that would, with today's operating practices, be needed as a reserve. Load will shift as a result of "real-time pricing" that will adjust the price of electricity at frequent intervals to reflect the marginal cost of production. Capacity that is now held in reserve for emergencies (the reserve margin) will be used by offering its output for sale at lower, interruptible rates. The ability to rapidly and selectively shed loads will allow utility customers to operate different loads on different priority schedules. For example, households will be able to operate their refrigerators with a rate that permits short interruptions for emergencies. By such means even the traditional "spinning reserve" can be displaced by rapidly interruptible loads. The automation of utility operations and the more efficient use of plant will save utility customers many billions of dollars annually. But the impact of other new utility services may be even greater. Foremost among these services will be energy management. The computer that replaces the electricity meter will transform information from the utility's communication network, sensors at the customer's premises, and databases describing the customer's preferences into control signals for the equipment (e.g., lights, air conditioners) that provides the customer with energy services. Experience to date suggests that good control can reduce energy consumption by 20 to 30 percent while improving the quality of service. Control capability opens the door for utilities to begin supplying energy services such as space conditioning instead of just supplying energy. The opportunities for reducing energy consumption and improving the quality of service multiply with this approach. Ultimately, the technological revolution in computing, communication, and control may mediate an institutional transformation of the utility industry–from energy suppliers to energy service companies.

OBSTACLES AND OPPORTUNITIES

There are some formidable obstacles along the path to our vision. First, it won't be cheap. For example, the investment for computing and control in each of California's more than 10 million households will be on the order of $500 per household. Add to this the costs for the commercial and industrial sectors and the costs for building and maintaining a communications network and pretty soon you are talking about real money. Second, it can't be fully demonstrated on a small scale. Many of the benefits of the system that is envisioned depend on its wide-scale application. Consider the case of real-time pricing combined with priority pricing for households. Optimizing energy usage under such a pricing regime would be greatly facilitated by appliances that could be controlled by signals from the customer's meter (e.g., a refrigerator that can alter the timing of its defrost cycle and can turn itself off for short periods in response to signals from the meter). But manufacturers are unlikely to develop such products until they are confident that a market for them will exist. A little reflection will produce numerous other examples of how the success of a UC-3C system may depend on its scale. Thus, incremental development of a new system will be difficult. We are talking not only about costly systems, but also about costly experiments to prove out the benefits.

Given these obstacles, one is tempted to opt for a simpler way of providing the services being considered at this meeting: buy a radio transmitter, broadcast the prices, and let market forces generate an appropriate response. This approach has some serious drawbacks both in potential losses in efficiency and, for utility companies, the loss of an immense business opportunity. Efficiency losses may occur because of the absence of two-way communication and because of higher equipment costs resulting from the separation between metering and computing and control.

Priority pricing provides an example of the possible advantages of two-way communication. Typically, priority pricing schemes envisage that customers will be committed to a priority level for an extended period. However, it is almost certain that there would be efficiency gains if, when the moment of truth arrived, customers with a low priority had the opportunity to make trades with higher priority customers (i.e., pay the higher priority customer to take the outage). With two-way communication it would be possible to develop a spot market for reliability to complement longer-term contracts. [This market might operate through a computer-conducted matching of buyers and sellers based on prices posted in the customers' computers.]

New pricing methods such as those being discussed at this meeting will require new metering technology. If the new methods are to be effective, automated customer response will also be necessary. This latter point derives from the fact that manual response will be too expensive and too slow. In households, we cannot expect that customers will routinely attend to the small tasks required to monitor prices (e.g., read a display in the kitchen) and to optimize consumption accordingly–this is too much time and trouble for too little gain. In larger facilities, where the gains would be larger, the number of actions needed is likely to be too great and the optimization problem too complicated for an effective manual response. In a simple "broadcast the price" strategy, utilities would be responsible for the new metering technology and the market would have to supply the means for automated response. But the technology needed for metering and the technology needed for automated response are closely related and have may elements in common. A single device that does both functions is almost certain to be less expensive than two separate devices.

The strategy of broadcasting prices and letting the market work implies that utilities will not be part of the market. But utilities would have some competitive advantages in such a market. They have regular transactions with their customers–the marginal cost of additional transactions should be lower than the transaction costs of competitors. They have a monopoly position in the metering business. And, the expense of developing a UC-3C system can be largely offset by gains from automating existing operations (meter reading, capacitor switching, etc.). The proper functioning of the market does not usually require participants with competitive advantages to opt out. Indeed, the competitive advantages that would be enjoyed by utilities in such a market seem to be so large that there is room for them to earn very substantial profits while, at the same time, leaving the economy substantially better off as a result of their participation.

GETTING FROM HERE TO THERE

Making the transition from the existing methods of operating the electricity supply system to operation with a UC-3C system won't be easy. As we have noted, these systems will be expensive and their benefits will be difficult to demonstrate of a small scale. The challenge is to find a path from here to there with steps that are large enough to produce real progress and yet are not too costly or too risky. It is not too soon to start. Indeed, utilities that hang back and wait for someone else to show that it works will be at a disadvantage. The utility of the future may not match our vision, but we think that it is inevitable that information technology will profoundly change the industry. Utilities that experiment with new methods and have a proactive stance toward new technology will be in a much better position to adjust to this change.

A Place to Start

One area in which we think early efforts should be concentrated is large commercial customers, particularly those whose facilities have energy management and control systems (EMCSs). EMCSs are becoming common in commercial buildings. The primary purpose of these systems is to reduce expenditures for energy and power. Among the energy-management and control strategies that are implemented by EMCSs are optimal stop and start, demand limiting, economizer control, and daylighting. They are a prototype for the customer response computers that we believe will be necessary if new methods of pricing electricity are to be fully effective. Establishing direct communication links to customer EMCSs appears an obvious first step on the path to the development of full-scale UC-3C system. This step would be (relatively) low cost and could have significant payoffs without having to involve very large numbers of customers.

Finding Allies

For the most part, those concerned with the development of UC-3C technologies and those concerned with new pricing methods have worked in isolation from each other. The continuation of this isolation is not in the interest of either group. The benefits from new pricing methods are probably not sufficient to justify the costs of a UC-3C system–other functions such as those we have listed will have to be performed by the system if it is to be cost effective. By the same token, the benefits from other functions alone are unlikely to be sufficient to justify the costs of a UC-3C system. Even if one or the other did provide sufficient benefits to justify the costs, the economies from combining functions would be compelling. The two groups need each other. Most of you at this meeting are interested in new pricing methods. You need to pay attention to the technology and the technologists: you need to understand the technical possibilities and limitations, you need to help the technologists understand your technical requirements, and you need to encourage and support technical research and development.

INTEGRATED UTILITY COMMUNICATIONS AND DISTRIBUTION AUTOMATION; BUILDING THE FRAMEWORK FOR DIFFERENTIATED PRODUCTS

by

Wade P. Malcolm, P.E.
Electric Power Research Institute

INTRODUCTION

Today, utilities are facing increasing pressures of deregulation, competition, changing business conditions and varying customer requirements.

Existing computers and communications systems were installed with limited capabilities to communicate with other systems. The result, say many utilities, is an electronic Tower of Babel among computers that are unable to readily talk to one another or, if they can, haven't much to say because of vastly different database structures.

Estimates of the industry's operating costs for telecommunications range from $2 billion to more likely $5 billion a year, with some individual company budgets growing as much as 25% a year. A typical medium-size utility will spend $35 Million in annual telecommunication expenses.

EPRI has been tasked by its member utilities to develop guidelines and specifications that would support the development of integrated nonproprietary, interoperable utility communications systems. Dramatic cost savings and improved performance are the key reasons for communications systems integration. Further, opportunities for new products and services result when one can now share information, across all operations in a company, in an effective and timely manner.

PROJECT OBJECTIVES

EPRI's undertaking is known as the Integrated Utility Communications Project. The objectives of this project are: 1) develop a communication architecture tailored to the utility communication needs and based upon the ISO Open System Interconnection (OSI) reference model depicted in Figures 1; 2) develop database access procedures and methods that are compatible with the communication architecture; 3) implement several pilot demonstrations of the architecture and/or database procedures at host utility sites; and 4) develop analytical models and methods to plan, design and maintain communication systems, given a variety of available communication media. Early in the project development, a fifth objective had existed to incorporate expert system technology into communication network planning and operation. This project has been consolidated into the analytical tools development project. These developments will permit information exchange between all elements of a typical electric utility system and between utilities without employing expensive custom software bridges between different vendor's equipment. Significant cost and operations benefits will result from the applying of existing and emerging standards to future communications procurement.

RESEARCH APPROACH

EPRI's research approach is depicted in Figure 2. The integrated communications effort is currently focused on two major funded projects. The first is the development of a utility communications architecture (UCA) that provides the guidelines and specifications necessary to link dissimilar data communications systems throughout a utility. Our second funded effort is an extension to the architecture development allowing for the access and sharing of data across connected computers at a utility.

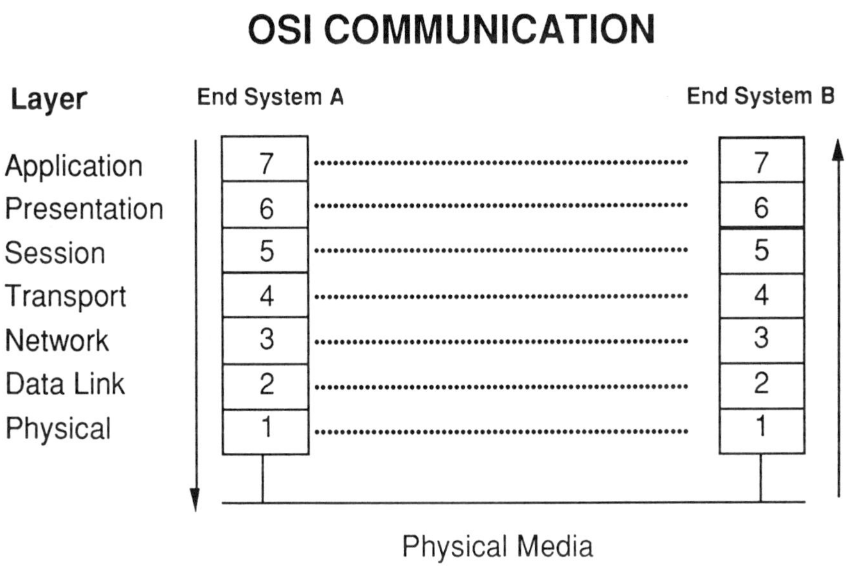

Figure 1 - OSI reference model:

A model for describing and distinguishing between the different functions required for communication.

As part of the pending project phases, EPRI will fund further demonstrations of the UCA/DAIS technology at EPRI member utility sites.

Also, we are starting to formulate the plans to develop analytical tools, similar in nature to those used by today's utility system planners, such as load flows, that will enable utility personnel to effectively install, operate and maintain integrated utility communications systems.

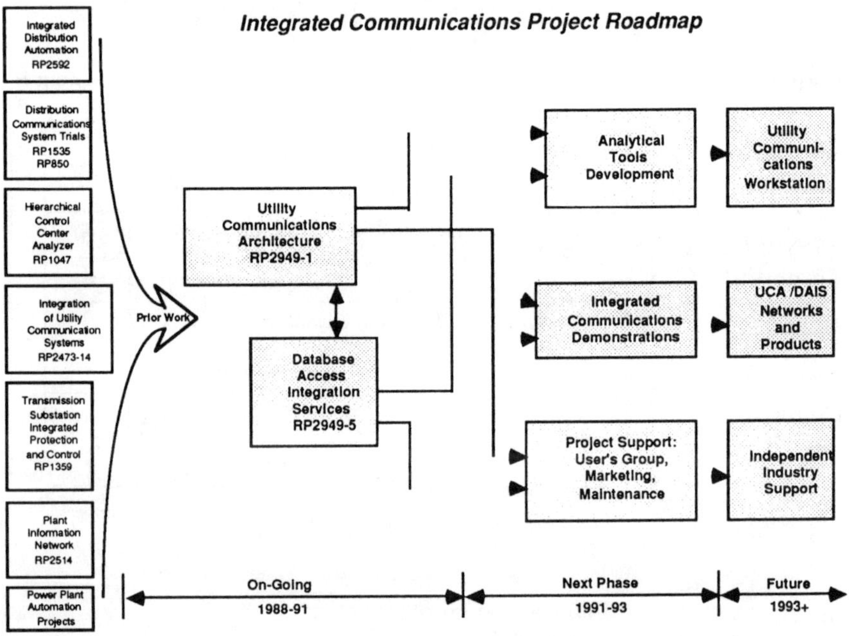

Figure 2 - Integrated Utility Communications Project Roadmap

Throughout all of these efforts we have, and will, maintain interaction with both the utility industry and the vendor community in a series of seminars and workshops that allow input and review of the EPRI work, and facilitate technology transfer. To extend this commitment, EPRI has established an Integrated Utility Information Users' Group. The intent of the group is to facilitate the transfer of the technology to the utility industry and be the focal point for interaction in the future.

The Integrated Communications effort is based on two major goals:

- That the systems developed to conform with EPRI's guidelines and specifications be nonproprietary.
- And that elements of the systems be interoperable.

To accomplish this, we are basing our specifications on international standards that have applicability to other industries, thereby broadening the market base of products for utilities to consider. More details on the individual projects follow.

UTILITY COMMUNICATIONS ARCHITECTURE

The Utility Communications Architecture is a specification that provides an overall framework, based on international standards, for the interconnection of all the data communications systems within and external to a utility company. The concept is portrayed in a philosophical fashion in Figure 3.

The Utility Communications Architecture development has produced several deliverables, as seen in Figure 4. Two primary host utilities have participated. Houston Lighting and Power and Pacific Gas and Electric have hosted the architecture work. Andersen Consulting, the Contractor, has been heavily involved with the host utilities.

The first deliverable is called the UCA Functional Definition which is a compilation and description of all the functions occurring within a utility that requires the exchange of information. In essence, who talks to whom and how. Over fifteen utility interviews to determine communication needs and requirements were conducted. A workshop to review early results was held and was attended by over 100 utility engineers, communication systems suppliers and integrators.

The Functional Definition document, was completed in draft form in 1989. It provides the most comprehensive information model of an entire utility developed to date, and has proven to be very popular as a reference with utility functional and telecommunications analysts. Over 600 copies of the draft have been distributed to date. It serves as an excellent educational tool for those trying to understand the basics of utility communications.

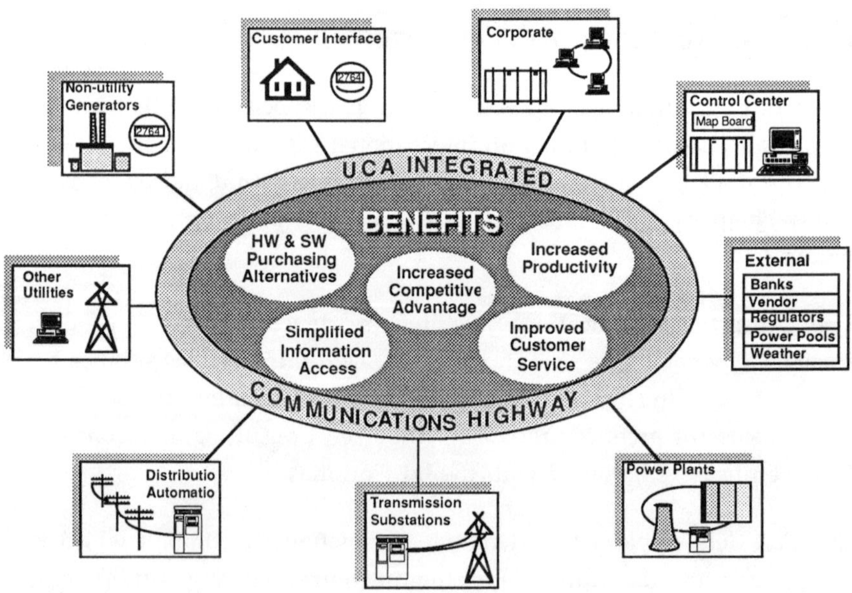

Figure 3 - UCA Conceptual Objective

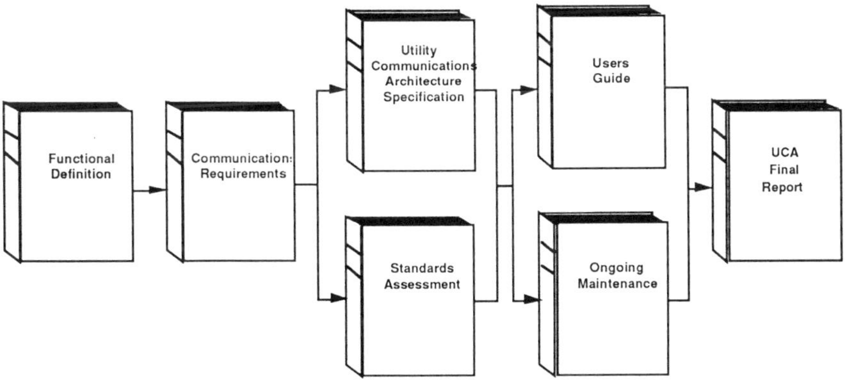

Figure 4 - UCA Project Deliverables

The second deliverable is known as the Communications Requirements document. This document presents the current and future communications requirements, and important attributes, of the data exchanges described in the functional definition. This document serves as the utility industry's technical requirements for which today's international standards are assessed. Forty-five utility companies participated in the development of the document.

The Communications Requirements report has been called the most ambitious characterization of an industry's communications requirements to date by those outside our industry in the standards community and serving on our advisory committee. The document is currently being published.

The third deliverable is called the Standards Assessment and it provides the listing of international communications and utility industry standards assessed with regards to our communications requirements and also an audit trail of the assessment results. The document also serves as a good tutorial on both OSI and the international standards process. The final version of this document is currently being published.

The forth deliverable is the actual Utility Communications Architecture Specification that is based on the assessed international standards and published in the form of a technical specification that could be used for procurement. Over 600 copies of the UCA Specification have been distributed to utilities and vendors. The UCA Specification will be available to the general public and can be freely reproduced in order to make it widely available for consideration by both utilities and vendors.

A supporting Users Guide is being readied for published that describes the intent and relationship of the project deliverables and guides the utility personnel to determine the cost benefits and migration strategies from existing communications systems to those that best suit their companies. It also contains supporting material for procurement and usage of UCA compliant systems.

An ongoing maintenance memorandum has also been produced that will address how the UCA will be updated, as requirements, standards and technologies change.

Executive summaries of the deliverables are compiled into a final report. All of the reports will be available through normal EPRI distribution.

DATABASE ACCESS INTEGRATION SERVICES

EPRI has contracted Honeywell, Inc. to develop DAIS (Database Access Integration Services). The project is the second of the planned projects comprising EPRI's Integrated Utility Communications effort. DAIS is a collection of services that facilitate access to data among diverse data systems in an electric utility communications network as portrayed in Figure 5.

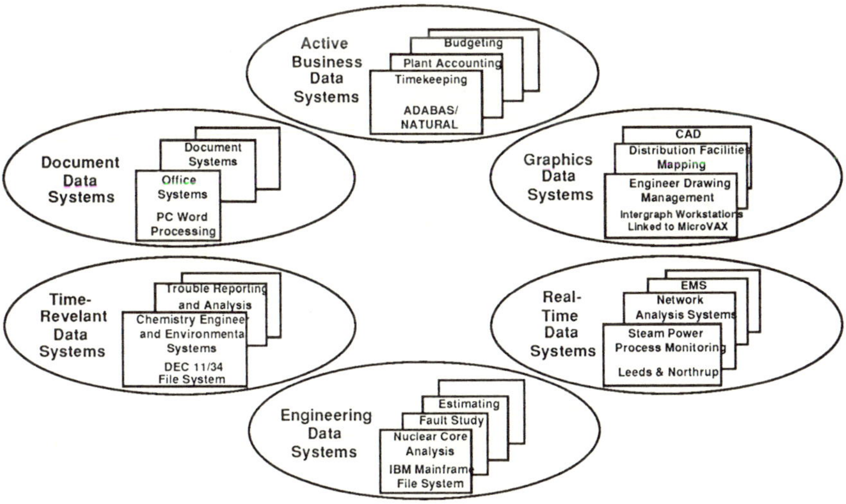

Figure 5 - A "Typical" Utility Data Environment

DAIS will provide access to data in distributed heterogeneous data systems that include relational database management systems, other database management systems, control systems, file systems, and application systems. It provides a common method for describing data, common data access operations and essential support services including a data dictionary, a data directory and distributed data access management capabilities. A simplified view of the DAIS concept is seen in Figure 6.

The DAIS project has developed draft specifications intended for vendor and third-party implementation, and will only develop software to implement a data access demonstration at the primary host utility, Northern States Power Company, as part of the current effort. One important consequence of this strategy is that most actual software development will be performed by vendors, not utilities.

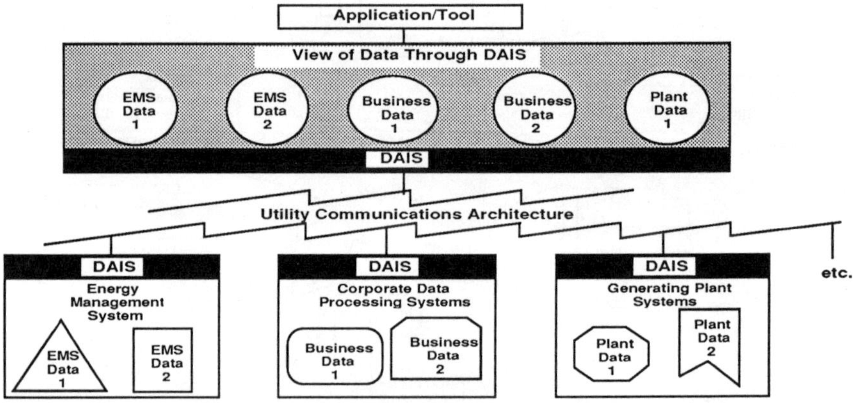

Figure 6 - DAIS makes the diverse data systems depicted by the differing geometric shapes appear as a common system to the example application.

DAIS is a tool to support data access. It is policy neutral regarding issues such as local or central administration of data or standardization of informational model contents. As a tool, it can be used to help realize such policies. DAIS provides an evolutionary approach as it can either be incorporated directly into a newly developed application or could exist as a software database access gateway module for use with existing applications, enabling them to share data on a network.

DAIS will not provide data storage facilities, schema integration, distributed query processing, distributed transaction management, distributed applications or cooperative processing. Rather, DAIS is complementary to these functions and can be used with other software that does provide these functions.

Similar to the UCA in project approach, the DAIS project is generating several deliverables.

Like the UCA, DAIS is based on the utility industry's functional requirements. The DAIS Requirements Analysis document was completed in January and is currently being readied for publishing. The Requirements Analysis is the basis for the design of the DAIS specifications. The DAIS *key* requirements are:

- Uniform access to heterogeneous utility data systems,
- Remote update,
- Coexistence with local data systems,
- Local autonomy,
- Security and access restriction enforcement,
- OSI and UCA compatibility,
- Open architecture and extensibility,
- Operating platform independence.

A technology assessment has been performed and draft reports developed in February 1990 are currently being readied for publishing.

International standards (OSI and utility) have been assessed for applicability and incorporation into DAIS, as part of the developing specifications. Over 100 EPRI member utilities have been surveyed about the data integration products they currently use. The information has assisted the DAIS project team in determining migration issues.

A draft DAIS specification is being made available for public comment and review. The draft specification will be tested at Northern States Power Company in a funded demonstration. Any appropriate modifications to DAIS from the public input and demonstration will be made. Scheduled completion date for the demonstration is in the third quarter of 1991. The finalized DAIS specification will also be available to the public in the third quarter of 1991.

In summary, the DAIS project is defining, developing and demonstrating techniques that support uniform data access across the various data and control systems employed by a utility. DAIS will help substantially reduce operating costs, increase operational flexibility and decrease the installation and integration costs of new components in a utility data communications system. UCA and DAIS will jointly provide a uniform platform for tools and applications development for the utility industry

INTEGRATED SYSTEM DEMONSTRATIONS

As the architecture has been completed, and the database access work is nearing completion, we have developed an integrated communications demonstration plan that will enable EPRI, the utility and vendor communities to quantify the economic and technical advantages of installing integrated communications. A Request for Proposals solicitation is currently being readied for release.

INTEGRATED SYSTEMS ANALYTICAL TOOLS ASSESSMENT AND DEVELOPMENT

Also, a follow-on project will identify and/or develop a set of tools that will aid users and prospective users of the UCA and DAIS specifications to design, implement, analyze, manage and optimize their utility data communications systems. The work will be based on and use the results of the UCA and DAIS projects. The software tools discussed would provide utility communications planners and operators the analogous tools that our power system planners have today such as load flow and stability assessment programs. The major steps associated with this effort are:

- Evaluate products and standards against the UCA and DAIS requirements.

- Identify and/or develop required software tools.
- Test the software tools and integrate them into a "workstation" with associated guidelines for use.

Another Request for Proposals solicitation is planned for release.

INTEGRATED UTILITY COMMUNICATIONS PROJECT SUPPORT

Because of the nature and scope of this project, many activities must be carried out to effectively transfer the technology to the industry.

To facilitate the process, an Integrated Utility Information Users Group has been formed to provide a forum for those who are interested and for those implementing the specifications. EPRI's involvement in the users group is to initiate it and plan for its independent operation, possibly linked to a standards related body by the mid-1990s.

UCA AND DAIS IN THE POWER PLANT ENVIRONMENT

Figure 7 illustrates the functional decomposition of the power plant functional area from a communications perspective. Functions specific to nuclear plants are shaded. While each individual utility company will differ in the way it views power plant functions, Figure 7 was most widely accepted as a generic decomposition. The functions and subfunctions listed were analyzed in detail. The network architecture that best represents the determined requirements is shown in Figure 8 along with some of the sample requirements. The figure shows the devices and connections of the power plant network and how it is integrated into all the other networks within the utility, and connected to external entities. The standards that support

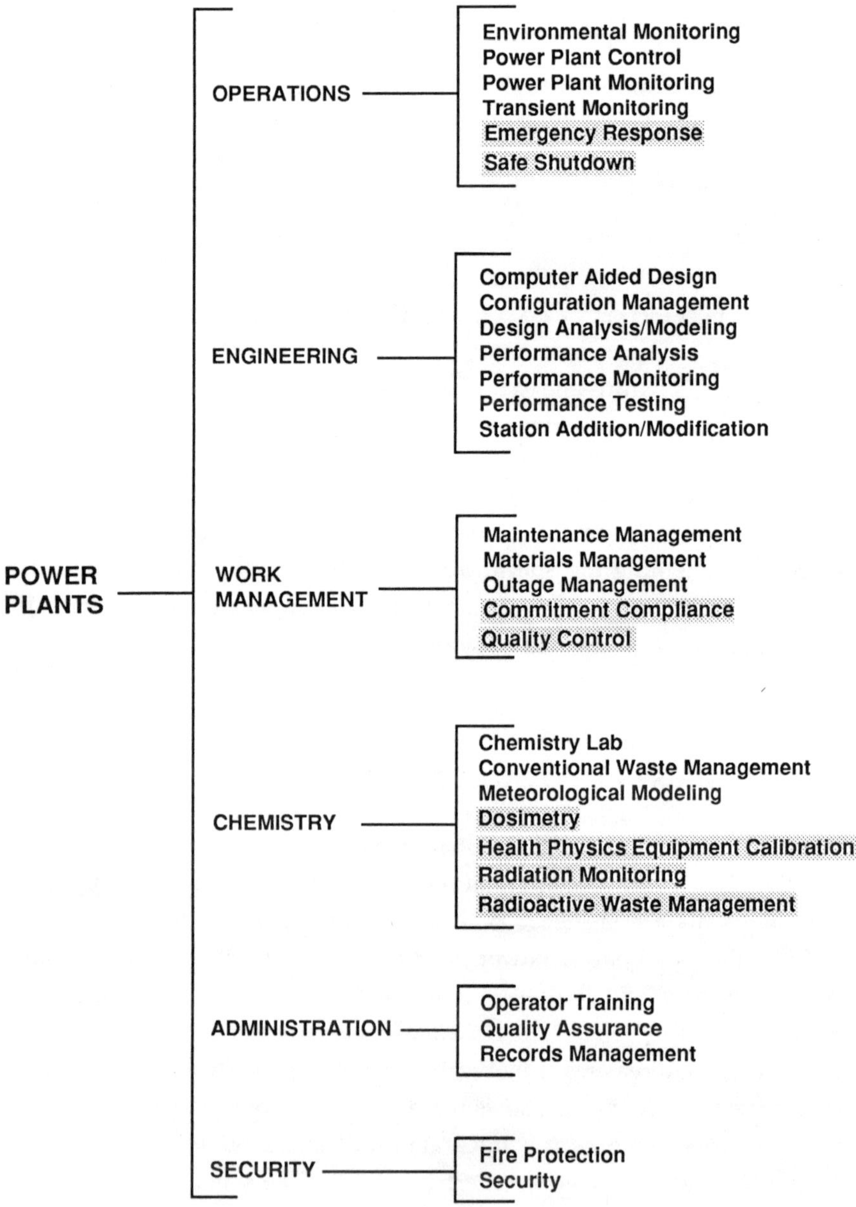

Figure 7- Power Plant Functional Schematic

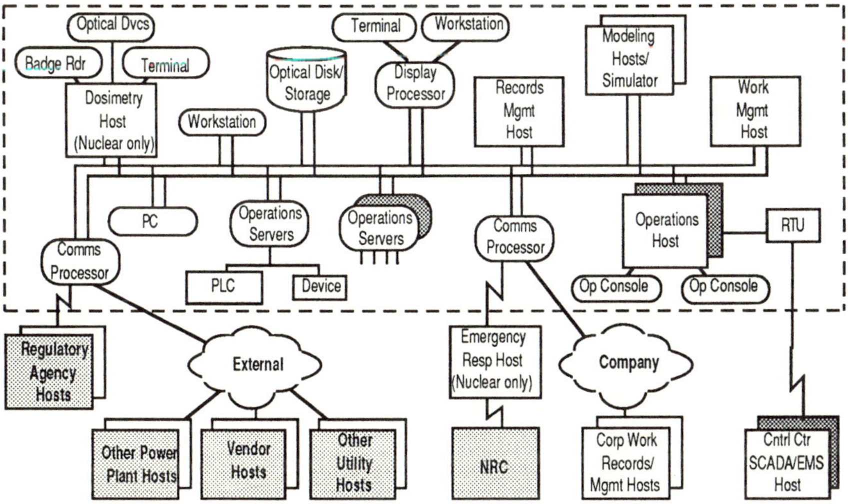

- Requires a hierarchy of distributed subsystems including a variety of devices.
- Requires a concurrent access by terminals to multiple on-line applications.
- Requires journaling of transmitted commands.
- Requires incorporation of images and graphics with product specifications and plant procedures from distributed systems.

Figure 8 - Power Plant Network.

Some of the sample requirements associated with the power plant network appear below the drawing.

the equipment and systems depicted in Figures 7 & 8 are listed in the UCA and DAIS specification documents.

The figure shows the devices and connections of the power plant network and how it is integrated into all the other networks within the utility, and connected to external entities. The standards that support the equipment and systems depicted in Figures 7 & 8 are listed in the UCA and DAIS specification documents.

UCA AND DAIS IN THE POWER DELIVERY ENVIRONMENT

The network architectures that best represent the determined requirements for power transmission and distribution are shown in Figures 7 and 8, respectively, along with some of the sample requirements.

The figures show the devices and interconnections of the power delivery network and how it is integrated into all the other networks within the utility, and connected to external entities. The standards that support the equipment and systems depicted in Figures 9 and 10 are listed in the UCA and DAIS specification documents.

CONCLUSION

We have accomplished these results thanks to an extraordinary level of utility support. We are grateful for the established host utility team for both funded projects comprised of Houston Lighting and Power Company, Northern States Power Company and Pacific Gas and Electric Company. These utilities have provided man-years of support and on-site resources for our project teams' use.

Through our own efforts in the industry, and our follow-on work this year and beyond, we plan to further promote the industry acceptance of this project. We will also establish on-going support for the architecture to ensure that it continues to properly represent the utility industry's needs.

We encourage you to acquire, review and comment on the project results, become involved in the Users' Group and make UCA and DAIS part of your strategic computing and communications plans.

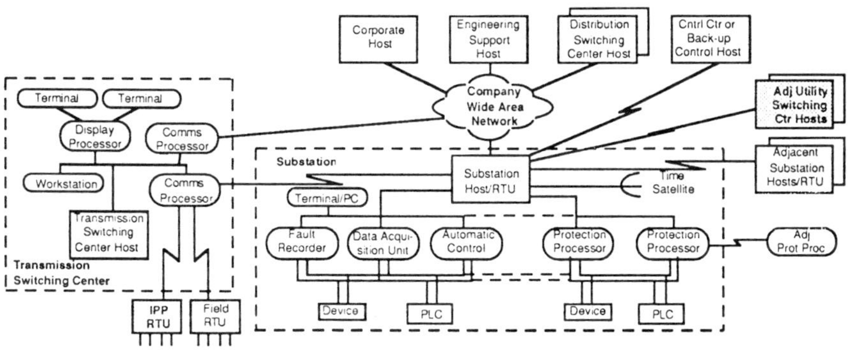

- Fiber optic LANs desirable for EMI immunity.
- Requires high speed continuous communication from transducers to fault recorders.
- Requires 2 milliseconds (1/8 cycle) protection response after detection of a fault.

Figure 9 - Transmission Substation Network.

Some of the sample requirements associated with the transmission substation network appear below the drawing in summarized form.

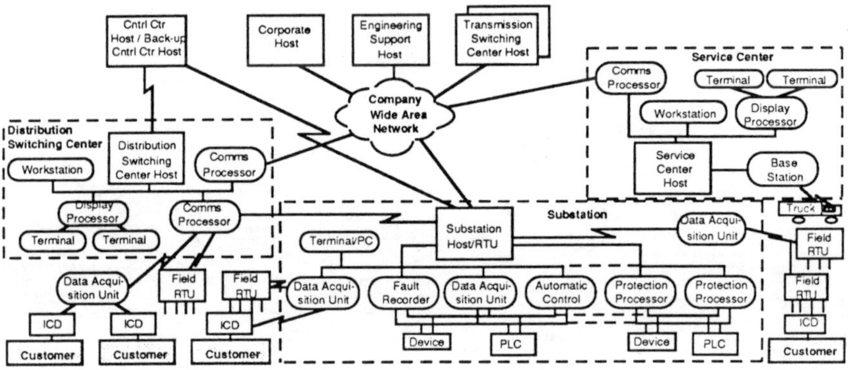

- Requires simple protocols for simple microprocessor-based field devices.
- Must accommodate a variety of transmission techniques (radio, PLC, telephone, satellite, fiber).
- Must accommodate a variety of radio schemes such as spread spectrum, cellular, 800 and 900 MHz radio.
- Requires prioritized processing of messages in order to allow higher priority messages to be processed first.

Figure 10 - Automated Distribution System Network.

Some of the sample requirements associated with the automated distribution network appear below the drawing in summarized form.

VI. UTILITY EXPERIENCE WITH PRODUCT DIFFERENTIATION

RELIABILITY SERVICE OPTIONS AT PG&E

by

Dennis M. Keane and Michael J. Sullivan
Pacific Gas and Electric Company

INTRODUCTION

PG&E has been developing the ability to offer differential levels of service reliability for about fifteen years. In that time, reliability service options have gone from research and development status, to fully operational, and then back to research and development status. Much has been learned by PG&E about the operational and technical characteristics of these programs over the years. This paper attempts to summarize that knowledge. In addition, it suggests several changes in strategic direction that are appropriate in light of PG&E's experience. Finally, it describes research underway at PG&E designed to develop the next generation of reliability service options.

RELIABILITY SERVICE OPTIONS

An electric utility can differentiate its product in either direction along the dimension of service reliability. Customers can be offered reliability service options with discounted prices and lower reliability than the standard level of service. Alternatively, utilities can offer premium service with price and reliability higher than for standard service.

Customers can then choose either standard service or the option that best meets their particular needs.

Most utility experience to date has been with offering discounted rates for reduced levels of reliability. This is true of PG&E, as well. Although efforts are underway to develop premium service programs,[1] PG&E has limited experience in marketing "super-high" reliability service.[2] In contrast, PG&E has offered various forms of lower reliability service to retail customers for more than ten years. Consequently, this paper focuses on utility service offerings at the low end of the reliability spectrum, and the term "reliability service options" will be used throughout to denote options for lower than standard levels of reliability.

The basic idea of reliability service options is simple: customers are offered monetary incentives to take actions that will reduce peak loads and provide cost savings for the utility. PG&E offers two basic types of programs: load curtailment and dispatchable "super-peak" price signals.

Customers participating in load curtailment programs receive lower rates or incentive payments) in exchange for volunteering to take the risk that the utility may curtail their loads (i.e., interrupt part or all of their service) during periods when it has difficulty supplying power to all of its customers.[3] To limit the customers' exposure, PG&E agrees to a set of dispatch constraints. Specific system operating conditions must be met

---

[1] Premium service programs can vary from selling engineering services to improve power quality (e.g., monitoring customer facilities and recommending technical solutions to problems) to charging premium rates for high reliability power delivery systems (e.g., premium service industrial parks or utility-owned back-up generation).

[2] Like most utilities, PG&E normally offers very high reliability service. The term "super-high" refers to service reliability above this very high standard.

[3] Since PG&E is a summer-peaking utility, the curtailment periods generally occur on hot summer weekday afternoons.

before PG&E is allowed to dispatch curtailments. In addition, PG&E agrees to limit the duration of curtailments and not to exceed specified numbers of curtailments annually.[4] Load curtailments are implemented via direct or indirect control methods. With direct control, PG&E installs equipment that enables it to interrupt customer loads when curtailments are called. Interruptions occur automatically, and the customer has no latitude in deciding to comply. With indirect control, PG&E does not possess this type of "push button" control. Instead, when PG&E requests curtailments, the customers can decide which (if any) actions to take to curtail load.[5]

The "super-peak" rate options are similar in nature to load curtailment programs. Most of the time, the customer pays rates that are below standard rates. However, during periods of high customer demand, PG&E dispatches a very high price signal that is applicable to energy consumed for the duration of the specified super-peak period. As with load curtailment programs, the super-peak price can only be dispatched when certain system operating conditions exist, and upper limits are specified on the number and duration of super-peak periods that are permitted. Customers are free to adjust their load however they wish (or to not respond at all, if they so desire) when the super-peak price is dispatched. The customer's load response determines the amount of bill discount, if any, that it receives for participating in the program.

It is worth noting that the super-peak price signal option is very similar to a load curtailment program under indirect control. In both cases, the utility dispatches a message during critical periods that it is in the customer's financial interest to curtail its load. And in both cases the customer has to decide whether to respond by curtailing its load or, instead, to pay a very

---

[4] For some programs, limits are also placed upon the number of curtailments that can occur in any week. PG&E may also promise not to dispatch curtailments on consecutive days.

[5] PG&E typically notifies the customer of an impending curtailment by telephone or some other means of communications. Non-compliance penalties are assessed to customers that refuse to curtail their loads.

high price (either the super-peak rate or the non-compliance penalty) for continuing to consume electricity. The difference between the programs is a matter of customer perception. In the case of the load curtailment program, PG&E specifically requests that the customer curtail load. Consequently, the customer may feel more obligated to do so than with the super-peak program, where PG&E merely sends out a high price signal without making an explicit request for load reduction. In either case, the ultimate decision to reduce or maintain its load is the customer's to make.

PG&E's RELIABILITY SERVICE OFFERINGS

Table 1 shows the reliability service options that have been offered to date by PG&E. These programs historically have been marketed to customers in all sectors, industrial, commercial, residential and agricultural. During the 1980s, PG&E experimented extensively with these programs and evaluated their cost-effectiveness. Some programs are still ongoing, others are not. In the remainder of this section we briefly describe each program.

Load Curtailment Program

In the industrial sector, PG&E offers a Non-Firm Rate program to its largest customers. In terms of load curtailment capability, this program is PG&E's largest by far, with more than 500 MW of subscribed load. Customers choosing this option receive rate discounts on the portion of their load that they designate as curtailable (all or part of their load, but at least 500 kW, can be so designated). In return PG&E can curtail these loads (up to a maximum number of days and hours per year) when capacity conditions dictate. Customers are provided with one-hour advance notice of any curtailment and the duration of the curtailment cannot exceed six hours. Failure to comply with requests to curtail will result in customers being assessed stiff financial penalties. Customers may also earn an additional incentive by agreeing to the installation of an under-frequency relay that interrupts their load for brief periods when system frequency drops below a threshold level.

Table 1

PACIFIC GAS AND ELECTRIC COMPANY
RELIABILITY SERVICE OPTIONS
1977-1991

Customer Class	Program	Load Controlled	Type of Control	Dates Offered	Number of Customers	Load Shifting Capability (MW)
Load Curtailment Programs						
Industrial (>500 kW)	Non-Firm Rates	Customer-Specified	Indirect	1981-Present	230	500
Commercial (<500 kW)	Group Load Curtailment	Customer-Specified	Indirect	1981-Present	40	15
Commercial (<500 kW)	Small Commercial Interruptible	Customer-Specified	Indirect	1986-Present	13	3
Commercial (<500 kW)	Commercial Air Conditioning	Air Conditioning	Direct	1982-1984	630	2
Residential	Residential Peak Load Reduction	Air Conditioning	Direct	1977-1988	60,000	53
Residential	Residential Peak Reduction	Water Heating	Direct	1981-1984	2,200	0
Agricultural	Agricultural Interuptible	Irrigation Pumping	Directr	1983-1991	212	2
Super-Peak Rate Option						
Industrial (>500 kW)	Real-Time Pricing	Customer-Specified	Indirect	1986-Present	14	2

For smaller, commercial customers with loads below 500 kW, PG&E offers the Group Load Curtailment (GLC) program and the Small Commercial Interruptible Program (SCIP). These programs also require customers to curtail loads to designated firm service levels on hot summer afternoons. GLC relies on cooperative groups of participants to provide load relief, rather than individual customers. Each group must curtail its aggregate load upon request, and customers are connected with communications equipment to others in the group to facilitate success in meeting the group's curtailment obligation. This program is capable of producing approximately 15 MWs of load relief. The SCIP program, on the other hand, is designed for individual customers, and is marketed primarily to those with some form of backup power supply. SCIP is still a small program in the experimental stage, with 13 customers providing about 3 MW.

The final four load curtailment programs in Table 1, the Commercial and Residential Air Conditioner Control programs, the Residential Water Heater Control program, and the Agricultural Interruptible program, were extensively tested by PG&E during the late 1970s and 1980s, and are currently not offered to customers. All involved direct control by PG&E of specific customer end-use loads. This control, which was implemented by sending a radio signal that switched off the customer equipment, caused customers to incur outages for a limited period of time on hot summer days.[6] With the severe "shedding" control strategy, customers would lose control of their equipment for the entire curtailment period (typically four hours). Alternatively, PG&E might employ a "cycling" control strategy, turning their equipment off and on intermittently for short periods of time (e.g., every half-hour) for the duration of the curtailment. At their peaks, these programs were subscribed to by 60,000 residential, 600 commercial, and 200 agricultural customers. They delivered a combined 57 MW of load relief.

---

[6] In the case of the Agricultural Interruptible program, farmers were provided with the ability to override the radio control and continue pumping. There was a financial disincentive for doing so, however.

Super-Peak Rates

The only program offered by PG&E with a super-peak rate feature is the Real-time Pricing (RTP) program. RTP customers are charted prices which vary from hour to hour according to PG&E's cost conditions. Usually, PG&E sends customers the 24 hourly prices for a day on the afternoon of the previous day. However, if PG&E's spinning reserve margin is forecasted to fall below a specified threshold on any particular day, customers are immediately sent a very high price (from $0.50 to $0.75 per kWh), termed the "load management pricing signal". This load management pricing signal feature imparts to RTP the character of a dispatchable load curtailment program. PG&E's RTP program typically provides about 2 MW of load relief, at present.

THE CHANGING CAPACITY ENVIRONMENT AT PG&E

From a utility's point of view, the desirability of offering reliability service options to customers is, to a large extent, dependent on its capacity situation. When capacity is in short supply, the ability of reliability service options to limit demand during peak periods make them very attractive to utility decisionmakers. Conversely, during periods of capacity surplus, these options are perceived as largely unnecessary and of greatly reduced value as a means of ensuring that the utility can meet customers' power demands.

In the past fifteen years, PG&E has experienced both extremes of the capacity spectrum, and it is interesting to trace the history of its reliability service offerings over this period. During the late 1970s and early 1980s, PG&E had ample capacity reserves to meet customer demands. Load curtailment programs were viewed by utility decision makers as a possible resource for the future, and it was in this era that the first program designs were formulated and offered to customers on a limited basis. There was little pressure, either internally or from regulators, for rapid development of these customer options.

During the early and mid-1980s, the capacity situation changed. PG&E was nearing the completion of three major generating units (the Helms pumped storage plant and the two units of the Diablo Canyon nuclear plant) and capacity was in very short supply. To help alleviate the shortage, PG&E accelerated the development of reliability service offerings. Many new load curtailment programs were begun and existing programs were rapidly expanded. These programs were viewed as insurance by PG&E against unexpected growth in peak demands or delays in bringing plants on-line. California regulators, too, assisted in the expansion. Both the Public Utilities Commission and the Energy Commission were very supportive of PG&E's demand-side efforts to solve the capacity shortage.[7]

By 1986, PG&E had completed and brought on-line its three major plants, and the capacity picture had changed once again. From 1986 to the present, capacity has been in ample supply, and load curtailments have been virtually non-existent. Once capacity was no longer in short supply, PG&E began de-emphasizing reliability service offerings. Efforts to rapidly expand load curtailment programs were halted and, in some cases, existing programs were cancelled. These options once again began to be viewed as possible "future resources", to be held ready in case another capacity shortage developed.

Table 2 dramatically illustrates PG&E's changing generation capacity conditions from 1980 to the present. In the three-year period from 1983 through 1985, when it was short on capacity, PG&E called 18 curtailments. In the five years since, it has called just one, and none in the last three years. Capacity has been plentiful, load curtailment programs have not been needed, and their value as a demand-side resource has declined.

---

[7] The California Public Utilities Commission regularly approved budgets for implementing reliability service option programs, while the California Energy Commission mandated minimum participation rates for residential customers on PG&E's air conditioner direct control program.

For PG&E, the predictions for the immediate future are for a continuing capacity surplus. The 1990 Electricity Report published by the California Energy Commission forecasts that PG&E will not have a systemwide need for additional generation capacity for the rest of the 1990s.[8] So, as a means of avoiding generation capacity costs, the value of load management program will likely continue to be low for the foreseeable future.

Table 2

PACIFIC GAS AND ELECTRIC COMPANY
HISTORY OF EMERGENCY LOAD CURTAILMENTS

Year	Curtailments
1980	0
1981	0
1982	0
1983	10
1984	7
1985	1
1986	0
1987	1
1988	0
1989	0
1990	0

8 The repot forecasts PG&E's first systemwide addition in the year 2003. See California Energy Commission (1990), p. 6-3.

COPING WITH CHANGING CAPACITY CONDITIONS: LESSONS LEARNED

The conventional wisdom is that, compared to supply-side alternatives, reliability service options are a very flexible resource. Unlike power plants, which can take many years to plan, site, and build–and then represent sunken investments for many more years–reliability service options are touted as being easily and quickly expanded or contracted according to a utility's needs. In a world where demand forecasts are uncertain, and power plant siting and cost recovery subject to regulatory risk, this flexibility is regarded as one of the major selling points for demand-side programs.

PG&E's experience casts some doubt on the conventional wisdom, at least as it pertains to contracting existing programs when capacity shortfalls disappear. In this section we describe PG&E's efforts since 1986 to "ramp down" its programs. We then draw some lessons regarding the true level of flexibility of these programs and the implications for utility planners.

PG&E's Response to Capacity Surplus

By enabling a utility to curtail some customer load that it would otherwise have had to serve, reliability service options reduce generation capacity costs.[9] These reduced, or avoided, costs provide a measure of the benefits from offering a program,which must be balanced against the costs of the program (administrative and equipment costs, plus the costs of the rate discounts received by participating customers). If the benefits exceed the costs, then the program is cost-effective and should be pursued.[10] For

[9] For some load curtailment programs, there may be energy cost savings as well. These are typically small, though, if they exist at all, and some programs may result in an increase in energy usage.

[10] Cost-effectiveness is frequently examined from a number of perspectives (e.g., the utility perspective, the ratepayer perspective, the societal perspective), and utilities' and regulators' evaluations generally take into account multiple perspectives. These perspectives differ from each other in the list of items that are considered to be program benefits and costs. For

PG&E, avoided generation capacity cost is the primary factor influencing a program's cost-effectiveness. In 1986, after the addition of the three large power plants, PG&E's declining generation capacity costs drastically reduced the cost-effectiveness of its reliability service options.

In response, PG&E began to scale back programs and reduce program costs to improve cost-effectiveness. The easiest to phase out was the residential air conditioner direct control program. It was "mothballed" in 1988, with PG&E halting load curtailments and virtually eliminating the rate discounts.[11] These actions significantly reduced the major operating costs of the program. PG&E's program contraction efforts met with little resistance. Few, if any, residential customers objected to the withdrawal of this rate from the market.

In the agricultural sector, PG&E was not as successful in shutting down its load curtailment program. In its 1990 General Rate Case filing, PG&E requested permission from the California Public Utilities Commission to eliminate the Agricultural Interruptible program due to its poor cost-effectiveness. But, because of opposition to the proposal by its staff, the Commission ordered PG&E to continue offering the option to customers. In 1991, however, PG&E finally prevailed, convincing the Commission to authorize termination of the program.

PG&E employed a different strategy for its large commercial/industrial curtailment programs. Instead of phasing out the programs, PG&E tried to

---

example, the cost of the incentive paid to participants is paid for by non-participants (in the form of higher rates). This cost will appear in a cost-effectiveness evaluation from the ratepayer perspective, but will not appear in one from a societal perspective (since it represents a transfer from one segment of society to another).

11 As a precautionary measure, the radio control switches were left in place, so that the program could be made operational in case capacity conditions changed. In May 1991, however, the California Energy Commission granted PG&E approval to terminate the program and remove the control switches.

improve the cost-effectiveness of the Non-Firm, Group Load Curtailment, and Small Commercial Interruptible programs by reducing the rate discounts paid to participants. In its 1990 General Rate Case filing, PG&E requested Commission approval to realign the discounts downward commensurate with its low avoided generation capacity costs. PG&E's request was strongly opposed by customers participating in the program who did not want their discounts reduced. These customers and their representatives strenuously lobbied utility management and regulators to continue these uneconomic programs, in part because they claimed to have become economically dependent on the associated rate discounts. These powerful business interests (many as large or larger than PG&E) were quite effective in blocking and delaying PG&E's efforts to adjust incentives to levels more in accord with the value of generating capacity. After nearly three years of litigation at the Commission, PG&E to date has achieved only a modest reduction in the rate discounts, which still substantially exceed the value of the curtailment program in terms of avoided costs.

Lessons Learned

Back in 1986, when PG&E was making its major resource additions, reliability service options were viewed by operations personnel as an emergency resource–an insurance policy–which could be cancelled or scaled back after planned capacity became available. The strategic plan after new capacity additions became available was to "stay the course", reducing the scope of the programs and focusing instead on research and development objectives. The idea was to shelve these options until the time in the future when they would again be needed to fill in the gap between available generation and growing loads.

Unfortunately, it turned out to be very difficult to scale these programs back. Despite the fact that PG&E was awash in generating capacity after 1986, and load curtailment programs were completely uneconomical, there were strong forces to maintain the status quo. Constituencies developed for these programs, composed of customers, regulators and even PG&E personnel, that actively lobbied for continued existence of these programs long after their usefulness as an emergency resource was past.[12] The result was that, despite their flexibility in the expansion phase, reliability service options were very difficult to remove or limit after they were underway.

The chief lesson drawn from this experience is that reliability service options should not be viewed as an emergency insurance policy. Insurance policies can be cancelled when the risk of an adverse event is past, or the policy can be continued at a greatly reduced premium. Reliability service options, though, involve human customers capable of effectively resisting having their terms of service modified by utilities when conditions change.

Many customers who initially subscribe to a less reliable service option do so because they have low outage costs or access to backup power. These underlying factors do not change simply because the utility adds generation capacity and no longer values the ability to curtail customer load. Nor do the changing capacity conditions affect program participants' preferences for lower reliability at a discounted price. So participants will naturally resist if the utility tries to eliminate the service option or reduce the discount, since they would be forced to take service under less satisfactory terms.

The effectiveness of customers in lobbying regulators to delay or block program downsizing and reductions in rate discounts can cause substantial increases in program costs.[13] Utility planners thus need to adopt a long-term perspective that factors in these costs at the outset when deciding

---

[12] For an interesting discussion of how these programs develop cadres of supporters within a utility irrespective of their economic benefits to the utility as a whole or its ratepayers, see Hennessy and Sullivan (1988).

[13] PG&E's Non-Firm Rate program for large customers is a good example. A 1990 PG&E report estimates that approximately $40 million was paid to program participants during 1990, a year in which no curtailments occurred. Roughly similar amounts were paid other years during the capacity-rich period since 1986. For details, see Pacific Gas and Electric Company (1990).

whether to initiate non-firm service programs. This requires a change in thinking away from the "insurance" paradigm towards one that regards reliability service options as permanent offerings that exist regardless of the utility's capacity situation.

With a long-term perspective, the programs would be considered a regular part of the resource mix, rather than as a "swing" resource that can be ramped up and down to offset fluctuations in the availability of supply-side resources. Utility planners would view these options as competitive alternatives to capacity improvements, and they would be fully integrated with supply-side resources in resource planning models. Customers could then look forward to the elimination of the "roller coaster" effect of wildly fluctuating rate discounts as the supply-side situation changes. With the reduced uncertainty regarding future rate discounts, customers would have greater incentive to make whatever adjustments in their operations are required to handle a lower level of service reliability. Of course, the *quid pro quo* for customers receiving more stable incentive levels would be the certainty that they would be curtailed a specified minimum number of hours each year. If utilities are to pay participants discounts befitting a permanent, useful resource, they must also have the ability to "dispatch" the program like a supply-side resource calling curtailments when it is most economic to do so, and not just under emergency conditions.

PG&E's FUTURE RELIABILITY OFFERINGS

Because of these lessons, a change in strategy is underway at PG&E regarding the offering of reliability service options to customers. Two basic principles are guiding the new strategic direction. The first is that, for PG&E, the highest value application of reliability service options is in avoiding local distribution costs. The second is that program design and marketing should be focused on customer groups that value of service (VOS) research has identified as most likely to subscribe because of low outage costs.

Local Applications of Reliability Service Options

For the foreseeable future, programs designed to offer reliability service options to customers should be focused on avoiding distribution system investments. In the near term (i.e., between now and the end of the decade), PG&E's avoided cost of generation capacity is expected to remain low, making programs designed to curtail load systemwide of little value. However, this is not true for PG&E's avoided distribution costs.

PG&E's distribution capacity costs are substantial, about $600 million on an annual basis, and expected to grow. As population and demand on the distribution system grow, investments must be made to improve or preserve local electric reliability. PG&E can offer economic reliability service options–principally load curtailment programs–which will reduce coincident peak load growth on the distribution system. If sufficient numbers of customers are willing to accept lower service reliability in return for price reductions, the utility can delay investment in distribution capacity needed to maintain existing reliability levels. By selectively lowering reliability for customers who do not value it, resources can be dedicated to areas where capacity requirements are more pressing.

Using Value of Service Information to Design and Market Programs

Program planning and marketing of reliability service options should explicitly take account of the economic value customers assign to their service reliability. Load curtailment programs should target customer market segments which place relatively low value on service reliability. Customers who do not value reliability highly are obviously better candidates for reliability service options than those who value it highly. A key to the success of offering stable and cost-effective reliability service options is to identify and target these options to the low VOS segment of the market.

Recent research by PG&E and others has demonstrated that service reliability needs to vary greatly across customer classes. Table 3 summarizes the estimated outage costs that PG&E customers experience as a result of various kinds of electric outages. The table shows that residential and agricultural customers have the lowest average VOS of PG&E's customer classes. Outage costs for these customers are roughly an order of magnitude lower than outage costs for commercial and industrial customers (i.e., small, medium, and large light and power customers).[14] All other things being equal, residential and agricultural customers are better candidates for reliability service offerings than are commercial and industrial customers.

However, reliability needs also vary greatly within PG&E's customer classes. Figure 1 displays the distribution of outage costs per event for small and medium light and power customers. Even in the case of a four-hour outage in the middle of a weekday afternoon, slightly over one-third of these customers report that they experience zero outage cost.[15] Thus, even for the customer class which, in the aggregate, values service reliability most highly, there appears to be considerable market potential for reliability service options designed to trade reliability degradation for price reductions. We have analyzed the distribution of outage costs for all customer classes at PG&E, and found similar distributions.

Because of their generally low outage costs, the residential sector seems to be the best market for reliability service options. However, the amount of load relief per customer tends to be small, resulting in relatively high per-point costs for control hardware. In addition, since these programs generally have a large number of subscribers, considerable effort is required to manage customer relations during program start-up and operations.

---

[14] Table 3 presents outage costs in units of dollars per kWh unserved. In terms of dollars per outage event, the difference between residential and commercial/industrial customers' outage costs is even more pronounced, with residential being several orders of magnitude smaller.

[15] It is unlikely that these customers really experience zero outage costs under the circumstances that occur in a four-hour afternoon outage. It is more likely that they experience some outage cost that is sufficiently small that they consider it insignificantly different from zero (i.e., too trivial to report).

Nevertheless, there are very compelling reasons to emphasize the development of reliability service offerings for residential customers–particularly in light of PG&E's interest in distribution system applications.

Table 3

ESTIMATED AVERAGE SUMMER OUTAGE COSTS

1990 Dollars per kWh by Customer Class
Time of Day, Duration and Extent of Advance Notice

	Residential	Small and Medium Light & Power	Large Light & Power	Agricultural
Without Advance Notice				
Morning				
3-4 hours				
12 hours				
Afternoon				
Momentary			$188.53	
1 hour	$5.26	$42.38	21.47	
3-4 hours	4.00	40.46	9.30	
12 hours	4.09			
Evening				
1 hour				
3-4 hours				
With One hour Advance Notice				
Afternoon				
1 hour	$4.36	$29.61	$10.77	$3.51
Voluntary Curtail	0.54	4.27		

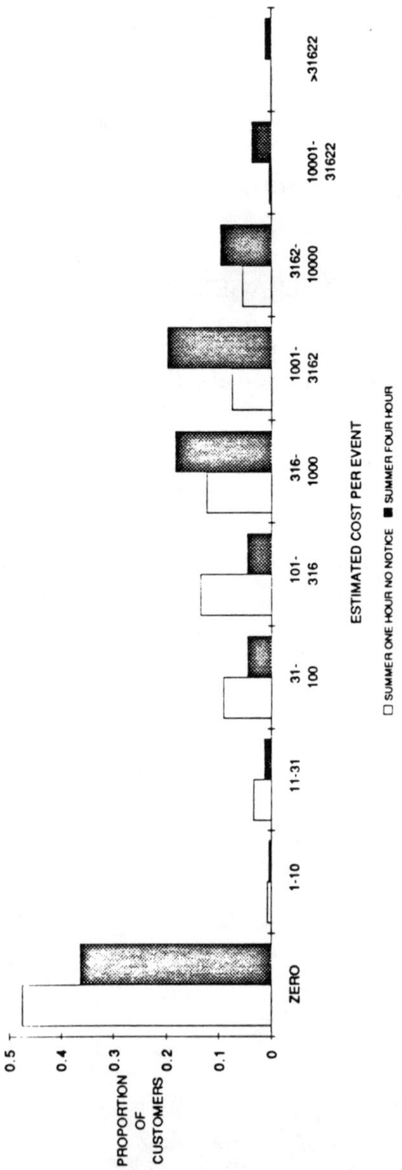

Figure 1. Distribution of Outage Costs ($ per Event)

Summer 1-Hour and Summer 4-Hour Outages
Commercial Value of Service Survey

Aside from their low VOS, residential customers tend to be situated in many cases on PG&E's constrained distribution circuits. If PG&E can successfully recruit sufficient numbers of customers on problem circuits to direct control curtailment programs, then distribution planners can be confident that predictable and reliable load relief will be forthcoming when curtailments are dispatched. In addition, with the development of new technologies capable of performing a variety of tasks (e.g., remote meter reading, fault detection, automatic service connections and disconnections), it may be possible to share the costs of direct control hardware with other utility applications and dramatically improve cost-effectiveness.

The picture is quite different in the commercial and industrial sectors. These customers' VOS is typically about ten times higher than that of residential customers. While they can provide higher levels of subscribed load relief per point (necessitating lower hardware and administrative costs per kilowatt), the amount of load relief actually obtainable is relatively uncertain. This occurs because indirect control is typically used in commercial and industrial curtailment programs.

Indirect control is highly undesirable in distribution applications. To truly avoid costs by deferring the upgrading of distribution facilities, planners must be certain that the dispatchable load relief available from program participants is reliable. However, there may only be a small number of commercial or industrial customers (in some cases, just a single large customer) on a given constrained circuit. With indirect control programs, where the customer ultimately decides whether to curtail, a distribution planner cannot be sure what will happen when a curtailment is requested, and so cannot count on obtaining the subscribed load relief. In the absence of direct control programs (which generally do not appeal to these types of customers, because they surrender control over the customers' operations to the utility), reliability service options for distribution applications do not seem feasible for commercial and industrial customers.

FUTURE RESEARCH

Several research projects are underway at present at PG&E which will facilitate the above described strategic direction. They are described briefly below.

Development of Area-Specific Marginal Costs

To target reliability service options on specific distribution system locations, the utility must be able to identify the local area benefits that will be obtained and the costs that will be incurred as a result of implementing the options.

As described in Section V, the benefits of reliability service options are usually measured by estimating the system average capacity costs that they allow the utility to avoid. This is a reasonable approach to evaluating programs which are intended to impact the entire electric system. However, it is not appropriate to apply these system-level costs to specific areas within the utility service territory (i.e., at the level of the distribution circuits).

System-level marginal costs are essentially averages of the utility's costs of servicing many local ares. These disaggregated local area costs may vary dramatically in either direction from the system average. By assuming that the system-wide figure accurately reflects the true marginal costs of capacity in each individual area, serious decision making errors can result–particularly in areas where the true marginal costs are extremely high (i.e., where there are opportunities for cost-effective reliability service programs) or in areas where the true marginal costs are very low (i.e., where reliability service options are not needed).

Recognizing this problem PG&E has undertaken an extensive study designed to estimate area-specific marginal costs. The study involves development of marginal transmission and distribution (T&D) costs for each of the approximately 200 planning areas in the PG&E service territory. These costs will be used in a variety of applications including:

- identification of locations in which reliability service options might be used to replace or supplement investments in conventional T&D equipment;
- identification of specific demand-side management alternatives best suited to solving area-specific capacity problems;
- calculation of area-specific benefits for demand-side management programs; and
- calculation of rate discounts and super-peak prices for reliability service options targeted to specific areas.

Measurement of Customer Value of Service

PG&E has conducted detailed VOS studies for all of its major customer classes. The residential customer class was studied in 1985-86, the small and medium light and power class in 1987-88, and the large light and power class in 1989-90. A study of the agricultural customer class is underway at this time. PG&E's approach to VOS measurement involves performing recurring measurements for each of its customer classes over a cycle of about five years. In this way, new VOS measurements are made for each class about every five years.,

VOS measurements are used in a variety of applications throughout PG&E. They are used by resource planners as an input to reliability planning models which forecast generation reserve margin requirements. VOS results are also employed by T&D planners to assess the cost-effectiveness of investments designed to improve reliability in substation and distribution systems. And, as discussed in Section VI, VOS estimates help PG&E to identify and target customer market segments that are likely to be attracted to low reliability service options.

Market Research

As indicated in Section VI, VOS measurements suggest that residential customers may be highly attracted to lower reliability service. To further investigate this hypothesis, PG&E conducted a focus group research study in 1990. In this study, groups of homeowners were asked to discuss their reactions to the following service options:

- Residential Interruptible Service

  With this option, the customer's service is completely interrupted (i.e., a full power outage) for a period of one hour between the hours of 5 and 8 p.m. on up to ten evenings per summer. This option provides a very close approximation to "real" outage, except that customers are given 30 minutes notice of the impending interruption. By signing up for the program, customers agree to have their entire power supply reliability become less reliable.

- Power Subscription Service

  With this option, the customer agrees to reduce its power demand to or below a designated firm service level (e.g., 1 kW) for a period of two hours between 5 and 8 p.m. on ten evenings per summer. This option is similar in concept to Demand Subscription Service offered by Southern California Edison in the late 1980s. The customer designates a portion of its load as "high priority", not to be curtailed by the utility. The remainder of its load is considered to be low priority and free to be curtailed. Direct control hardware is employed to prevent the customer from exceeding its firm service level during times of program operations.

- Residential Super Peak Price Signal

  With this option, the customer purchases and installs in its home intelligent communications hardware which is capable of receiving a super-peak price signal dispatched by the utility during critical peak periods. The hardware controls a thermostat which is programmed by the customer to raise or lower the household temperature, based on its relative preferences for comfort and a low electric bill. This service option is similar to the real-time pricing option offered by PG&E to large commercial and industrial customers.

The primary finding of the focus group study is that "money talks". When confronted with the first two options above, residential customers voiced all of the obvious objections that a customer might be expected to have. They didn't like the idea of having to reset their clocks. They thought it would be extremely inconvenient if the power went off in the middle of dinner or when they were watching something interesting on TV. They were afraid they might be using their computers when the outage or power reduction period commenced. In short, they didn't appear to like the idea much. However, when the focus group moderator indicated that participants could save up to thirty percent on their electric bills, most participants had a change of heart and said they would sign up for one of the programs.

A second interesting finding concerns the super-peak option. Residential customers do not seem very interested in the concept of real-time pricing. Instead, they would much prefer to be billed on a flat rate that they could predict from month to month. Most customers live on a monthly budget and they seek to remove uncertainty about their future electric bill in this budget, not increase it. The idea of the utility increasing the price rapidly and without warning distressed most of the participants. Based upon these responses, we conclude that it will be awhile before residential customers are ready for real-time pricing.

Demonstration Projects

The next step in development of reliability service options for residential customers involves demonstration projects designed to evaluate the practicality and attractiveness of these services to real customers.

The residential super-peak price signal concept is attractive from point of view of economic theory (i.e., it should lead to efficient use of resources). It is also attractive to utility management because it allows the customer to voluntarily choose a level of service according to the price. Under this system, the customers must decide for themselves whether or not to degrade their service in response to price changes. Whether it will reduce loads on substations and whether or not customers buy it remains to be demonstrated.

A 100-point demonstration project is underway at this time in PG&E's service territory.

Direct control technology appeals to utility planners and engineers because of its demonstrated ability to obtain reliable load relief. Despite this, and despite the apparent attractiveness of direct control load curtailment programs to residential customer focus groups, these programs are very difficult to "sell" to utility management and marketing personnel. Utility management is naturally reluctant to degrade the quality of customer service–even when customers volunteer for degraded service. The philosophy of these programs runs counter to the traditional utility business culture, and it will take time before a new culture develops that embraces the idea of offering customers a menu of reliability options. Meanwhile, efforts are underway at PG&E to find locations where the benefits of local area load curtailment projects can be demonstrated.

CONCLUDING REMARKS

In this paper we have described the reliability service options that PG&E has offered to its customers under a variety of capacity conditions since 1977, and have attempted to draw some lessons from PG&E's experience. Our primary conclusion is that the conventional wisdom regarding the offering of such options–the insurance model–is wrong. Reliability service options are not easily scaled back in response to changing capacity conditions, because of resistance from program constituencies (composed primarily of program participants but also, sometimes, of regulators and utility personnel) that develop once they are offered. Consequently, utilities are ill-advised to think of these options as insurance policies to reduce risks related to load growth and plant construction timelines.

Instead, utilities should view reliability service options with a long-term perspective, as an integrated part of their resource mix. These options should be offered to customers on a permanent basis, not just temporarily as a "swing" resource that is later withdrawn when additional supply-side capacity becomes available. The programs should be operated a guaranteed minimum number of hours each year, dispatched like supply-side resources whenever economic conditions warrant. Customers with a preference for lower reliability at a discounted price could then be assured of receiving such service without concern that the utility might subsequently modify their terms of their service (i.e., raise the price and offer more reliable service) as part of a capacity boom-bust cycle.

We have also discussed a shift in strategic thinking at PG&E regarding the use of reliability service options, and we have summarized recent research efforts to develop programs based upon that strategic shift. PG&E currently has ample generation capacity, but is facing large distribution-related investments in some local areas. Because of this, PG&E is shifting its emphasis away from systemwide programs in favor of local area curtailment programs. Residential customers, with their high tolerance for outages, are prime candidates for area-specific reliability service options. If inexpensive direct control hardware can be developed, local area load curtailment programs for residential customers offer a promising, cost-effective, way for PG&E to defer or avoid costly investments in distribution capacity.

REFERENCES

1. California Energy Commission. "1990 Electricity Report". California Energy Commission, October 1990.

2. M. Hennessy and M. Sullivan. "Implementing Dispatchable Load Management Projects". *Public Utilities Fortnightly.* April 14, 1988.

3. Pacific Gas and Electric Company. "PG&E's Non-firm Service Program Final Study and Proposal". Pacific Gas and Electric Company report submitted to the California Public Utilities Commission in response to Ordering Paragraph 28 of Decision 89-12-057, June 29, 1990.

MAKING THE TRANSITION: PREREQUISITES TO PRODUCT DIFFERENTIATION

by

Robert Mango[1]
Niagara Mohawk Power Corporation

INTRODUCTION

Much debate has taken place over the feasibility and merits of diversifying the electricity product (i.e., temporal and spacial product differentiation). Niagara Mohawk Power Corporation has engaged in numerous forms of electricity product differentiation, through real time pricing, priority service and advanced time-of-use offerings, and has gained a number of practical insights into making the transition from standardized service offerings to diversified ones. It is this practical experience that I wish to share with you through this presentation.

Essentially, my recommendation to utilities wishing to engage in diversified service offerings is four-fold. First, and foremost, I propose that the transition be an equitable one--the departure from a system of

---

[1] Bob Mango is the Director of Electric Rate Design and Evaluation at Niagara Mohawk Power Corporation, Syracuse, New York. The author gratefully recognizes the substantial contribution Bernie Neenan made to the formulation and refinement of these ideas. The author remains solely responsible for any errors that this manuscript contains.

traditional offerings must be conducted with care. Second, the allocation and production efficiency objectives of product differentiation can best be realized through adherence to some form of *short -run marginal* cost based pricing principles. Third, customer segmentation associated with diversified offerings is better realized through market response than through utility imposition. And, lastly, innovative product offerings require a commitment to increased levels of customer service that not only have to be fulfilled, but need be cost-effective.

BACKGROUND

Niagara presently fields three offerings, illustrated in Figure 1, that I will characterize as being of a non-traditional nature, that are directed towards realizing pricing efficiency and that have served as the test-bed for developing the prerequisites proposed herein. The first, and the mainstay of our innovative offerings, is a real-time pricing program otherwise known as our Hourly Integrated Pricing Program or simply "HIPP". The second is our Voluntary Interruptible Pricing Program (VIPP)--our version of an efficient priority service program. And third, we have an advanced time-of-use offering (Residential S.C. No. 1-C) which is characterized by its highly differentiated rating periods and uniquely high access charge.

HIPP is a two-part pricing program that communicates twenty-four dynamic, marginal cost-based prices to participating customers by 4 p.m. each previous business day. It is a four year experimental program with fourteen participants who account for Company revenues in excess of fifty million dollars annually. HIPP utilizes an access charge to ensure customer specific revenue neutrality and to collect participant contributions to embedded revenue requirements.

VIPP, our reliability-differentiated priority service offering, utilizes a seasonal contract mechanism and a menu of service offerings to provide customers with a number of options for selling short-term capacity back to the Company. It incorporates both a price rationing scheme--a temporary

Figure 1. Niagara Mohawk Innovative Pricing Family Tree

version of HIPP--and a stricter quantity or contract rationing scheme that are both designed to appeal to varying levels of customer risk preferences and desire for accompany remuneration.

Our S.C. No. 1-C TOU offering is a mandatory program targeted towards our largest residential customers. It incorporates seasonal, off-peak, shoulder-peak and super-peak rating periods which contain highly differentiated, marginal cost-based prices. Its thirty-five dollar customer charge contributes to its distinguishment as a relatively unique offering.

Niagara Mohawk's HIPP, VIPP and S.C. No. 1-C offerings are three active and successful programs that, when combined with a number of additional innovative offerings that are in the contemplative stage, make up what we refer to as our innovative pricing family tree. It is our collective experience with these programs that serves as the basis for the recommendations contained herein for making the transition to product differentiation.

EQUITY

Development and implementation of diversified service offerings effectively constitutes a migration from one pricing system to another. Inherent in such change, particularly that characterized by a movement towards marginal cost, is a potential fairness problem. I propose, to any utility who seeks to move towards efficient pricing, that the basic fairness problem be adequately addressed both before and during such a transition. I further assert that fairness will be judged from the standards of the *old* system and that requisite standard of the old system is that of inter-class parity on an embedded cost basis.

Niagara Mohawk has been fortunate enough to enjoy reasonable revenue-to-revenue requirement parity amongst its residential and commercial/ industrial classes prior to pursuing innovative rate structures. We did, however, experience what could be considered to be a fairly significant intra-class disparity amongst high- and low-use residential customers prior to devising our S.C. No. 1-C offering. With this as an exception, we were left for the most part with preserving equity in our innovative rate designs and not with acquiring it. In maintaining and achieving some notion of reconciliation schemes which relied upon access charges and historical consumption profiles as described in the two examples which follow.

HIPP

The equity provisions of HIPP are best illustrated through its rather simple but significant algebra. The two-part provision of HIPP billing utilizes an access charge (AC) in conjunction with short-run marginal cost-based energy charges (SRMC) in order to collect a fair quantity of contributions to embedded revenue requirements. It further uses individual customer's historical consumption patterns, what we refer to as customer baseline load's (CBL's) to ensure that reconciliation is revenue neutral for each customer relative to the standard rate offering (R)--at the customer's CBL. In so doing, actual load (AL) is always priced at the margin, thereby allowing us to realize our efficiency objectives, and equity is preserved through the access charge. When displayed in equation format, HIPP looks like this:

$$AC = R(CBL) = SRMC(CBL)$$

$$\text{HIPP Bill} = AC + SRMC(AL)$$

Residential TOU

Fairness considerations were of tantamount concern in developing the Company's mandatory residential time-of-use rate as well. Here, fairness considerations were extended to address what effectively was a pre-existing disparity between high- and low-use customers. As with many utilities' residential rate structures, sensitivity to the magnitude of customer charges relative to lower income users' bills created a situation where high-use customers were effectively charged a disparate amount of fixed charges that were under-recovered through depressed customer charges.

Design of our TOU rate required reservation of equity in one sense and achievement of a greater fairness in another.

Time-of-use energy charges were developed to reflect short-run marginal costs to the fullest extent possible in a static rate offering and, as similar in the design of HIPP, an "access charge" was utilized for revenue reconciliation. Once established as a separate class, large mandatory time-of-use customers were then targeted for relief from historical disparities through exemption from upcoming class level increases associated with general revenue requirement proceedings. It is the latter, gradual treatment of this class that has allowed the Company to effectively pursue movement of this class towards more efficient consumption behavior in response to highly time-differentiated rates.

In any event, whether it be a large commercial/industrial real time pricing offering or a residential time-of-use offering, I reassert that adherence to some notion of fairness, as judged by the standards of the system being departed from, should necessarily serve as a prerequisite to any form of an efficient design process.

EFFICIENCY

Few people would argue the merit of pursuing efficient, differentiated service offerings, whether they be intended for welfare objectives or more narrowly for competitive advantage, but many may argue how best to tactically proceed. I argue that utilities interested in product differentiation, whether it be temporal or spacial, acquire a comprehensive working knowledge of short-run marginal costs (SRMC) and an ability to estimate them. They are the utilities first and best weapon towards combating inefficiency and they can be utilized in a number of different means.

Before citing a few examples of ways in which SRMC can be formulated into product offerings, I suggest that they be viewed as being comprised of two components--(1) hourly operating costs, and (2) hourly congestion costs as illustrated in Figure 2. The hourly operating costs are essentially direct, fuel-related costs and are commonly referred to as system lambdas or in this case marginal energy costs (MEC). The congestion costs are less direct, but real none the less, and are a function of some estimate of the probability of unserved energy in a given hour and the cost that would accrue to an average customer should an outage occur. I will refer to these costs as marginal outage costs (MOC). The two cost combined form aggregate short-run marginal costs (SRMC or just MC) and can be useful in either an hourly, an average or "contract" forms.

HIPP (Hourly MC's)

Hourly marginal costs remain closest to their pure form (i.e., five-minute or instantaneous) and are easiest to use because they require little re-formation to incorporate into the HIPP price quote. Niagara Mohawk's HIPP offering is our most straightforward example of the use of short-run marginal costs and it serves as a reference for the development of derivative programs. The graph below illustrates the highest price day in the history of HIPP where MEC slightly exceeded $.10 per kilowatt-hour and MOC approaches $.40 per kilowatt-hour. Such a distribution of costs is somewhat anomalous for us given that most hours are predominated by MEC and only a relatively few critical hours reflect significant congestion costs.

S.C. No. 1-C (Average MC's)

Alternatively, short-run marginal costs can be expressed in an expected average format and can serve as the basis for highly differentiated time-of-use offerings as illustrated in Figure 3. The shape of Niagara's S.C. No. 1-C TOU energy prices can be seen to closely resemble that of the actual Summer of 1989 HIPP marginal cost based prices as illustrated in Figure 3.

VIPP (Contract MC's)

VIPP, through being a menu of offerings, simultaneously incorporates both price and quantity rationing principles. As such it utilizes SRMC in two

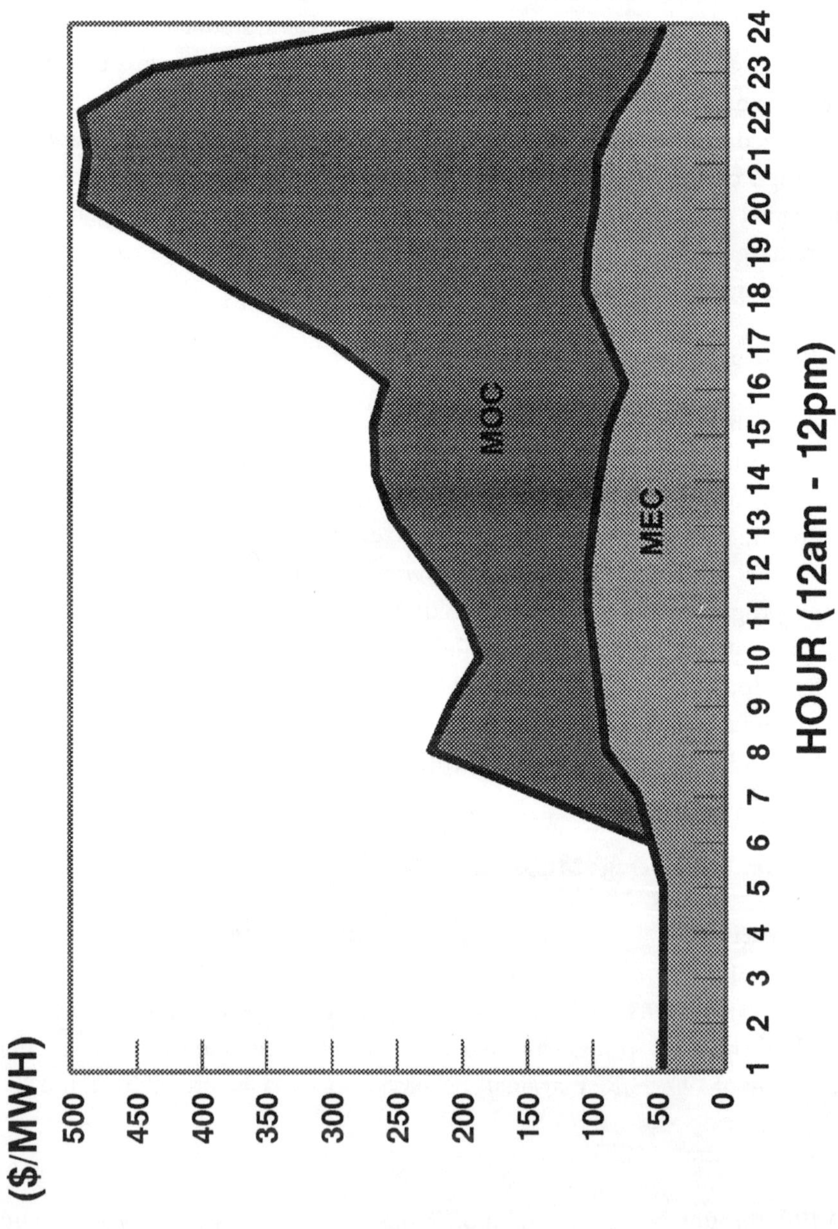

Figure 2. HIPP/SHIPP (Hourly MC's)

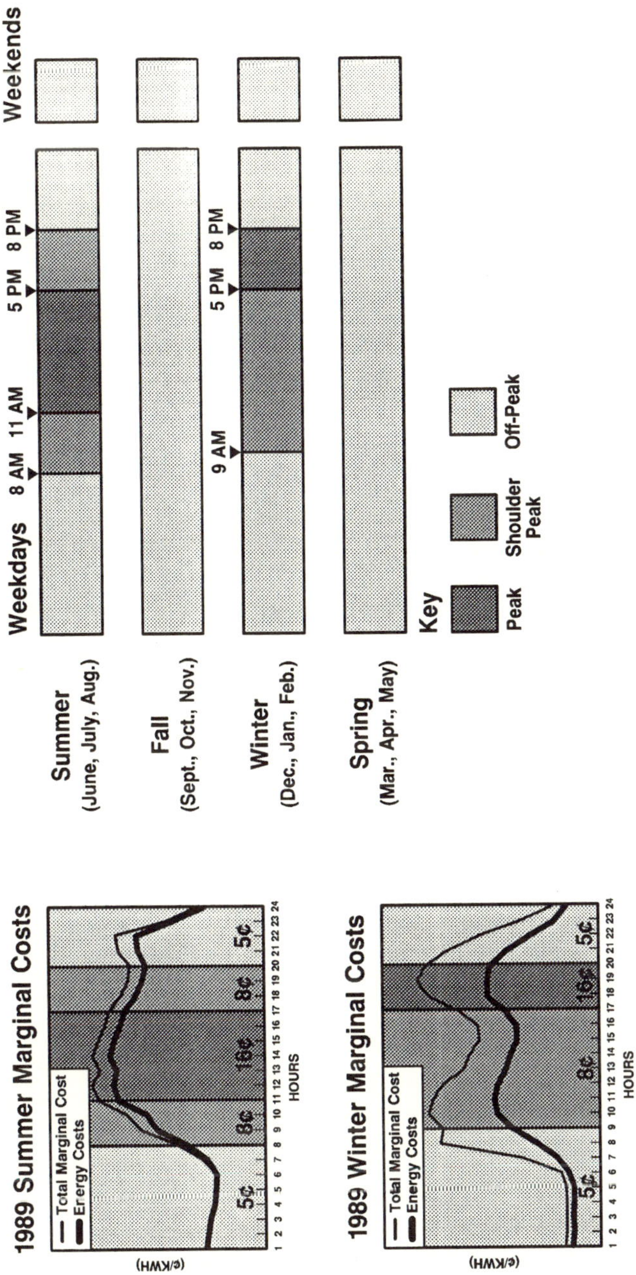

Figure 3. TOU (Average MC's)

similar but distinctly separate ways. One version, the price rationing variety, is simply a temporary form of our HIPP offering which uses the HIPP prices directly. Conversely, the other requires the Company to anticipate the occurrence of anomalous SRMC in advance, package a portion of them into a lump sum payment to purchase options to that allow it to quantity ration capacity--if and when the need materializes.

In the former, customers are enticed onto the program with a relatively small, up-front payment for nominated curtailable load and, if system conditions warrant, notified or a curtailment event. In notifying participating VIPP customers of a capacity need, the Company also communicates that day's HIPP prices. If a customer complies with the notice down to their predetermined firm power level, they retain their up-front incentive payment. If they do not comply, they pay prevailing marginal costs. Alternatively, customers anticipating high HIPP prices can elect high firm power levels and receive per-kilowatt hour payments at HIPP prices for load curtailed below firm levels during an event.

In the latter option the onus is on the utility to anticipate capacity deficiencies, whether they be physical or economic, and to convert a portion of the expected variance that exists between the SRMC and tariff prices into a contingent contract payment in exchange for the right, but not the obligation to restrict load at a later time. This concept is illustrated graphically in Figure 4.

Again, whether your utility's interest lies in time or reliability differentiated service offerings, I suggest that the best avenue to such diverse services will be found through a thorough understanding of the nature of your utility's short-run marginal costs.

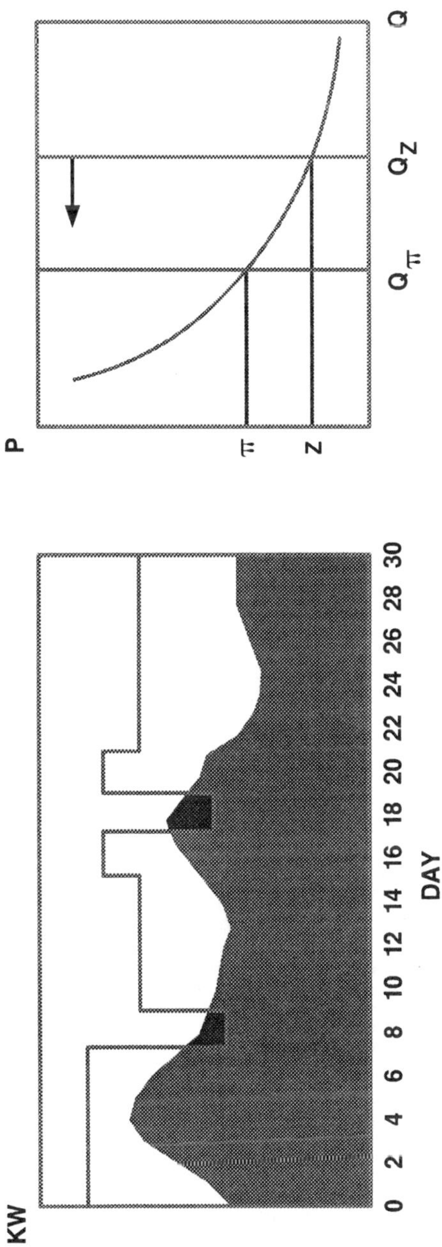

Figure 4. VIPP (Contract MC's)

SEGMENTATION

I propose that a third, and essential, prerequisite to product differentiation is the utility's preparedness for managing market segmentation issues that will either precede and/or result from diversified service offerings. I propose further that this preparedness be focused on three considerations--(1) that the ultimate outcome of any segmentation be that of the alignment of varied customer preferences with the utility's cost structure; (2) that market based segmentation be considered in light of its potential superiority to imposed segmentation; and (3) that if and when imposed segmentation is desirable, and it may be for target recruitment purposes if nothing else, that it be conducted in a way that is consistent with identifiable and measurable cost characteristics.

SERVICE

Fourth and not necessarily last in terms of importance, I suggest that a final prerequisite for engaging in a product differentiation strategy is a utility's commitment to fulfilling the promise of service and the realization that the attendant service function must be performed cost-effectively in order to maintain the economic viability of differentiated offerings. In other terms, do not underestimate the magnitude of ancillary service obligations and make certain their fulfillment is performed in a cost effective fashion.

Niagara's experience with differentiated service offerings indicate that these obligations fall primarily into two categories--recruitment and operations. On the recruitment side, often because we are dealing with contingent products, we have encountered a rather strong demand for informing customers. This can be labor intensive, both in terms of face time with the customer and material preparation beforehand, and usually involves briefing material that includes program descriptions, illustrations and bill comparisons. On the operations side, the service obligations involve interval metering, monitoring and communication equipment that provide customers with knowledge of the composition of their load and how to modify it.

The message of ancillary service obligations is not intended to discourage product differentiation, rather it is intended to ensure that service requirements are planned for, integrated into programs and hence anticipated to be cost-effective. We have developed a simple cost-effectiveness planning model for our VIPP offering that takes into account the tradeoffs between the costs of recruitment and incentive payment and further how both relate to the potential value of individual load subscriptions and ultimately the value of the program. In utilizing this model, we hoped to refute the hypothesis that only large industrial customers make good candidates for reliability differentiated programs. Savvy recruiting makes possible and preliminary results indicate that larger numbers of relatively small customers (500 kW - 1000 kW) may make for an economic program.

The three graphs in Figures 5, 6 and 7 illustrate the model. Figure 5 simply plots the relationship of both program total and variable costs, on a unitized basis, against the size of the average customer interruptible load nomination. Not surprisingly, given fixed program costs, unit costs increase as customer nominations decreases. The interesting aspects of the model are illustrated in Figures 6 and 7, which reveal the tradeoff between incentive costs and recruitment costs. If it is accepted that utility planners indicate a $25 per kW-cycle value of capacity, and if you accept that the average customer's willingness to accept payment for curtailment is $19 per kw-cycle then the model indicates in turn how much you can afford to spend on recruiting relative to expected nomination rates per customer.

The model can be used in a number of alternate fashions--say for example, solving for the "affordable" level of incentive payments given anticipated subscription rates per customer. Whatever the specific application, the important point is that there exist a number of trade-offs between customer size, recruitment costs and customer willingness to accept payment that can be evaluated and an optimal mix that can be economically harvested. As a note, the difference between Figures 6 & 7 is essentially an assumption about the treatment of "sunk" costs. In Figure 7, the highlighted or darkened area of the graph is shifted to the left to show the greater prospective cost-effectiveness of the program if and when you assume that fixed program development costs are indeed sunk and no longer recoverable.

SUMMARY

In very brief summary--any utility wishing to engage in a program of differentiated electric service offerings should (1) give full consideration to fairness and start from a position of equity; (2) understand their utility's marginal cost structure and build their programs around short-run marginal costs; (3) strive for a sustainable market segmentation, preferably one that evolves through market forces; and (4) not underestimate the commitment to providing ancillary services in support of differentiated service offerings while integrating the anticipated cost of such services into benefit/cost evaluations of programs in their entirety.

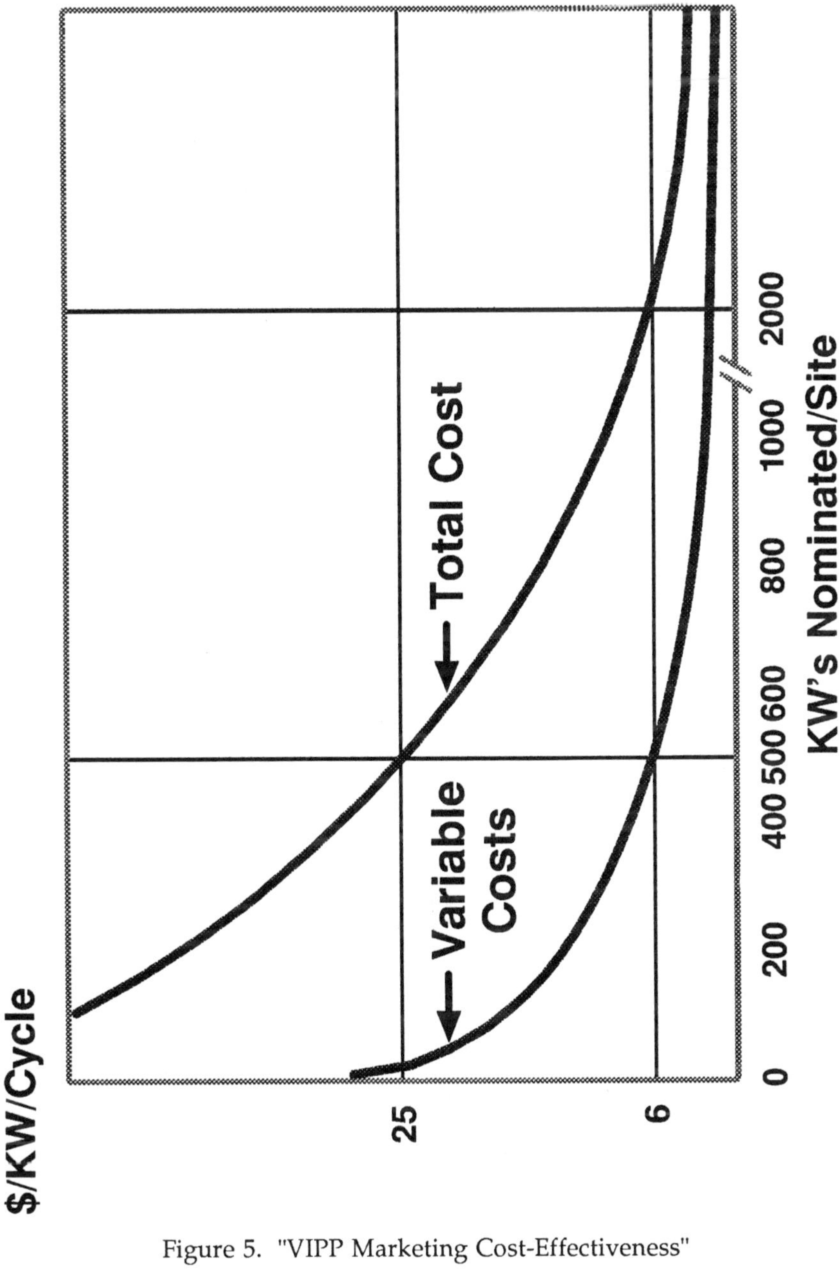

Figure 5. "VIPP Marketing Cost-Effectiveness"

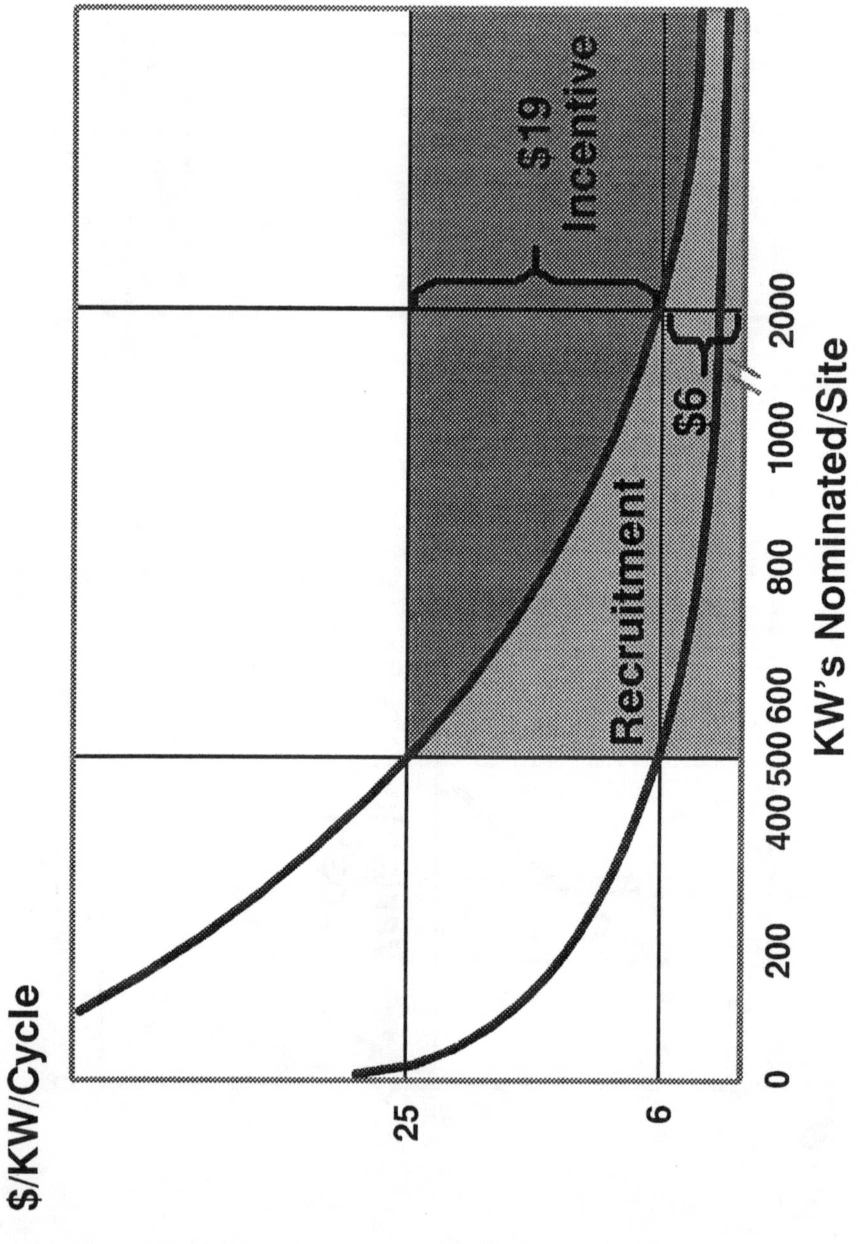

Figure 6. "VIPP Marketing Cost-Effectiveness"

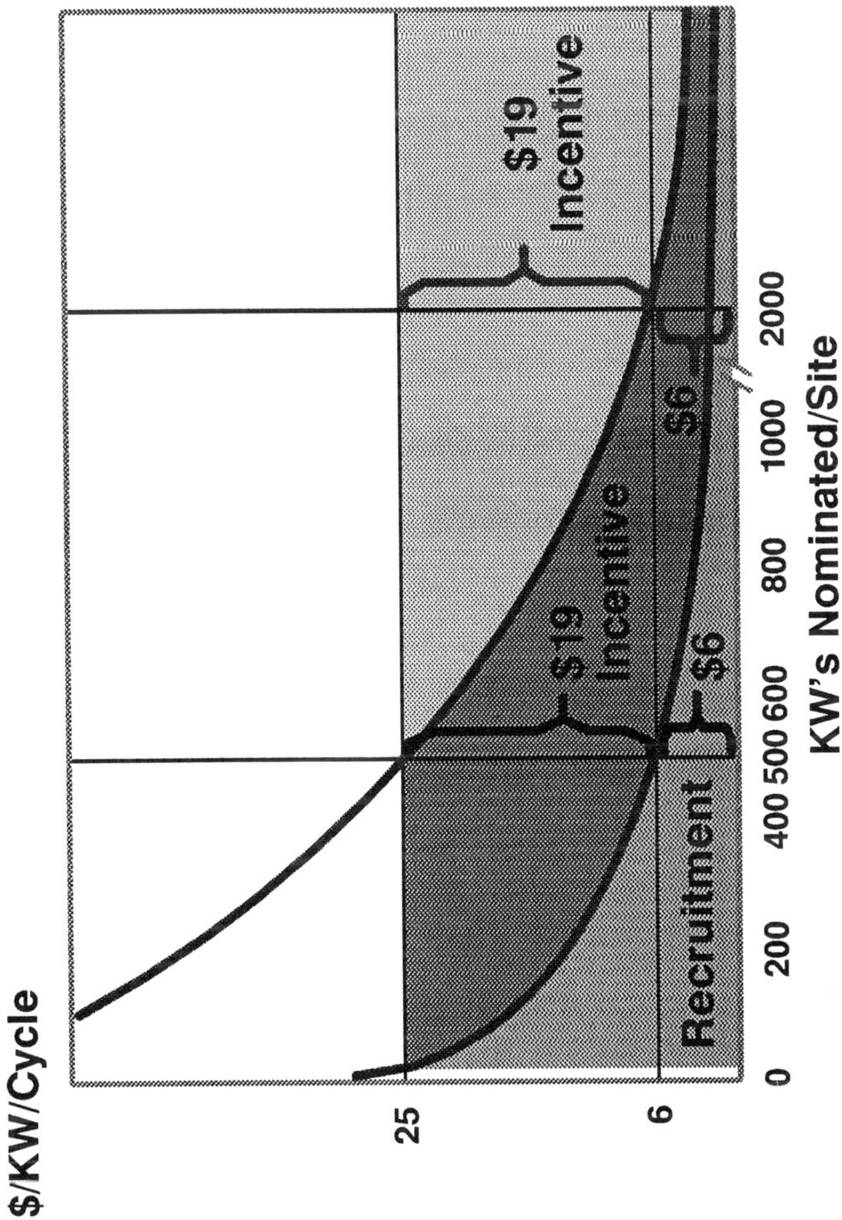

Figure 7. "VIPP Marketing Cost-Effectiveness"

PRIORITY SERVICE AND OUTAGE COSTS IN THE POWER SECTOR: THE TAIWAN PERSPECTIVE

by

George J.Y. Hsu
Chung-Hua Institution for Economic Research

and

Tser-Yieth Chen
Chung-Hua Institution for Economic Research and
Institute of Management Science
National Chiao-tung University

INTRODUCTION

Priority service is the new direction that many North-American utilities are moving in to cope with the ever increasing competitive environment and increases in production costs. Priority service is also applicable to electric utilities in other countries. For Taiwan, priority service promises to be a useful demand-side management instrument. Taiwan is a small island with a high economic growth rate, which has averaged 8.9% over the last four decades resulting in a 54 fold increase in electricity demand, from 1,420 GWh in 1952 to 76,909 GWh in 1989. The increase in the supply of electricity, without a doubt, has been one of the most critical factors in Taiwan's achieving such a remarkable level of economic development. However, since reaching a respectable level of per capita income ($6,942 in 1989), the people in Taiwan have been becoming more and more concerned with the quality of the environment, which has been significantly sacrificed in Taiwan's quest for economic growth. Moreover, during the last few years, many power plant development programs have been postponed due to the opposition of the local population near the proposed plant sites. As a result, the reserve margin of Taiwan's power system has significantly dropped; there are just not enough power plants on line. Being an island, also requires Taiwan to generate all of its own power needs. Therefore, Taiwan is not interconnected with other power systems allowing it to buy power in times of shortage. Over the last three years, several large scale black-outs have occurred in the peak summer period. Obviously, the implementation of a priority service rate program would be one feasible solution to the power shortage problem in Taiwan.

Another reason for Taiwan to implement a priority service rate program is by looking at the problem from the viewpoint of Taiwan's electricity sales structure. Taipower's industrial power users (including agriculture, manufacturing, and the service industry) account for 71.1% of total electricity sales, while these users represent only 3.2% of the total number of users. General users, whose consumption of electricity is primarily for the purpose of lighting (residential and commercial), account for 28.9% of total electricity sales, and these users make up 96.8% of total users. This is quite different from the situation in the United States and other OECD countries, where about one-third of electricity sales goes to the industrial, commercial and residential sectors respectively. In addition, in Taiwan, manufacturing industries account for 79.3% (38,997 GWh/49,209 GWh) of total industrial power sales. Because electricity users in the manufacturing sector are, as a whole, the major consumers of electricity, they should be the focus of attention of a priority service rate program. Obviously, the transaction costs involved in implementing a priority service rate program are relatively low and the rewards would be high. Moreover, Taipower is the sole power company on the island, and it is run by the government; therefore, it would be relatively easy to implement and enforce a priority service program once the regulatory body of the government makes the decision to do so.

According to the above background information, the purpose of this study is, thus, to investigate the relationship between priority service rates and power outage costs in Taiwan. The structure of the paper is as follows: Section two introduces Taipower's three rate schedules for its curtailable rate program. Section three presents three sets of data on outage costs in Taiwan, based on surveys carried out in 1986 and 1989. Section four presents the model developed to quantify the relationship between priority service rates and outage costs. Taipower's curtailable rate schedules will then be utilized to calculate the upper bound of the outage cost functions of customers; then, the model's estimated upper bound for outage costs will be compared with the outage costs presented in section three. In the final section, some conclusions will be drawn and some areas for further research will be suggested.

TAIPOWER'S PRIORITY SERVICE CURTAILABLE RATE PROGRAM

Priority service programs come in a variety of forms, differentiated in terms of utility rate schedules. Time-of-use and interruptible rate programs are two of the most fundamental approaches quite frequently adopted by utilities. The former bases its charges for electricity on demand at the time of consumption while the later bases them strictly on the amount of electricity consumed. In the second tier, real-time pricing and curtailable[1] rate programs are also used by some utilities. And in extreme cases, spot pricing is employed for either capacity or time-of-use charges. However, the following discussion on Taipower's current priority service pertains only to the curtailable rate program.

In 1987, Taipower first launched its curtailable rate program. This program has been modified twice to increase its flexibility and to alter the various rate schedules. Currently, there are three Rate Schedules under this program as shown in Table 1. It should be noted that Rate Schedule I is

---

[1] The curtailable program calls for partial outages while the interruptible program allows for total outages of the customers' electricity service.

designed for large power users whose consumption is more than 500 kW. Under this rate schedule, customers have to routinely curtail the level of their contracted load five working days a week during the peak summer period, no matter whether Taipower suffers a capacity shortage or not. This method is, of course, not efficient from the viewpoint of power resource utilization, because, when load demand still has not reached Taipower's full capacity, this idle capacity could be utilized to generate electricity for distribution to customers, so as to maximize consumer and producer surplus, and, hence, increasing social welfare. However, the benefit of implementing such a program is its ease in managing from Taipower's viewpoint, i.e., the transaction cost is relatively low.

Note that Rate Schedule II is more flexible than Rate Schedule I in terms of the customer's selection of the day of curtailment. Under this schedule, the problem associated with idle capacity, that was mentioned above, can be mitigated by reducing the curtailment period from five days to just two days a week. Rate Schedule III is different from Rate Schedules I and II because it only applies to the off-peak period and is, therefore, much more flexible than either of the other two rate schedules.

INDUSTRIAL OUTAGE COSTS SURVEYS

This section analyzes three industrial outage cost surveys conducted in Taiwan in 1986 and 1989. The first two surveys looked into the problem of outage costs from an ex-ante or hypothetical standpoint, while the third survey was conducted from an ex-post or factual-case-study point of view. All were based on high tension power customers with electricity consumption of 1000 kW or greater. The questionnaires focused on partial outage costs, the impacts of the outage ratio pertaining to the customer's contracted capacity in kWs, i.e., 20%, 40%, or 60%, and the outage duration, i.e., two-hour, four-hour or eight-hour. The outage costs are then broken down into

Table 1

TAIPOWER'S CURTAILABLE RATE PROGRAMS

Rate Schedule	CONDITIONS Curtailed Period	Curtailed Hours	Curtailed Load	Incentives
I	*June 10 to Sept. 9 *every Monday to Friday excluding holidays.	10 a.m. to 12 p.m. 1 p.m. to 5 p.m.	*For 500 kw and above, at least 4500 kw should be curtailed. *For 100 kw to 4999 kw, at least 900 kw should be curtailed. *For 999 kw and under. at least 450 kw should be curtailed.	50% discount on demand charge for the curtailed load for 12 mths.
II	*June 10 to Sept. 9 *Any two days a week.	10 a.m. to 5 p.m.	*at least 50% of customers' contracted capacity.	50% discount on demand charge for the curtailed load; incentive given only for the month when the curtailment occurred.
III	*Sept. 10 to June 9, next year	*4 hours advanced notices *total curtailment not more than 180 hours and less than 15 curtailments	*at least 20% of customer's contracted capacity; at least 4500 kw.	40% discount on demand charge for the curtailed load for 12 months.

Note: Rate Schedules I, II, and III were launched in 1987, 1989 and 1990 respectively.

Sources: Taiwan Power Company, *Rates Schedule*, 1990.

those components that can be associated with production loss, such as the quantity of the reduction in output, the quality of output, clean up, the cost of restarting operation after the power outages, over-time wages, and "others", the latter including costs associated with damage to the environment or people's health.

The first survey was conducted in 1986 utilizing stratified random sampling; 140 power users in the manufacturing sector were surveyed. Of these 140 surveys, 40 were conducted by personal interview and the remaining 100 via mail. The number of valid questionnaires collected totalled 111, for a validity rate of 79.29%. The firms in the sample were further categorized into the following seven industries: basic metals, fabric products, cement, metallic products, petrochemicals, food products and electronic machinery. The average outage cost of the seven industries range from $0.5/kWh to $1.2/kWh as shown in the second column of Table 2.

The second survey was conducted in April 1989. 239 firms were surveyed. The reply rate was 45.2%, that is, 108 firms answered the survey. Among those surveys returned, 91 were acceptable and constitute the effective sample size of the study. To be more comprehensive, firms were categorized into nine, instead of seven, industries--adding the paper products and transport equipment industries to the seven used in survey 1. The average outage costs of the nine industries range from $0.8/kWh to $5.6/kWh and are shown in the third column of Table 2.

The third survey was conducted in August 1989; it included 1093 firms who had their electricity curtailed or interrupted from June to September that year. The reply rate was 24.4% and the effective sample size was 201. The firms were also categorized into the previously mentioned nine industries. The estimated average outage costs range from $1.2/kWh to $5.8/kWh and are listed in the last column of Table 2.

There is one point that should be stressed concerning these surveys, that is, the surveys all focus on the cost of partial outages. This is because, as pointed out in EPRI (1989), most of the outage cost literature is focused on

Table 2.

THREE SURVEY'S AVERAGE OUTAGE COST BY INDUSTRY
(Unit: $/kWh)

	Year Surveyed		
Industries	1986	1989a	1989b
Basic metals	0.5	0.8	1.2
Fabric products	0.7	1.2	1.8
Cement	1.0	1.3	2.0
Paper products	–	1.4	1.6
Metallic products	1.1	2.1	1.8
Petrochemicals	0.9	3.2	3.1
Food products	0.5	3.3	3.4
Electronic machinery	1.2	4.0	4.5
Transport equipment	–	5.6	5.8
Weighted average	0.9	2.4	2.8

Note: The exchange rate, U.S. dollar vs. N.T. dollar, was 40:1 in 1986 and 27.5:1 in 1989a and 1989b.

measuring the impact of total power interruptions, without investigating how outage costs change with the depth of the outage. The lack of partial outage cost information is a significant shortcoming in the literature–in terms of value to priority service pricing. Basically, priority service programs require customers to divide their loads into different reliability levels. These divisions are determined in a large part by how customer outage costs change with the depth of the interruption/curtailment. Therefore, our surveys deal with this specific issue; a summary of the survey results are shown in Table 3.

Table 3.

POWER OUTAGE COST UNDER VARIOUS OUTAGE DEPTHS
(Unit: $/kWh)

	Outage Depth		
Industries	20%	40%	60%
Basic metals	0.98	0.77	0.72
Fabric products	1.13	1.10	1.13
Cement	1.31	1.23	1.24
Paper products	1.58	1.41	1.41
Metallic products	2.39	2.18	2.10
Petrochemicals	3.19	3.32	3.27
Food products	3.46	3.50	3.44
Electronic machinery	4.20	4.54	4.39
Transport equipment	6.24	6.46	6.27
Weighted average	2.21	2.27	2.18

Note: 1. The exchange rate, U.S. dollar vs. N.T. dollar, was 27.5:1 in 1989.
2. Based on the data of the second survey in April 1989.

Note that the figures for outage costs for 20%, 40% and 60% curtailments do not show an apparent downward or upward trend. This is not consistent with our prior knowledge of priority service programs average outage cost should increase as outage depth increases. The underlying reasons behind this phenomenon may be the lack of customer's experience in responding to questions concerning their estimation of outage costs. Another reason may be that, for most customers, any curtailment greater than 20% is beyond the customer's tolerance limitations and, therefore, the incremental cost thereafter is seemingly a linear relationship.

EMPIRICAL RESULTS

Theoretically, a customer will join the priority service program if he can enjoy benefits greater than his expected cost due to the inconvenience of the power outages (i.e., outage costs). Expressing this in a functional form, we can assert this decision mechanism using the following equation.

$$R_i > OC_i = N_i H_i C_i$$

where:

- OC is the outage costs under a specific priority service rate schedule.
- R is the rate incentive given by the utility under a specific priority service rate schedule.
- N is the number of expected outages under a specific priority service rate schedule.
- H is the expected duration of power outages under a specific priority service rate schedule.
- C is the average outage cost of the customer.
- i represents the ith priority service rate schedule.

By rearranging the equation, we obtain:

$$C_i < \frac{R_i}{N_i H_i}$$

where the right-hand side could be considered as the upper bound of the outage costs of customers who are eligible to participate in the priority service program.

Figure 1 illustrates the process that is involved in calculating the relationship between outage costs and the priority service rate schedule. Based on the above formula, and utilizing the data from the three surveys on Taiwan's outage costs, we derive the upper bounds of outage costs which range from \$0.06/kWh to \$0.10/kWh. By comparing these figures with those in Table 2, it is found that, since these figures are much smaller than those presented in Table 2, the customer's in Table 2 will not participate in the priority service program. However, over sixty customers have joined the program so far. Three possible reasons could explain this phenomenon. First, the outage costs provided by the customers in the three surveys may have been exaggerated. Second, since the priority service program is arranged to regularly curtail the customer's load no matter whether Taipower has idle capacity or not and since most customers have already adopted a modified production pattern, it is in their interest to take advantage of the rate incentives, as outage costs in this case would be lower than those revealed in the surveys. Third, most of the customers can receive tax exemptions from the government as a result of their participation. The government gives importation tax exemptions to these firms because most customers who join the program import products to substitute for the loss in production due to the curtailments. This regulation was passed by the government to encourage customers to joint the curtailment program so as to mitigate power shortages. Therefore, the loss to the customers who join the priority service program may be less than the outage costs shown in Table 2. In order to further analyze this issue, a separate, in-depth study is required.

It is worthy to note that the figures in Table 2 are also much greater than the outage costs of United States customers who have joined priority service programs. From data on the New England Electric System (1990) and Niagara Mohawk Power Corporation (1990), we can derive that the upper bounds of outage costs are \$0.18/kWh and \$0.20/kWh, respectively,[2] for each of these utilities.

[2] In the Niagara Mohawk Power Corporation's Same-Day Program, they provide an incentive rate of \$6.33/kw in their curtailable demand program and cut off 96 hours over 3 months so the upper-bound of the attender's outage cost is \$0.20/kWh, i.e., \$6.33*3/96.

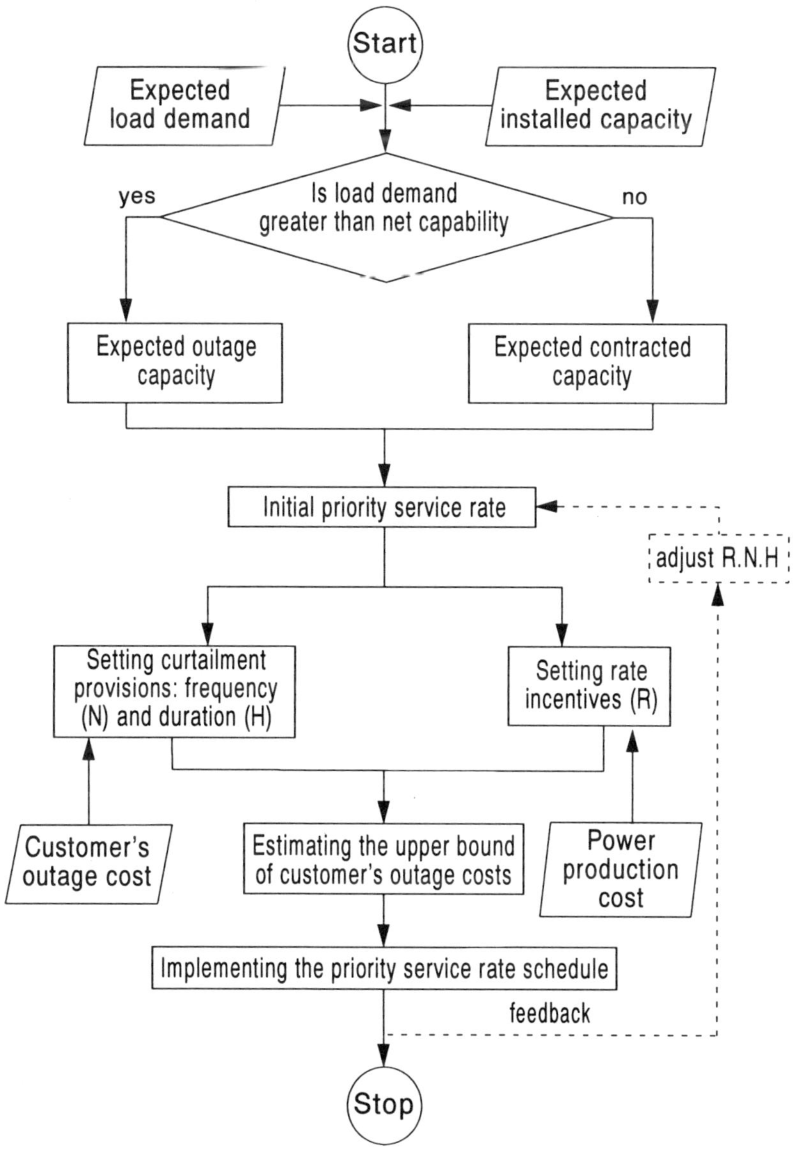

Figure 1. The Relationship Between Outage Costs and the Priority Service Rate Schedule

CONCLUDING REMARKS

This paper has investigated the relationship between priority service program and outage costs in Taiwan. A brief description of Taipower's curtailable rate schedules and of the three outage costs surveys conducted in 1986 and 1989 are given. The surveys focus on the industrial sector and on customer's responses to question concerning their partial outage cost. Based on the findings of the previous section, outage costs of the surveyed firms may have been greatly overstated. This may be due to the fact that the customers may wish to get a better rate by giving an overly large figure to their outage costs. In fact, the magnitude of the outage costs have to do with the production characteristics of the industrial customer, e.g., production technology, product features, and scales of production. From the viewpoint of the end-consumer, there are both external and internal differences among the various types of power outages. The external differences can be characterized by whether there is a "warning" before the outage occurs, while the internal differences can be characterized by what time the outage occurs (e.g., daytime or night-time), or maybe by outage length (e.g., two-hour or four-hour). In other words, there may be quite a different set of results for the same kWh outage based on which type of outage occurs. Therefore, when one estimates outage costs, the important determinants, such as the power-outage depth, outage duration, and the types of industries affected, must be specified. These various type of outage costs may be adaptable to provide different priority service menus.

In short, priority service rates should not display a linear relation in terms of the customer's outage cost at various outage depths; in general, outage cost is expected to increase with an increase in outage depth (since customers would curtail their loads so as to minimize cost, selecting the least costly first, the next costly second, etc.). Furthermore, there normally is a discrete parametric form, rather than a derivative form, to outage costs relative to the outage depth because most equipment is turned-off by the same switch, that is, runs on the same system. All of these areas need further research.

REFERENCES

1. H.P. Chao, S.S. Oren, S.A. Smith and R.B. Wilson. *Priority Service: Unbundling the Quality Attributes of Electric Power*, Palo Alto, CA: Electric Power Research Institute, Report EA-4851, 1986.

2. H.P. Chao, S.S. Oren, S.A. Smith and R.B. Wilson. "Priority Service: Market Structure and Competition", *The Energy Journal*, vol. 9, pp. 77-104, 1988.

3. H.P. Chao and R.B. Wilson. "Priority Service: Pricing, Investment, and Market Organization", *The American Economic Review*, vol. 77, no. 5, pp. 899-916, December 1987.

4. *Environmental and Socioeconomic Consequences of a Shortage in Installed Generating Capacity*, Palo Alto, CA.: Electric Power Research Institute, 1982.

5. *Customer Response to Interruptible and Curtailable Rates*, Palo Alto, Calif.: Electric Power Research Institute, 3 vols. EM-5630, 1988.

6. *Customer Demand for Service Reliability: Existing and Potential Sources of Information*, Palo Alto, CA.: Electric Power Research Institute, 1989.

7. G.J.Y. Hsu. "The Cost of Power Outages on Taiwan's Industry". In *Proceedings: The 12th Annual North American Conference*, Ottawa, Canada, pp.215-26, 1990.

8. G.J.Y. Hsu and T.Y. Chen. *Electricity Economics: Theory and Application* (in Chinese), Taipei: Hua-Tai Book Co., 1990.

9. G.J.Y. Hsu, C.L. Zheng, W.C. Chou and T.Y. Chen. *An Analysis of the Cost of Electricity Outages in Taiwan* (in Chinese). Taipei: Chung-Hua Institution for Economic Research, 1989.

10. M. Munasinghe and A. Sanghvi. "Reliability of Electricity Supply, Outage Cost and Value of Service: An Overview". *The Energy Journal*, vol. 9, pp. 1-18, 1988.

11. *A Report to the New England Power Service Company on the Structure and Results of Interruptible/Curtailable Rate Programs at Other Utilities,* Madison, WN.: Christensen Associates, New England Electric, 1987.

12. *Voluntary Interruptible Pricing Program,* Syracuse, New York: Niagara Mohawk Power Corporation, 1990.

13. *Ontario Hydro Survey on Power System Reliability: Viewpoint of Large Users,* Ontario Hydro. PMA 76-4, 1977.

14. *Ontario Hydro Survey on Power System Reliability: Viewpoint of Small Users, Ontario Hydro.* PMA 76-5, 1978a.

15. J.B. Wharton. "Customer Response and Appropriate Credits for Interruptible Rates". In *New Dimensions in Pricing: Proceedings,* pp. 155-164, EPRI CU-6300, 1989.

16. C.K. Woo and K. Train. "The Cost of Electric Power Interruptions to Commercial Firms". *Energy Journal - Special Issue on Electricity Reliability,* vol. 9, pp. 161-172, 1988.

17. C.K. Woo and B.M. Gray. *An Econometric Analysis of Industrial Firms' Power Outage Costs in Northern California,* PG&E Working Paper, 1987.

VII. EXPERIENCE FROM OTHER INDUSTRIES

PARCEL/MESSAGE DELIVERY SERVICES

by

A.L. Kolbe and R.W. Hodges
Putnam, Hayes & Bartlett, Inc.

OVERVIEW

In recent years, the options available to deliver parcels and messages have expanded dramatically. At one time, the U.S. Post Office had a legal monopoly for most messages, sent as letter mail. It shared a near monopoly for parcels, at least on a nationwide basis, with the now defunct Railway Express Agency (REA), a freight service owned by a consortium of railroads (and therefore also constrained by regulation). Its successor, the U.S. Postal Service (Postal Service), still enjoys an effective and legally guaranteed monopoly for ordinary letters, but overnight letters, facsimile and electronic mail compete for parts of the message business; for parcels, competitive options abound. In short, a regulated entity has turned into just another competitor for many of the basic services it once dominated, and there are an enormous number of new variations of those services available.

How did this happen? What new "flavors" of service eroded postal market share? How did competitors know to offer those services, and why was the Postal Service unable to preempt these offerings with services of its own? Most important, what lessons are there for today's electric utilities in the evolution of parcel and message delivery services? We cannot and do not claim to be able to answer these questions fully, but we believe that there are important lessons in the partial answers we have found.

Historical Summary

The development of competition in parcel/message delivery seems to have followed three distinct phases. Originally, both businesses and the general public had very limited options for moving small packages and messages. Although the Postal Service offered a variety of services, the only national competitor for the parcel business was REA, which shipped parcels as rail freight. The modern era of competition developed in the 1950s, when United Parcel Service (UPS), a regulated motor carrier that delivered department store packages, decided to compete with the Postal Service for the general delivery of parcels. UPS had dramatic success. Its revenues went from $4.9 million in 1960 to nearly $528 million in 1971, despite a market for small parcels that grew only moderately [1]. Eventually the majority of the surface parcel business would be served by private competitors, principally UPS (now a $9 billion company [2]), but also by companies such as Roadway Express that focus on specific market segments defined both geographically and by type of business. The Postal Service lost most of its parcel market share, while REA went out of business entirely.

The year 1973 ushered in the second phase, a new era of competition for the expedited parcel delivery business. In that year Federal Express (FedEx) introduced its guaranteed overnight package delivery service. FedEx saw an undeveloped market of customers that would pay a relatively high price for absolutely dependable, on-demand overnight delivery. Within 15 years, FedEx has grown to be a highly profitable firm with annual revenues greater than $3 billion. The success of FedEx rapidly attracted competition and today many private firms compete fiercely for all or part of this market. A particularly important development occurred in 1980 when private delivery services were granted a waiver of the private express statutes by the Postal Service. The waiver permitted entities other than the Postal Service to carry expedited mail that previously was legally restricted to delivery by the Postal Service, providing the price was a multiple of the Postal Service's priority mail rate. FedEx and other overnight package firms found their market effectively redefined from packages to both packages and letters. The growth in this combined market in the 1980s has been dramatic, as Figure 1 illustrates. Figure 2 shows the breakdown between letter-sized and other packages for some of the carriers: both have grown materially, but the overnight message business has exploded.

Today a third phase of competition has emerged. In the package market, instead of developing major new services, the focus is on the fight to expand the share of existing services, by filling "gaps" between these services, adding new features and/or price competition. For example, UPS offers "2nd Day Air" at a lower price. The Postal Service is moving to upgrade its Priority Mail parcel delivery to a second-day standard. It has reshaped its services to present the customer with three parcel shipping options: Express Mail, Priority Mail and Parcel Post. Other private firms, such as Federal Express, are moving to offer a wider menu of options as well. Thus, entities are moving from their positions of strength to challenge other entities in their positions of strength. This is leading to consolidation within the industry–the merger of Emery and Purolator for example–and increasing competitive pressures for the competitors that remain. Revenue per package has been flat or falling since the early 1980s, even controlling for the growth difference in message and package service [3].

The message market benefits from the competition over service features, but is benefiting as well from facsimile machines and electronic data transfer. The traditional transportation market for messages now overlaps with the telecommunications market, and at least one major carrier (UPS) sees electronic data transfer as a major growth area and plans to be "a big player in the field" [4]. At the same time, the explosion in private facsimile machines and electronic mail has cut into the overnight letter delivery market [5]. Although there will remain a substantial market for which facsimile is not an alternative [6], some think as much as 30 percent of the market may eventually be lost. ZapMail, FedEx's attempt to preempt this

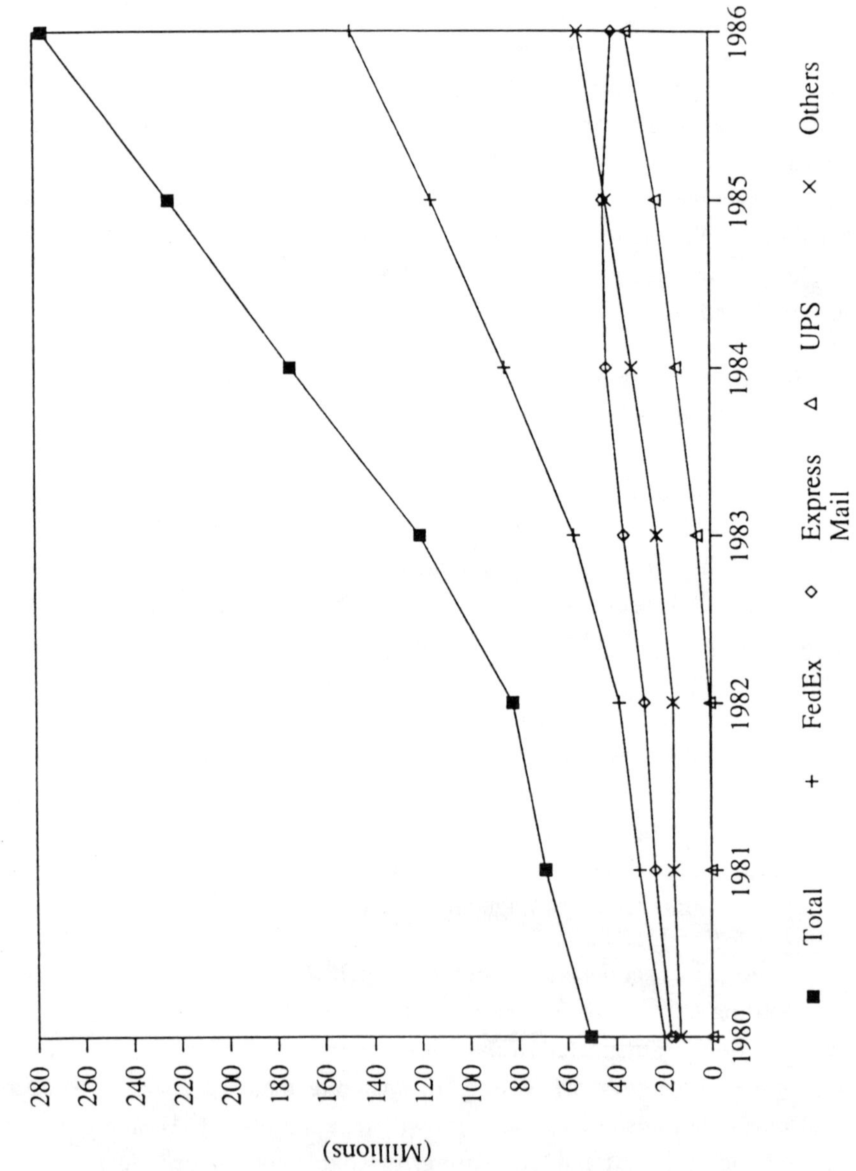

Figure 1. Overnight Packages for Top Six Carriers*

* Year Ending in May for Federal Express.
Source: Clifford D. Currier, Rebuttal Testimony before the Postal Rate Commission, *Postal Rate and Fee Changes, 1987*.

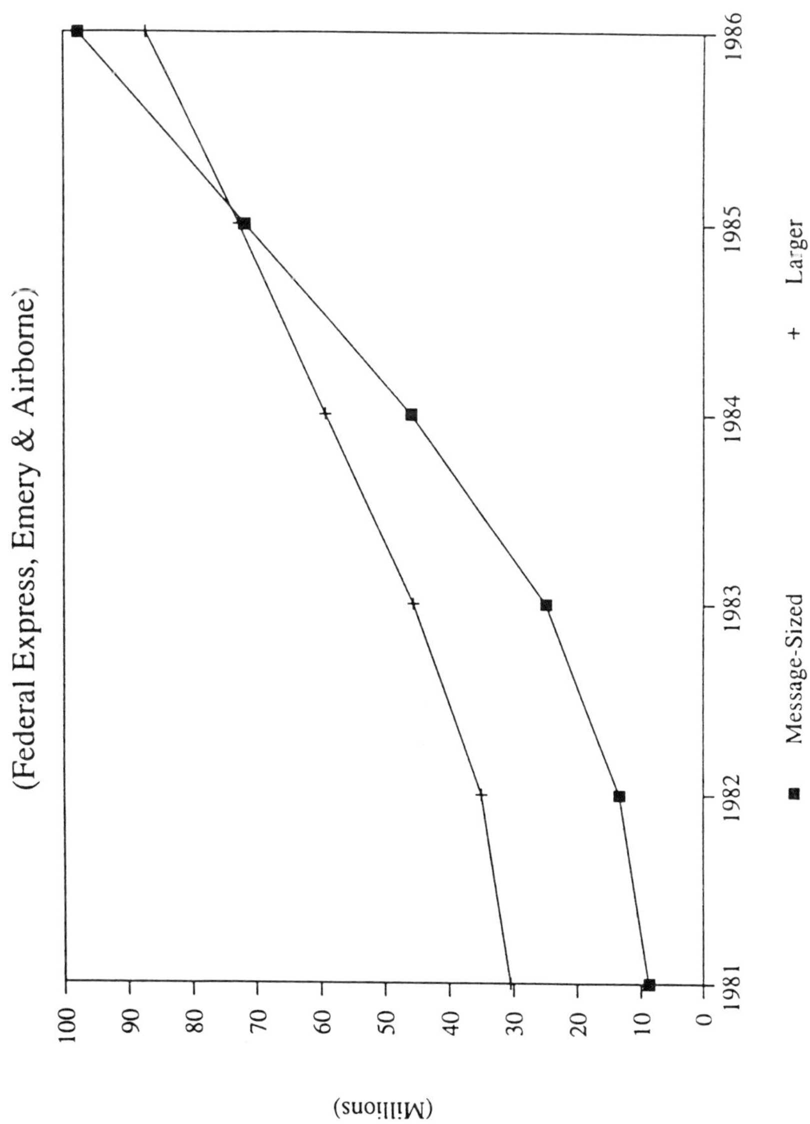

Figure 2. Message-Sized vs. Larger Parcels*

* Year Ending in May for Federal Express.
Source: Clifford D. Currier, Rebuttal Testimony before the Postal Rate Commission, *Postal Rate and Fee Changes, 1987*.

alternative to its traditional market, lost $350 million before it was abandoned [7].

Thus, the outcome of this competition has sometimes been hard on the companies, but it has been highly beneficial for customers. They now enjoy an extremely diverse set of choices for getting a message or a parcel from point A to point B, at widely varying but generally declining prices. They also benefit from fierce competition to find still newer varieties of service. In addition, customers of package and message delivery services and the firms that serve them are finding new ways to use the delivery capabilities that now exist as well as the technologies of the future. These developments have the potential to redefine the boundaries of the delivery business in ways that were unforeseen as the industry developed.

Summary of Findings

The principal findings of this report may be summarized as follows.

- Product diversity often springs from competition. Profitable product niches created by regulatory pricing can permit competitive entry into a regulated entity's markets, as can inefficiency by the regulated entity.

- Once the competitive process begins, the regulated entity must become adept at many competitive skills–identifying customer needs, marketing, modifying or dropping product lines, cutting costs, value-pricing,–or lose substantial market share. Surprises *will* occur, either unexpected failures or unexpected successes, and the surviving companies will be those that can respond quickly and appropriately. Rate regulation makes this task extremely hard, and the parcel/message business teaches that regulated entities that cannot adapt do very poorly indeed.

- Markets for different levels of reliability can start with better provision of existing services or with a whole new service. But electric utilities today, unlike the parcel/message carriers described here, start from a highly reliable service with cost-based, rather than value-based, prices. There is probably more "unexplored territory" in electric markets at the low-quality end of the spectrum.

- Profitable service innovations at the low-quality end of the spectrum must pay particular attention to cost control, UPS's path to success. At the high-quality end–exemplified by FedEx–technical innovation is more important than cost control, since price is relatively less important for high-quality services (at least initially).

- Customers care about many product dimensions, not just price and reliability. The PRISM focus on a price-reliability schedule must not cause other product dimensions to be overlooked.

- Once a new service begins, its evolution is often unpredictable, for several reasons. An important one is that customers cannot know their own tastes until they have experience with the product. Another is that neither companies nor customers can know what extra features will turn out to be important once the service is in operation. This suggests that attempts to design an "optimal" service schedule in advance are: (1) guaranteed to fail; and (2) likely to be counterproductive, since they delay the introduction of good, if not optimal, services that let companies and customers learn what products customers really want.

The introduction has provided a brief historical perspective and summarized the main findings. The next section of this paper, Relevant Practices, examines in greater detail the industry practices that have allowed competitors to successfully encroach on the services for the delivery of messages and parcels that were once dominated by the Postal Service. These practices are of interest because they help explain how companies learn what products customers want. Additionally, they shed light on the generic strategies that are available to competitors to carve away market share from the regulated entity. Section II also looks at lessons to be learned from these practices. The final section will discuss some overall conclusions drawn from the study of the parcel/message delivery business.

RELEVANT PRACTICES

Research into the management of the package/message delivery business has produced relevant practices that can be grouped into five major categories:

- Competitive positioning of services
- Reliability of service
- Cost control
- Special customer services
- Evolution of service applications

Competitive Positioning of Services

In the first era of competition, as outlined in Section 1 above, the new services that developed were for the surface delivery of parcels and small packages. During this period UPS was very successful in introducing new services while another competitor, REA, ended up in bankruptcy. In the next era, Federal Express saw the potential in high-priced, reliable overnight delivery, a market that the Postal Service says it founded but which clearly never amounted to much before Federal Express. The end result in both cases is that the successful firms managed to build large and profitable businesses based on services that would previously have been considered to be within the domain of the Postal Service. The successes and failures of these firms offer valuable insights into the competitive positioning of services in "monopoly" markets that are opening up to competition, such as electricity.

One practice tends to characterize entry into this market: successful competitors have usually employed a niche strategy. The initial niches exploit differences between the regulated price and the cost of providing service. Such differences are common in regulation: for example, a first class stamp costs the same whether it is on a letter that moves within one large city or between two rural farms a continent apart. Thus, a new service initially may be restricted to major population centers since rural areas are too expensive to serve. Or, packages over a predefined size or weight may be excluded because they are uneconomic to deliver. Note that the competitor is able to enter because regulated entities often offer the same rate for services of widely varying cost, either in the name of "equity" (e.g., cross-subsidizes for residential or rural customers with prices far above cost for business or urban customers) or "rate simplicity". This becomes especially troublesome for the regulated entity once competition begins because of requirement to offer universal service, thus leaving the regulated entity with the most costly parts of the market.

The initial success of UPS in competing for parcel delivery customers was based on cost control and competitive pricing, attention to the service needs of the business shipper and marketing skill. For example, UPS pick-up at customer premises (for a weekly fee) was an important early advantage [8]. The market was low-cost, low-valued, unglamorous surface delivery. UPS originally targeted the low-price and price-sensitive end of the package business by providing superior service at a lower price.

During the first era of competition, cost mattered most, although reliability, convenience and similar features also served to differentiate competitors. Though price and service quality were major factors in determining competitive position, obtaining the right to operate in a given region and intervening in regulatory proceedings where others sought that right was also an important competitive activity.

During the same period that UPS was building its successful package delivery business, REA was dying. REA, jointly owned by a consortium of railroads, offered nationwide rail and truck freight service. Largely because of its ties to the railroad industry, REA suffered from a number of problems that other competitors did not. As competition emerged, REA failed to solve the problem of regulatory oversight. Further, while it was able to price flexible, change rates to meet market conditions and tailor its price-service schedule to cost differences among customer groups, its general rate level was so high and its service so poor that it could not compete. Because of its inability to be selective about the types of packages to carry, REA could not install the automated equipment required to reduce the cost of handling small packages. The strength of the railroad labor unions further hindered REA's ability to reduce costs. (UPS solved this problem by successfully negotiating productivity-enhancing work rules along with wage increases; today, UPS's labor force is widely regarded as one of the world's most efficient.) As rail service declined, so too did REA's business. UPS and other competitors successfully positioned their services with regular shippers of ordinary parcels. REA was left in the unenviable position of serving low-volume, low-margin customers that were shipping odd-sized, difficult-to-manage freight. By the late 1950s and early 1960s, when UPS began expanding its operations, REA was not a significant player in the parcel post market.

The rapid growth of FedEx beginning in the 1970s was powered by mass market television advertising, innovative application of high-technology, the deregulation of air cargo service in 1977 and the waiver granted by the Postal Service in 1980 that permitted overnight letter carriage. When it first began offering overnight package delivery service, FedEx threw price competition out the window and instead focused on other product attributes. The key product dimension was an absolute, money-back guarantee of overnight delivery to any destination FedEx served, made possible by the innovative "hub and spoke" transportation network. FedEx also won customers for its service by providing convenient desk-to-desk pickup and delivery, and special customer services like package tracing. After developing the package delivery system that could support its claims, FedEx aggressively marketed its new service using television advertising to create a dynamic image that stood in marked contrast to the general public perception of the Postal Service. Then, as regulatory restrictions were relaxed, FedEx was well positioned to provide a service that no other competitor could match.

The Postal Service responded to the initial success of FedEx's package service by introducing its own full-scale overnight delivery service, "Express Mail", in 1977. Express Mail had a three-year head start before FedEx was allowed to carry overnight letters, and during that timeframe it possessed 100% of the overnight letter market. Since that time, it has had to fight to maintain a steadily eroding market share of the overnight delivery business [9]. See Figure 1. Its loss of market share appears to be tied to the Postal Service's inability to offer the critical product and service dimensions that attracted customers to FedEx. The Postal Service's expedited delivery has not been able to match the reliability, convenience and special services provided by FedEx and other private carriers.

The rapid growth and relative price insensitivity of the market FedEx discovered naturally attracted more competition than just the Postal Service. Competitors included both new, start-up companies and existing package or freight carriers of various types, which competed on the basis of both price and service characteristics. These firms employed a variety of technologies and delivery systems to compete for segments and sub-segments of the parcel/message delivery market. Market entrants were firms like Emery/Purolator, Airborne Freight and DHL, as well as numerous smaller, more specialized carriers. As a result, prices and overall margins have continuously declined over the last decade and product offerings have proliferated. FedEx, however, has been able to maintain its competitive position by continually reducing costs and improving customer service.

Another major competitor that entered the market was UPS, and it is instructive to examine early UPS experience with expedited delivery. For several years, UPS offered a second-day air service known as UPS Blue Label. Only in the 1980s did UPS begin to offer an overnight delivery service known as Next Day Air. Initially, overnight delivery was viewed as an ancillary service to be offered if the normal UPS pickup schedule could be maintained. Surface parcel delivery was seen as the principal business, with overnight service to be offered only if it did not interfere with existing services. As demand grew and customers wanted more features, however, expedited delivery became a significant product in its own right. A corporation that took justifiable pride in its ability to offer "low tech" services with exceptional efficiency had to add "high tech" options such as parcel tracking. Customer demand and willingness to pay drove the company in a direction not foreseen by those initially planning the service offering. In this case, the company was forced to rethink its original strategy for the competitive positioning of its service.

More recently, FedEx has responded to UPS's entry into the overnight market with the introduction of a "second-day" air delivery service to compete with UPS's second-day service. The intention was to offer a less expensive product that would allow customers a broader range of choice in meeting delivery needs. However, customers quickly discovered that since the carrier's system was designed to guarantee overnight delivery, most packages sent by the slower service were actually delivered overnight. In this case customer behavior eliminated the distinctions between two competing products and forced the service provider to change operational practices in order to avoid losses of revenue and profit. It is reported that Federal Express is now having to intentionally introduce delays into the cheaper service [10].

Finally, timing may turn out to matter a great deal. FedEx introduced its ZapMail service for same-day delivery via high-quality facsimile in 1984. It turned out that the market just was not there, at least at the price FedEx charged, and the service was abandoned. But new, faster and cheaper facsimile machines are now "sweeping the business world ..." and "seem certain to replace a sizable portion of the overnight document delivery business ..." [11]. FedEx might or might not have been able to preempt this competition had its service been introduced a few years later, but it clearly did not do so with the actual introduction date.

LESSON: Firms offering a service in a competitive market must pay careful attention to the competitive position and pricing of their products.

- Initial competitive entry is made possible by three potential defects in a regulated entity's service offering: (1) overall costs may be too high, for any of a number of reasons; (2) average-cost pricing may create profitable niches for "cream skimming"; or (3) the regulated entity may simply fail to see the potential market for a new service.

- Products have to be designed and positioned to appeal to a particular target group of customers. In the early days of its parcel business UPS targeted "back-office" shipping managers. Advertising was relatively unimportant and limited to trade publications. FedEx did just the opposite when it entered the overnight delivery business; it used heavy mass-market advertising to reach customers who knew little about shipping but knew they wanted their package to get someplace in a hurry. In both cases the product being offered was packaged and priced to appeal to the target group.

- The history of REA shows that a competitive enterprise must be equally adept at identifying and avoiding or eliminating services that offer no long term prospects for covering the cost of providing them. "De-marketing" services that are not viable in a competitive market is likely to become an ever more critical skill for electric utilities as products and competitors proliferate. However, the special public role played by the utilities will certainly make it difficult for them to match competitors in this aspect of competitive positioning.

- Firms must be flexible in redesigning service offerings based on customer response. As was shown in the experience of the carriers with overnight and second-day air service, firms cannot always predict how customers will use their services. When initial predictions prove incorrect, competitors must adapt service offerings to meet customer needs. An especially important aspect of this flexibility is the ability to make timely adjustments to prices and terms of sale. Statutes or regulations may make this difficult or impossible for regulated entities.

- Competitors must also adjust to meet the challenge of new entrants to the market. The history of the package/message delivery business shows that when a competitor in the market introduces a new service or new features to an existing service, it is difficult for other competitors to avoid having to follow suit unless a choice is made not to compete for that business.sd Every new entrant, every new service and every new service enhancement requires competitors already in the market to make decisions on appropriate competitive responses.

In general, the discussion of competitive positioning shows that in the early days of priority services for electric utilities, much flexibility will be required from companies in designing, pricing and marketing their products.

Reliability of Service

An entirely new industry has been created in the last 15 years by firms that took a mundane, utility-type service and turned it into a high-visibility, high-margin priority service for which customers were willing to pay a premium rate. The value that the customer was paying for was not just the physical movement of a package but the convenience and peace of mind of absolutely reliable service.

The importance of reliability in the business of delivering parcels and messages is summed up by the now famous advertising slogan used by FedEx: "When it absolutely, positively has to be there overnight." Reliability of service is unquestionably the most important product attribute in the competition for expedited delivery. In a survey of Fortune 1000 company managers, conducted by Opinion Research Corp. for the Postal Service, 95 percent of the respondents said that "timely delivery is the key factor in choosing an overnight delivery service" [12].

In the expedited delivery business, FedEx sets the standard for speed and reliability. The firm claims that more than 99 percent of U.S. packages are delivered on the correct day. In addition to timeliness, reliability means the absolute assurance that the package will actually be delivered. In the FedEx system that means the odds against a package being lost, stolen or damaged are 4,5000-to-1 [13].

Customers who need an expedited delivery are more than willing to pay for timely, reliable service. In the same Opinion Research Corp. survey quoted above, "86 percent polled said the benefits of an on-time delivery are more important than cost". However, the phenomenal success of FedEx and its many imitators illustrates better than any survey the willingness of customers to pay a premium rate for absolutely dependable service.

Yet today, we see price competition becoming ever more important in the expedited delivery business. UPS and the Postal Service both have letter rates well below those once charged by FedEx, and discounting for high-volume users is becoming more common. Once competition for a high-reliability service becomes intense, price again becomes one of the battlefields.

It is less clear how valuable reliability is in the surface parcel end of the business. Price is the dominant variable here. Still, customers prefer more reliability to less, and a sufficiently unreliable service would presumably have trouble keeping business unless its price were far below those of the competition. UPS's growth was based on competitive or lower prices, equal or greater reliability and additional valuable service attributes (e.g., pickup, free insurance, two redelivery attempts, package tracing, etc.) [14]. Thus, even at the low-price end of the scale, service features such as reliability remain important.

LESSON: There can be a market for reliable, high-quality service where customers are willing to pay a price that more than covers the cost of providing such service. Furthermore, as the issue of reliability increases in importance, the issue of price relative to other service features decreases in importance. However, competition for the new service eventually brings back price competition. A low-reliability service, on the other hand, needs to be cheap from the start.

Electric utilities today start at the high-quality end of the spectrum. Because electric utilities are so reliable today, customers already expect premium service, and at a cost-based price. It is not clear how much opportunity there will be to offer a more reliable, premium product on a widespread basis, although niches for such service no doubt exist. Rather, the larger change from today's market seems to be to offer lower-quality products (e.g., 75 percent reliability) at lower prices. This seems to be the reverse of the package delivery market which started from low quality and moved up. It also means that any period of extreme profitability from a high-priority service is likely to be limited, simply because high reliability is already the standard.

Cost Control

Both the economic theory of competition and the actual practical experience of business managers tells us that the success of a firm in a competitive market is tied to the firm's ability to continuously reduce costs. To succeed, a firm must not only control costs but do so while maintaining and improving the level of service that customers expect. This is especially true for rapidly growing industries or markets with high profit margins. In the long run, price competition for comparable services can only be based on actual differences in cost. The practices of the competitors in the package/message delivery business illustrate how critical the cost-control function is to competitive success.

Since its emergence as an aggressive price competitor, as described in the section on competitive positioning of services, UPS has been notable in its ability to control costs. This has been achieved through careful engineering of work processes, efficiency and cost-conscious management and the productivity of employees. A good example of the attention UPS focuses on the design of work processes is its system for package pickup and delivery. Every working day, UPS's 47,000 brown delivery vans follow regular, preplanned routes for which stops have been analyzed and timed. "Each regular stop on each route is studied with a stopwatch, and supervisors periodically recheck to make sure conditions haven't changed" [15]. Drivers have detailed instructions on how to deliver efficiently. For example, drivers are required to take their keys from their pockets while walking back from the van, to avoid delay upon reaching it. The progress of each van through its daily routine is so predictable that managers usually know within six minutes how long a driver's route will take. The careful planning and constant evaluation of this basic function allows UPS to eliminate any excess costs in the process of picking up or delivering parcels.

The efficiency and cost-consciousness shown by UPS in its industrial engineering can also be found in every other aspect of the business. Package cars are washed every day and are so carefully maintained that they last an average of 22 years. Company offices are located in very "spartan" buildings. Senior officers of the firm, including the CEO, share secretaries, do their own photocopying and make their own travel arrangements. Lunches for the Board of Directors meetings take place in the company cafeteria and the Directors buy their own lunches. UPS maintains tight controls over every aspect of its business and, as a result, keeps tight control over costs.

In addition to cost-conscious management, UPS enjoys the benefit of an employee body with "an unusual mixture of passionate commitment to hard work and a strong identification with the company" [16]. Almost all of the stock in the company is owned by a group of 15,000 managers and supervisors; a large part of their compensation is tied to the quarterly stock price set by the board. This group supervises a work force of package car drivers that, although, highly unionized, "consider themselves [to be] small businessmen, who manage by pleasing customers, maximizing productivity and developing new business" [17]. High morale and a sense of ownership in the business are what make engineered efficiency and operational cost controls actually work in the day-to-day management of the firm.

FedEx has been equally successful in managing costs to maintain profits and competitiveness, but from a very different angle. Starting with the basic hub-and-spoke concept, FedEx has succeeded with innovative applications of new ideas and new technologies. The firm's role as the high-tech leader in its field has enabled FedEx to continuously reduce the cost of providing its overnight parcel delivery service.

The operational concept on which FedEx was founded is one that defies the simple logic that the farther a package travels, the higher the cost to transport it. In the FedEx hub-and-spoke system, even a parcel going to a relatively nearby destination must first travel to he sorting center in Memphis, Tenn. Six nights a week this center unloads, sorts, reloads and ships about 650,000 packages. The entire exercise is so carefully choreographed that every minute of delay means 20,000 packages will miss their 10:30 AM delivery deadline and 20,000 customers will not have to pay.

Despite the difficulty, FedEx manages the process so that more than 99 percent of the packages reach their destination on time. By designing and mastering this innovative system the company "cut out the middlemen and freed customers from the delays and inefficiencies inherent in forwarding and consolidation" [18]. Interestingly, both UPS and the Postal Service have followed FedEx in the use of hub-and-spoke transportation systems.

FedEx has mastered the complex logistics of its operations through the cost-effective application of the most advanced technology available. In only 15 years the company has become one of IBM's five largest customers worldwide. Most importantly, FedEx has applied its high-tech solutions to the basic processes of its business. Company drivers and foot-couriers are equipped with computers that log in all parcels and immediately radio that information back to the central database. This system is being further improved by the introduction of more powerful "Tracker" units that pick up information about a package by simply scanning with a light pen, thereby eliminating the entire process of manually entering data into the system. Though the up-front costs are high for such advanced systems, making the investment has allowed FedEx to continue to set the standards for service and cost-effectiveness in expedited delivery.

In contrast to the continuing successes of UPS and FedEx, the Postal Service has not been very effective in reducing costs to improve competitiveness. Though the "Postal Service has undertaken numerous efforts ... to control costs and improve operating efficiency, the results of these efforts are largely discouraging" [19]. Part of the problem for Postal Service managers has been the political opposition, both internal and external, to making *any* changes in Postal Service operations. Unionized Postal Service employees, for example, have opposed changes in work rules. The general public, and their political representatives, have successfully blocked attempts to curtail services such as Saturday deliveries and to close tiny rural Post Offices. The existence of statutory obligations, deeply entrenched traditions and interest groups has sometimes given the Postal Service little room to maneuver in trying to improve competitiveness.

Another major cause of its failure to significantly improve competitiveness has been Postal Service's inability to control labor costs and increase productivity. For the private companies in the expedited parcel/message delivery business it is estimated that 50 percent of their total costs are due to labor [20]. The comparable figure for the Postal Service is around 85 percent. Though UPS, with its unionized work force, pays wages 5-10 percent higher than non-union FedEx, salaries of Postal Service employees are 25-33 percent higher than those for workers in comparable private sector jobs. (UPS, in contrast, has been able to negotiate more productive work standards in its labor contracts.) Postal Service workers have been described as "the new aristocracy of American labor" [21]. During the many years when it was not challenged competitively, the Postal Service developed a tradition of constantly increasing wages and benefits that did not necessarily correspond to equivalent increases in productivity. Since the advent of competition and the reorganization of the Postal Service, the Postal Service appears to have been unable to break free from that tradition.

Increases in productivity and efficiency have also been very difficult for the Postal Service to achieve. "While other industries continually engaged in research and development to cut costs and improve operations, the Post Office did not even have a research program of its own until after World War II" [22]. Though in the 1960s and 1970s the Postal Service did make major efforts to introduce automated processes for sorting letters and processing bulk mail, the bottom-line benefits were always less than expected. For example, the National Bulk Mail System was inaugurated in 1975 to "improve bulk-mail handling enough to stem the flow of parcel-delivery business away from the postal system toward the United Parcel Service and other competitors in the market for shipping small parcels" [23]. Instead, due to poor design of buildings and equipment, the incidence of damaged and misdirected mail actually increased. In the process, the speed and reliability of delivery decreased. The overall result was that the investment of $1 billion had an insignificant impact on operating costs and actually caused service quality to decline.

LESSON: Cost control is a critical factor in offering priority services in a competitive market but there are a variety of strategies that firms can follow to achieve cost competitiveness.

- One approach that has been outlined above might be described as "cost management"; following this strategy, a company, through excellence in management, finds ways to constantly improve the efficiency of every aspect of its operations. This relentless drive for economy and efficiency is hard to achieve and harder to sustain, but it is also very difficult for competitors to imitate.

- An alternative strategy is one of constant innovation. If a company is able to successfully apply new ideas and new technology to keep itself on the leading edge of the market, the firm can set the standards that other competitors have to match. Some of these innovations may save costs directly, while others may improve the service and attract market share. Both types of innovation help the high-tech firm to maintain a relative cost advantage over its rivals.

- Following either strategy seems to be difficult for a regulated entity. Political constraints and labor and behavioral norms that evolved under "monopoly" conditions can impede cost-control activities. Electric utilities should pay particular attention to this danger as electric competition evolves. For example, particularly high-cost plants are likely to be just as much a handicap for utilities as unfavorable union contracts have been for railroads and, apparently, the Postal Service.

- The cost management and innovation alternative strategies are not mutually exclusive nor are they the only strategies to be followed. However, what is clear is that in a competitive market organizations must have *some* clear and effective strategy for controlling costs. Large investments that produce no return and a lack of discipline in managing costs will inevitably lead to deterioration of a firm's ability to compete for customers.

Special Customer Services

In response to intensifying competition, carriers in the parcel/message delivery market are seeking to differentiate themselves by offering customer services that go beyond the simple delivery of a parcel or message. In the last few years overnight air carriers have broadened their product lines to include less expensive, slower services and convenient drive-through or walk-by drop-off points. Surface carriers have added amenities such as on-demand pickup to their existing service lines and some have moved aggressively to compete for overnight deliveries. As competitors begin to look more and more alike and priority shipping service moves toward being a commodity product, "couriers are fiercely jockeying to position their services into a unique niche in order to segment their product from competitors" [24].

One aspect of customer service that offers opportunity for differentiation is providing information about rates and service conditions and assisting customers in making decisions about how to buy and utilize package delivery services. One of the first moves in this direction has been rate simplification for part of the market. "Virtually every air express company has worked hard in recent years to simplify tariffs by adopting one page national tariffs, reduced weight breaks, and reduced numbers of price zones in pricing formats" [25]. Simplified express rate schedules are intended to help customer service representatives quote rates more quickly and efficiently, aid customers in understanding what actual costs will be and facilitate the comparison of rates among various service options. Having easy access to comprehensible rate information enables customers to more intelligently manage use of shipping services by balancing levels of service and costs. Many companies are beginning to tighten controls on the use of priority shipping services and are emphasizing using lower-cost options whenever possible.

The drive for simplification has limits, however. Simplification is possible for express service in part because hub-and-spoke transportation networks weaken the relationship between cost and distance. But simplified rate structures in the presence of material cost differences create profitable niches for specialized carrier entry. Thus, some niche carriers such as the Eastern Connection, a surface overnight service in the Washington to Boston corridor, have arisen where simplified express rates exceed costs by enough to attract entry. And surface transportation rate schedules remain far more detailed because the cost/distance relationship is more important, and it is relative easy for new competitors to enter the market to exploit profitable niches created by mispricing.

Another facet of the drive to differentiate service is providing customers with specialized billing and management information reports. Roadway Package Service "is providing its customers with more management information on their parcel traffic. As part of this effort, the carrier generates reports and itemized billing for its clients, detailing all shipping information by week or by other specified period. These reports are designed to help shippers manage their small package flows more effectively ..." [26]. The computer terminals being provided to customers by other carriers allow them to offer an even greater range of management information services. The "Mercury" meter system consoles used by Purolator's customers calculates the lowest rate available for a parcel based on weight and destination. The system also provides hard-copy documentation and summary shipping reports. Other carriers' systems have features that provide customers with services such as real-time inventory management reports, on-site air waybill preparation and direct customer data links.

From a customer's point of view, the availability of detailed, up-to-date information, coupled with the capability to analyze and manipulate the information, means better management of the firm's resources. To the extent that competitors in the parcel/message delivery market can offer management information services unavailable from their competitors, they differentiate their package delivery services. They also provide customers with a way to verify the reliability of their service, to assess the value of such service to the firm and, if appropriate, to choose another service with a different level of reliability or probability of interruption. Ideally, a carrier will provide a customer with a complete menu of services offering varying levels of speed and reliability that meet any need. The customer can then use the information and analytical tools provided by the carrier to easily choose the most cost-effective mode of service.

Another area where competitors are making major efforts to distinguish their firms and products is in communications with customers. FedEx is the industry leader in this practice. In addition to an on-time delivery guarantee, FedEx customers are promised a full refund on overnight delivery fees if at any time their package cannot be located within 30 minutes. FedEx supports this promise with an automated order entry and tracking system that starts with hand-held data entry terminals used by pick-up drivers. Orders entered by the couriers are immediately transmitted by radio to a central database. Once a package has entered the system it continues to be tracked until delivered. Status information is instantly available on-line to customer service representatives at 11 customer service centers around the country. Customers can reach the service centers by calling toll-free telephone numbers. In addition, "for regular customers the company is installing numeric key pads in their offices to enable package collections to be booked by telephone without the bother of talking. Some major customers are even getting micro-computers with LCD displays to allow them to dispatch and trace their own packages ..." [27]

Competitors to FedEx are responding with their own computerized data collection and reporting systems. UPS has introduced an urgent inquiry service that provides customers with the location of surface parcels within one hour. Eventually UPS plans to equip all of its package delivery vans with on-board computer terminals that will plot routes and record all transaction data. Today, UPS vans follow regular pre-planned routes and have no on-board electronic data or communications equipment. Other competitors like Emery and Airborne still rely primarily on telephone contacts with customers for ordering, dispatch and tracking but are investing heavily in the technology required to match the advanced customer services offered by FedEx. Emery has already placed 100 computers in customer offices. Purolator provides customers of its two-day-or-less "Standard Regional" service with free, computerized shipping consoles that calculate rates, print shipping control labels and provide documentation for the shipment.

The importance of customer transaction communications was clearly stated by William Goins, FedEx manager of distribution sales systems: "We've found that it is just as important to provide information as it is to physically move goods" [28]. FedEx's ability to provide information on demand allows customers to find out whether there has been or likely will be any interruption or delay in the delivery of their package. Not only can customers access critical information about an ongoing service, but they can do so when *they* feel the need. This provides customers with reassurance about the reliability of the service being provided and a degree of control over how that service is executed. Furthermore, FedEx makes it as easy as possible for the customer to take advantage of the reporting service and guarantees a refund if the information cannot be delivered in a timely manner. Thus, the message delivery industry has gone from putting a message in a mailbox and hoping it will be delivered within a reasonable time, to sending a package via overnight delivery and having the option of determining its status/location in a matter of minutes.

The concepts are reliability, customer control and ease of use that are the basis for the special customer services offered today are being further extended by the application of developing technology. The computer terminals now in use by large customers will become more widely available. As electronic systems continue to develop, new services will be added, more customers will use computer terminals to access them and carriers will place even greater emphasis on providing transaction information to customers.

LESSON: Customers of parcel/message delivery services today are buying more than just a reliable service; they are buying up-to-date information on just how reliable that service is. Among other things, this allows customers to make intelligent and informed decisions on alternative courses of action depending on the status of the parcel/message.

When buying a priority delivery service, a customer expects not just reliable delivery but accurate and timely information about the execution of the service as well. The customer expects notification when the package cannot be delivered or will be delayed. Finally, the customer expects that the system for accessing that information will be geared to her needs and will be easy to use. Business practices in the parcel/message delivery business illustrate that providing information about the delivery of the product is as important to differentiating a priority service as is delivering the product itself.

Evolution of Service Applications

Once a system is in place, customers are accustomed to using it and the reliability of the service provider has been established, both customers and businesses begin to think of new ways to use the capabilities that have been developed. In many cases these applications are not ones that were anticipated or foreseen when the service was being designed. Evolutionary growth of this type can even force organizations to rethink and redefine what business they are in and what role they will play in the future.

An example of this in parcel/message delivery is the use of expedited delivery services as a "just-in-time" distribution system for high-cost goods that are critical to a customer's operations. FedEx "recently began warehousing parts for IBM workstations. By using Federal's airplanes and couriers, delivery costs were cut and IBM could begin closing 120 parts depots" [29]. Perhaps more important, IBM now can guarantee its customers that the parts they need to keep their computers running will be delivered by the next day. For FedEx, UPS and other competitors in the expedited delivery business, this could be just the beginning of an entirely new set of services that they can offer their customers.

In this new role, companies in the message/parcel delivery business would evolve from being just a delivery service to being "logistics firms" or "integrated distribution specialists". Chairman Smith of FedEx believes that "just-in-time" manufacturing joined with worldwide express delivery will become a major corporate strategy and he is preparing his firm to take advantage of the opportunity. Already all of FedEx's full-time sales representatives receive special training in "distribution problem solving".

They are supported by staff experts who specialize in fields such as network analysis, warehousing and finance. These FedEx employees work with customers to develop new uses and applications for the capabilities the firm has to offer. Together, the firm and its customers will create the new definition of the "parcel/message delivery business", a definition that was unforeseen in 1973 when FedEx delivered its first overnight package.

LESSON: Firms have to be prepared to change or expand the traditional definition of what their company is and what service it provides.

Planners, product designers and strategists cannot know all of their customers' businesses or the needs of potential customers well enough to predict how service offerings will be adapted to meet special requirements or new developments. Indeed, often enough customers do not know their own tastes for a new service until they have experienced it for awhile. Once a product is familiar, ideas for whole new ways to use it may occur. It is this constant process of adaptation to new discoveries, by the companies *and* by their customers, that distinguishes successful competitors from market failures.

In this process the unpredictable evolution of particular services plays an important role. Thus, in implementing PRISM, to try to design an "optimal" initial product offering may well be less productive than to simply implement a reasonable menu of choices and to be ready to modify it quickly and often. Utilities, with the tradition of long-term planning and the necessary focus on the regulator as well as the customer, may have difficulty taking this approach; if so, competitors may do so instead, to the utility's disadvantage.

CONCLUSION

At heart, PRISM is an attempt to unbundle and price electricity along service reliability lines. The parcel/message delivery business has exhibited considerable unbundling along the reliability dimension, but along many other dimensions as well. The experience in this market has lessons for PRISM.

One message is that competition forces product diversity whether a regulated entity is interested in such diversity or not. Electric competition is growing. Political, technological, social and economic changes are combining to alter the environment within which utilities operate. In a free-market society, change creates opportunities for innovation that will result in profitable new business ventures. Even a strong political bias toward maintenance of the status quo may not prevent the eventual emergence of competition in some segments of a controlled market. One impact of electric competition will be to increase the diversity of electric products offered.

Another message is that over the long-run, a "monopoly" franchise is no guarantee of market position–in fact, it can be more of a hindrance than a help. Regulation values simplicity and stability; competition thrives on change. Regulation creates niches where the regulated price is well above the cost of providing service. Regulation also makes introduction of new services more difficult. Both factors create profitable opportunities for non-regulated, or less regulated, competitors. One way to prevent such problems is to fill the niches in advance, through new service offerings such as PRISM envisions. Nonetheless, once competition develops, the "monopoly" service provider must adapt and meet the competitive challenge or risk losing its market position. Variants of the problems encountered by REA and the Postal Service can be expected to face utilities as well.

Analogies are never perfect, but utility managers could see a pattern of industry development similar to that of the parcel/message delivery business. First, the gradual opening of limited areas of competition for what may be perceived as standard, relatively unglamorous service. Competition in this stage is based mainly on offering customers equal or better service for a lower price. Competitors will go after the most profitable services, leaving the utility with the high-cost parts of the market. Then, as other firms see the opportunities that exist and regulatory restrictions are loosened, there would be periods when competitors and new products proliferate. In this phase, competition is based more on differentiation than price. This would in turn be followed by a period of consolidation when the number of competitors shrinks, product offerings become more standardized and competition focuses once again mainly on price. New services or new uses for existing services are then required to open new markets and maintain high profitability.

The electric industry today seems most like the parcel/message delivery market in the 1950s and 1960s. An industry long dominated by regulated entities with legal franchises is starting to face material competition, due both to economic and political changes. At the moment, competition based on price/cost seems to dominate, with cogeneration and self-generation perhaps the leading forms. But proposals to increase the permitted scope of electric competition abound, and intervention in regulatory proceedings over the rules governing competition is as important for utilities now as it was for parcel carriers in the 1950s and 1960s.

If the analogy holds, price competition and cost efficiency will be the key to success in the near term. Utilities have to worry about the REA example: political and other constraints may keep a utility from charging full cost for unprofitable services and cutting prices to match the competition for profitable services. Another competitive activity will be debate over the rules under which competition is allowed. The successful firms will be those like UPS, who offer an equal or better product at the same or lower price, but are also efficient that profits and growth are high.

PRISM will initially be implemented in this phase, and much of its success will thus depend on a utility's ability to track the cost and value of the services offered. Utilities should also be alert for whole new markets, however, particularly markets where value is so high that price is relatively unimportant. Success in this phase turns on knowing what your customers want and need before your competitors, or even your customers themselves, do.

Finally, the parcel/message delivery market teaches that surprises end up driving competitive service offerings, at least where the type of service offered forms the competitive battleground. Companies may enter a market with one strategy in mind and end up delivering a different service in a different, more profitable way. Product design in competitive markets comes from market research and from responses to both competitors and customers, not from long-lead-time economic studies. PRISM needs to develop tools that help utilities to be flexible and to move quickly. An "optimum" service offering is impossible until companies and customers know customers' true tastes and needs. A PRISM manual that helps design an "optimum" schedule is likely to be a good deal less helpful to utilities than one that helps design a "good enough" schedule quickly and then shows how to learn and profit from the resulting experience.

ACKNOWLEDGEMENTS

Putnam, Hayes & Bartlett, Inc., (PHB) gratefully acknowledges the comments on an earlier draft made by Robert L. Kendall, Jr., Esq. Of course, the views herein do not necessarily reflect those of Mr. Kendall. Those views and any errors remain the sole responsibility of PHB.

Within PHB. the authors would like to thank their colleagues, George Hall, Matthew O'Loughlin, Christopher Pleatsikas, William Tye and John Weber, for their contributions to this document.

REFERENCES

1. D.H. Nissen and A.M. Lago. "Price Elasticity of the Demand for Parcel Post Mail", *The Journal of Industrial Economics*, vol. 23, p. 282, June 1975.

2. *Business Week*, p. 62, November 9, 1987.

3. Clifford D. Currier. Rebuttal Testimony Before the Postal Rate Commission. *Postal Rate and Fee Changes, 1987*, Docket No. R87-1, Exhibits 5 and 7.

4. *Fortune*, p. 64, January 18, 1988.

5. *The New York Times*, p. 1, May 6, 1988.

6. Goldman Sachs & Co. Research Brief. Federal Express Corporation, pp. 5-6, December 19, 1988.

7. *Business Week*, p. 62, November 9, 1987.

8. Nissen and Lago, p. 283.

9. *Fortune*, p. 102, July 21, 1986.

10. *Flight International*, reprint. p. 5, March 28, 1987.

11. *The New York Times*, p. 1, May 6, 1988.

12. *Traffic World*, p. 8, March 30, 1987.

13. *Dun's Business Month*, p. 68, December 1981.

14. Nissen and Lago, p. 283.

15. *Fortune*, p. 58, January 18, 1988

16. *Fortune*, p. 58, January 18, 1988

17. *Fortune*, p. 58, January 18, 1988

18. *Flight International*, p. 1

19. John T. Tierney. *Postal Reorganization: Managing the Public's Business.* Boston: Auburn House, p. 73, 1981.

20. *Fortune*, p. 106, July 21, 1986.

21. *Wall Street Journal*, p. 6, May 27, 1987.

22. Tierney, p. 52.

23. Tierney, p. 59.

24. *Handling & Shipping Management*, p. 21, June 1987.

25. Currier testimony, p. 21.

26. *Traffic Management*, p. 77, November 1987.

27. *Flight International*, p. 5

28. *Handling & Shipping Management*, p. 21.

29. *Business Week*, p. 66, November 9, 1987.

VIII. REGULATORY PERSPECTIVE

ARE RELIABILITY-DIFFERENTIATED PRODUCTS UNDULY DISCRIMINATORY?

by

Robert E. Burns, Esq.
The National Regulatory Research Institute

Today there are increasing indications that instead of increasing kilowatt-hour sales, electric utilities are beginning to monitor their customers' services, changing needs and desires and adjusting their products, and methods of distribution to meet these new needs and wants of the marketplace. This is marketing, and is what product differentiation is all about.

To the extent that it is technically feasible, electric utilities are considering implementing reliability-differentiated electric services. Some services are not new; interruptible-service rates have existed for decades. Other services such as special rates for residential customers that permit load control devices, while not new, have been under active consideration since Purpa was enacted. Providing higher reliability power for some commercial customers who have a high cost of outage is, however, a relatively new idea (see EPRI journal, March 1986) that will increasingly be placed before the public service commissions.

Three possible reasons for a change from the status quo of few, undifferentiated "white bread" services that are priced based on cost are (1) changes in technology which make it possible for utilities to identify and distinguish customers with different values of services, (2) changes in technologies that allow the electric utilities to offer differentiated services of greater value to their customers, and (3) an increasingly competitive environment that motivates the utilities to offer these new services to compete. Are these reasons sufficient to justify offering new services? Regulators would frame the question: Are reliability-differentiated electric products unduly discriminatory? The answer is, it depends. To understand the answer, one must first understand what the prohibition against undue discrimination in rates and services means.

The explicit prohibition against undue or unreasonable discrimination or preference in rates or services is one of the universal obligations imposed by state and federal public utility laws. The prohibition is a legal term of art that is rooted in English and American common law. It is intimately tied to the utility's obligation to provide service to all who request it. The requirement that rates be reasonable follows from the requirement that anyone requesting service must be served, since the ability to charge an exorbitant rate is equivalent to the power to deny service. In early English common law, the requirement that rates be reasonable only prohibited extreme forms of price discrimination. Differences in rates based on value of service were permitted.

But the common law has evolved such that while not all discriminatory rates or services offerings are unduly so, undue discrimination is explicitly forbidden by public utility law. The word discrimination itself is synonymous with any kind of rate or service difference not based on cost differences. What makes specific differences undue? Interpretations of undue price and service discrimination statues have been developed by state commissions and the courts on a case-by-case approach. Even so, there are many common themes. These are (1) that similarly situated customers should be treated equally; (2) that unequal treatment of similar customers constitutes discrimination; (3) that undue price discrimination depends on whether there is a reasonable basis for the discrimination, that is, whether the discrimination is predicated on differences in costs or service; (4) that the presence of anticompetitive harm resulting from cross subsidies be considered; and (5) that any basis for discrimination be clearly articulated.

In particular, state commissions are sensitive to price discrimination that results in one rate class subsidizing another. Of particular concern is the protection of captive customers. Typically, a utility proposing a reliability-differentiated product can expect a state commission to begin its inquiry by asking whether the service and its price are discriminatory, and, if so, whether the discrimination is undue. We can start with a presumption that reliability-differentiated services, as their name implies, can be discriminatory. They often are based on value-based planning that differentiates or discriminates between customers (who are otherwise similarly situated) according to their value of service, which typically is measured according to the cost of outage. These new service offerings are not necessarily unduly discriminatory. If the services are offered to all similarly situated customers so that customers can self-select whether or not they want the service according to their own assessment of whether they have a high outage cost, such a service would not be unduly discriminatory, unless its price led to undue discrimination. The price of the service would not be discriminatory if it were based on the cost of the unbundled service offering. It is important that the utility not engage in value-of-service pricing, even though reliability-differentiated service may be based on value-based planning. If the price of the service is not tied to its cost but to its value, a state public service commission may find a cross subsidy and decree the service unduly discriminatory.

However, without some method of calculating the cost of service, one is left with the essential question of how to allocate joint costs in a fair and equitable manner that also maximizes efficiency. Public utility law's implicit limitation on price discrimination is the requirement that rates be just and reasonable. Typically, electricity rates that are found not to be cost-based are held to be unjust or unreasonable and, therefore, unlawful. Rates that vary significantly from the cost of service are also held to be unduly discriminatory as well as unjust and unreasonable. The argument is that rates that vary significantly from cost-based rates lead to cross-subsidization. But again, how does one divide joint costs in a way that promotes economic efficiency and still provides for equity? Many economists prefer Ramsey pricing as a means of allocating joint capacity cost to maximize economic efficiency. However, Ramsey prices are faulted by many analysts as being inequitable or, at the very least, at the extreme bounds of equity.

Traditionally, state commissions have used embedded or average cost-of-service studies to measure whether prices are just and reasonable. Although there if often controversy over what cost-of -service method (e.g., coincident peak, noncoincident peak, or average and excess demand) is most appropriate. These cost-of-service study methods contain familiar assumptions about how to allocate joint capacity costs between customer classes. These assumptions are not based on an attempt to maximize economic efficiency by spreading costs to inelastic (captive) customers. In many respects, these cost-of-service studies serve the commissions as a silent surrogate method of balancing efficiency and equity concerns, especially when the results are used to determine whether there has been any cross-subsidization between customer classes.

As long as utilities use value-based planning and refrain from resorting to value-based pricing in differentiated reliability service offerings, the state commissions are likely to be supportive of the new services, especially if the new services would increase consumer surplus for customers opting for the service. But, utilities can expect state commissions to take a hard look at these service offerings to make certain that the price for the service is cost-based and that it does not result in cross subsidies that will harm captive customers.